To John —

You made my day
with your comments!

Tide will ?
to you!

Advance Praise for
When Politicians Panicked

"A society or a civilization which is poorer will be less capable of coping with a public health crisis. Now, if that seems like a commonsense observation, well that is because that is exactly what it is. To anyone who has lived through what passes for health and economic policy in 2020, though, John Tamny's provocative book—based as it is on that observation—will come as a shock. Tamny's book is an excellent contribution to the conversation that the world will need so that the mistakes made during this epidemic are never made again."

—Jay Bhattacharya, Professor of
Medicine, Stanford University

"John Tamny bravely describes the terrible and senseless economic pain caused by politicians panicking in the face of a health concern that—let's be real—is no worse than a bad flu season."

—Rich Karlgaard, Publisher of *Forbes*

"The response of governments around the world to the coronavirus has been a colossal policy error—probably the worst in humanity's history. We'll be struggling to understand what went wrong for the next fifty years. *When Politicians Panicked* will bring essential clarity."

—Toby Young, LockdownSceptics.org

"John Tamny's myth-shattering new groundbreaker, *When Politicians Panicked*—isn't really about COVID-19 but a radically yet stunningly older, better way to envision it, innovation, healthcare and its evolution, economics, wealth creation, and our overall culture—both by what is normally seen and unseen."

—Ken Fisher, Founder and Executive
Chairman, Fisher Investments

"Tamny writes a provocative book exposing critically important issues arising from the coronavirus pandemic, beyond the destruction of families and tragic loss of life."

—Scott Atlas, Hoover Institution, Former Chief
of Neuroradiology at Stanford Medical Center

"John Tamny makes a convincing economic case for lockdowns being suicidally self-destructive."

—Lionel Shriver, Author of *The Mandibles*

"The intellectuals often get things wrong but it is the politicians that weaponize their errors. Read Tamny's riveting account of what is surely the greatest failure of politics in many generations. And work to make sure nothing like this ever happens again."

—Jeffrey Tucker, Author of *Liberty or Lockdown*

THE NEW CORONAVIRUS,
EXPERT OPINION, *and a* TRAGIC LAPSE OF REASON

WHEN
POLITICIANS
PANICKED

JOHN TAMNY
foreword by *WEALTH AND POVERTY* author
GEORGE GILDER

Post Hill
PRESS

A POST HILL PRESS BOOK
ISBN: 978-1-64293-837-1
ISBN (eBook): 978-1-64293-838-8

When Politicians Panicked:
The New Coronavirus, Expert Opinion, and a Tragic Lapse of Reason
© 2021 by John Tamny
All Rights Reserved

Cover art by Cody Corcoran

Post Hill Press
New York • Nashville
posthillpress.com

Published in the United States of America

For Reed, who entered the world in March 2020. May your generation turn its collective nose up to panic as the response to problems, real and imagined.

CONTENTS

FOREWORD

I'm relieved to report that righteous scriveners and saner doctors, academics, and statisticians across the land are publishing books debunking the tragic COVID madness that needlessly wrecked the lives of so many. With cogent authority, these books present all the statistical arguments on the insignificance of COVID compared to earlier, more deadly epidemics that brought no lockdowns or mask edicts.

Now John Tamny, Director of FreedomWorks' Center for Economic Freedom, and libertarian star of *RealClearMarkets*, has unleashed a devastating tract that you now hold in your hand, *When Politicians Panicked*.

Naming names and describing the endless carnival of outrageous overreach, Tamny vividly details the doings of politicians and experts reveling in power like so many Charlie Chaplin Fuhrers. To Tamny, the centralization of power in the hands of the very few was and always will be the definition of crisis. Markets work precisely because they factor in the decentralized knowledge of millions, and realistically billions. This is a lesson members of the political class have never learned, and didn't learn in 2020.

Having decided that the spread of the new coronavirus was a crisis, politicians and their expert enablers quickly fulfilled their prophecy with lockdowns, stringent rules for businesses "allowed" to operate, and other decrees from the Commanding Heights. It turns out central planning still doesn't work.

Tamny is not much interested in COVID-19 data not because it doesn't discredit the breathy alarmism of the Ruling Class, but because he reasonably fears that a debate won with statistics sets the stage for future lockdowns. Politicians embody "this time is different," and as there will always be camera-addicted experts ready and willing to gull the elected, Tamny argues that freedom must be the first and last answer to any governmental response.

At the same time, Tamny uses data to help readers understand that the political panic had no reasonable basis. Nothing offers any answer to the all-cause death data that show COVID to have been a trivial event in medical terms, with perhaps a million lives lost, average age over eighty, in the face of some 58 million global all-cause deaths in 2019. COVID deaths, even according to the Imperial College of London, were going to be quite a bit fewer in 2020 than the some 1.4 million new tuberculosis deaths resulting from the lockdowns and COVID hospital distortions.

As Tamny points out, the relative triviality of COVID-19 was blatantly evident as early as March 18, 2020, when Fred Smith, the venerable FedEx founder-CEO, was interviewed by Fox News' Bret Baier. Smith had extensive operations in the epicenter of the virus in Wuhan, China, and 907 employees there, delivering packages for weeks all over the stricken city. All employees were tested for the virus and only four tested positive. Of those four, two proved to be false positives. None of the FedEx workers got exceptionally sick and all recovered.

Adding to Tamny's point, Tesla founder Elon Musk's early skepticism about lockdown hysteria was similarly rooted in his company's extensive operations in China. Tesla has a major supply chain in China that employs thousands, yet like Smith, Musk thankfully encountered a virus that was rather meek.

Tamny concluded: "That [Smith's Wuhan] employees were largely spared the virus's spread, and that none had died from it, reads as a reasonable market signal going back over two months (and realistically much longer than that) [discrediting] the presumed lethality of COVID-

19." COVID seems chiefly to threaten people already dying and physicians who expose themselves repeatedly to a load-dependent viral attack.

What we have undergone is an egregious and perhaps criminal and certainly unconstitutional power grab by politicians. Whether merely stupid or demagogic or driven by polls or by a nefariously political media, the politicians from Trump on down simply blundered like no others in the history of public policy.

"Proper history," Tamny writes, "will indicate that what happened in 2020 was a global debacle.... The reaction by pols...amounted to the biggest crime against humanity [in two centuries]. When politicians panicked, those with the least suffered in unimaginable ways.... According to a UN study he cites, some 285 million people may die of starvation [because] of "an American upper middle class that was making decisions for everyone and for whom lockdowns were merely an inconvenience or vacation."

Tamny understands economics with an intuitive and uncanny contrarian eye that penetrates beyond all the macroeconomic fantasies of conventional economists. He points out: "If the virus had been lethal, the lockdowns would have made even less sense.... The biggest enemy of life is *poverty*." Lockdowns simply cause poverty without relieving disease in any way.

"Let's never again fight disease with the taking of freedom and wealth so essential to knowledge, prosperity, and by extension life itself."

Tamny is giving us a heroic book just in time. We suffered not a medical crisis, but from a political and economic and institutional crisis. We have undergone a vast breakdown of moral, educational, intellectual, and journalistic standards. Tamny tells this story better than anyone else. All should read his shocking tale.

—George Gilder

INTRODUCTION

*"Universal poverty isn't an acceptable solution
to any problem that I can think of."*

—Robert G. Brown, *Wall Street Journal,*
letter to the editor, May 16, 2020

"It doesn't make sense." Those were the words of Las Vegas resident Valicia Anderson to *New York Times* reporter Sabrina Tavernise. In the April 27, 2020, edition of the newspaper Tavernise reported that Anderson quickly ran out of fingers when she attempted to list all those she knew who were suddenly jobless.

Keep in mind that less than two months before, unemployment in the United States as reported by the Bureau of Labor Statistics was 3.5 percent. Yet suddenly seemingly everyone Anderson knew lacked a job.

As Tavernise went on to report, victims close to Anderson included "her husband, the breadwinner of her family and a restaurant worker in the Rio casino. All 25 of his co-workers. Her grown son, in a temp agency. The technician who does her nails. The barber who cuts her husband's hair. Her best friend, a waitress. The three servers and a manager at the TGI Friday's that is her family's favorite treat."[1]

On the very same day, the *Wall Street Journal's* Ben Kesling authored a piece with a headline right out of the 1930s. Titled, "Farmers Forced to Destroy Their Crops," Kesling indicated farmers were destroying their harvests on account of there existing "no market to buy them."[2]

Keep in mind that less than two months before, U.S. stock markets had been at all-time highs to reflect broad optimism about the future. Stock markets are never a barometer of the present; rather, they're a price signal about how investors see the future. This is an important distinction in consideration of the 3.5 percent jobless rate that prevailed in February 2020.

This is all a way of saying that the U.S. economy not only looked largely healthy in February 2020, investors were also confident that the economy would continue to grow as evidenced by the direction of the stock market. U.S. equities specifically reached an all-time high on February 17, 2020.

So what's the riddle here? What happened that the U.S. economy seemingly fell off a steep cliff in such a short amount of time? Economies don't just collapse on their own. They don't simply because economies are people, and it's the norm for people in free societies to get up each day and go to work.

Yet by April unemployment around the United States was rampant, business bankruptcies had surged, and this fed a feeling of mass desperation in what has long been the world's most prosperous and optimistic country. "It doesn't make sense," the quote that begins this book, in many ways doesn't do justice to what took place after February.

Which brings us to the answer to the supposed riddle. What could possibly have happened that the U.S. economy contracted so gruesomely and so quickly? The answer is that politicians on the local, state, and national levels in the U.S. panicked in response to the discovery that the novel coronavirus, a virus with origins in the Chinese city of Wuhan, had found its way around the world.

At which point it's useful to pause. The book you're reading is realistically not about the new coronavirus, the novel coronavirus, COVID-19, the Wuhan virus, or SARS-CoV-2 as some of the more scientific minded refer to it. For one, readers can rest assured that there will be hundreds, and realistically thousands of books that cover the voluminous history of pandemics, the intricacies of the coronavirus, why doctors, scientists, and politicians well understated its threat, along with why doctors, scientists, and politicians well overstated it. Though references will regularly be made to the virus, illness, and death rates throughout, it would be a major mistake to write about subjects that I have no reasonable understanding of. I'm not a doctor or scientist, so it would do readers no good for me to presume to write about something medical.

With the above in mind, it's also worth pointing out what this book will conclude on occasion: more often than not, medical specialists themselves have misunderstood illnesses and disease, or they've under- or overestimated them. About the previous statement, it should not be construed as a specific knock on experts, doctors, scientists, or all three. Nor is it a suggestion of medical knowledge. In truth, it's an expression of reality: while it's a known quantity that the future is exceedingly hard to understand or predict, the present is similarly no walk in the park. In relying on experts to understand the present, we're expecting them to digest voluminous information produced around the world on the way to coming to some kind of knowledgeable conclusion. We ask too much of experts, but we also rely on them too much as this book will eventually argue.

But the main reason *When Politicians Panicked* won't focus on the coronavirus in substantive fashion is because the act of doing so would thoroughly insult what actually took place. Consider what *Wall Street Journal* deputy editorial page editor Daniel Henninger wrote in April 2020: "Coronavirus is a grim reaper, an indiscriminate destroyer leveling businesses large and small."[3] Except that the virus did no such thing. And it did no such thing anywhere. Henninger would likely agree.

What happened was that politicians *panicked about the coronavirus*, proceeded to shut the global economy down to varying degrees, and to varying degrees it collapsed. So while this book's first chapter will make a case that by March 2020 there was already screamingly loud evidence that the coronavirus wasn't very lethal (evidence that required no medical or mathematical knowledge), the following chapters will broadly accept that the virus was a major killer in order to illustrate a larger point—the more threatening anything is, the more important it is that politicians do nothing. Translated, the more lethal the virus is presumed to be, the less need for rules and laws in a vain attempt to force behavior. When it comes to illness and potential death, people don't require force. At all.

So while statistics are starting to come out that support Chapter One's assertion about a virus that was much less than lethal, and while some of this will as mentioned be referenced on occasion, this book will conclude that debates made by lockdown critics that are backed by numbers win battles at the expense of winning long-term wars for freedom from politicians who panic.

Lockdowns shouldn't happen, period. They violate our individual right to live and work. They're horrendously cruel to those with the least. In 2020 they amounted to a global human rights tragedy that was staggering in scope. That they also make us less safe and less capable of protecting ourselves from illness and potential death is a conclusion this book will ultimately arrive at, but hopefully readers will have already concluded the same well before reaching the concluding chapters. For now, it should just be said that a focus on death rates and mortality when it comes to the coronavirus is a winning argument that loses the long-term war for freedom from panicky politicians.

So there we have it. Though this book can be reasonably billed as a coronavirus book, it's really a story about politicians losing their wits, reacting rashly after losing their wits, and creating a global economic contraction in the process. To blame this on the coronavirus is to excuse ineptitude that is the norm when the combined, decentralized knowledge of millions and billions of humans is ignored in favor of the centralized and highly limited knowledge of very few politicians, and even fewer experts. The ideal response to the chapters ahead will be not just that politicians reacted in tragic fashion to a virus, but that this reaction is what we can always expect unless we change the narrative away from expecting politicians to have an answer to societal problems real and perceived, and instead turn to free people to solve what comes their way.

To see why this is true, it's important to begin this book in mid-March of 2020, when the panic really started to take shape.

Chapter One

THEY ALREADY KNEW IT WASN'T LETHAL, DIDN'T THEY?

"I guess other people expect us to set our futures on fire to keep their fear warm. I think that's incredibly selfish—if you're that fearful, just stay home."

—Rashell Collins Bridle,
forty-two-year-old mother of five[4]

On March 18 FedEx founder and CEO Fred Smith was interviewed by Fox News Channel's Bret Baier about the new coronavirus. Smith's entrepreneurial brilliance makes him an interesting interview at any time, but the one on the 18th was particularly important.

That's the case because FedEx had 907 employees based in Wuhan. Wuhan is an increasingly prominent city when it comes to production, and as FedEx moves production and packages around the world, it was only logical that Smith's company would have a big presence there.

What Smith relayed to Baier was very eye-opening, which is why it's surprising the interview didn't achieve more play than it did. Smith indicated to Baier that all 907 of his employees in Wuhan had been tested for the virus, and four were initially diagnosed as having contracted it. Smith went on to say that two of the four positive diagnoses were later revealed as false, but the main thing was that those who contracted the virus were fully recovered.[5]

From there it's worth considering the Smith interview on March 18 relative to when the virus first became news in the United States. It was in early January that readers started to read about it, which means it likely had been working its way through Wuhan for quite some time.

The point here is that FedEx's complex in Wuhan is hardly some kind of micro warehouse employing very few. One imagines that at 907 employs it's fairly large relative to other employers in Wuhan, not to mention that Smith's employees were actively handling packages presumably touched by residents of the city that's known as the epicenter of the virus's breakout. Translated, Smith and FedEx's experience with the virus as of March 18 was much more than anecdotal. That his employees were largely spared the virus's spread, and that none had died from it, reads as a reasonable market signal going back over two months (and realistically much longer than that) that the presumed lethality of COVID-19 was thankfully quite a bit less than substantial.

Thinking about China more broadly, much noise was made by the left and right at the time about how China's death rates from the virus required an asterisk next to them, that Beijing's Communist Party leadership couldn't be trusted, that the country's economic figures are fudged, and so on. For the purposes of this chapter, let's agree that all that's assumed is true.

If so, it doesn't alter the reality that assuming massive numbers of deaths in Wuhan and elsewhere from the coronavirus, this truth would have quickly reached the media. In a world in which information travels at the tap of a smartphone, there's no way to hide what's happening. Or for that matter, what happened. Along these lines, it's been documented that Chinese history books and the country's internet are scrubbed of information about the bloody 1989 Tiananmen Square protests. At the same time, it's also well known in China that anyone with passable computer skills can pull up the truth about what happened *on the internet in China* with ease.[6]

In short, if the coronavirus had been a major killer in a country with hospitals that don't hold a candle to U.S. hospitals, and in a country where smoking is at least visibly quite a bit more common, we would have known about it months before the lockdowns and shelter-in-place decrees began to wreck U.S. cities, counties, and states. Baier's interview of Smith, along with the speed at which news travels, tells us there was fairly reliable information going back quite a while that this wasn't the bubonic plague. Not even close.

It's something to think about in consideration of the economic impact of the lockdowns. Patricia Cohen reported in the May 29, 2020, edition of the *New York Times* that "more than 40 million people—the equivalent of one out of every four workers—have filed for unemployment benefits since the coronavirus pandemic grabbed hold in mid-March."[7] In Cohen's case, let's first excuse her reportorial error of blaming the virus for the onset of the sick-inducing job loss, while also correcting it. What happened was that by mid-March, much of the U.S. was locked down or on the way to being locked down. With streets and businesses empty, and with other businesses increasingly shut down by decree, unemployment soared.

This is important simply because we knew by mid-March that the virus had in no way exhibited killer qualities of any kind. Think about it. Just as the old Soviet Union couldn't keep the Chernobyl nuclear incident off the front pages of U.S. newspapers at a time when communications technology was much more primitive in comparison to today's, there's no way that the Chinese could have hidden mass death in Wuhan or elsewhere.

Which means that it was also well known by mid-March that some who contracted the virus experienced a lot of discomfort, some very little, and some seemingly none at all. But the main thing is that if it had been a major killer, the previous truth would have been a known quantity.

Which brings us to an early and fairly easy to make conclusion about the lockdowns that began in March, followed by layoffs that took off at a rate no American has realistically ever seen. Politicians will claim they had no choice, that the virus was an unknown, that "China" wasn't forthcoming with the truth about it such that stateside politicians had to fly a little bit blind.

Let's please not let their attempts to deflect the hotter light stand. The very technology that enables rapid-fire communication among readers, the very technology that enables long-lost and geographically distant friends to stage Zoom parties amid the errant lockdowns, is the same technology that would have alerted us to a killer long before mid-March.

Politicians panicked. Plain and simple. And in doing so their panic led to exponentially more unemployment and long-term agony than would have been the case had they simply suggested to us adults that we might profit from being careful. In short, let's not let the political class hide behind an information deficit, "China," reasonable fear of a new virus, or all three.

At the same time, the certainty that a truly killer virus would have long been known by mid-March wouldn't excuse limited action any more than it would excessive action. The simple truth is that any government force is excessive in response to something said to cause illness and, in some instances, death. It will be said throughout this book, but people don't need a law.

Where this book is arguably different is in its assertion that the lockdowns were never justified. Looking back to Imperial College and Neil Ferguson's famous prediction of 2.2 million American deaths in response to the virus, predictions that were subsequently walked back, the answer still should have been no lockdowns and no response from politicians.

Really, what about the high possibility of death as a consequence of virus exposure also requires government command? It cannot be said enough (this book will say it a lot) that the more lethal something is presumed to be, the less authorities need to do or say anything.

Returning to the *Wall Street Journal*'s Daniel Henninger, whom readers were introduced to in the introductory chapter, if the virus itself had been an indiscriminate destroyer of all around it, then logic dictates that it would have had an enormous death count where it began to reflect its ability to destroy businesses of all sizes. Yet the virus quite simply wasn't a mass killer where it originated, nor was it globally. As Lionel Shriver put it in London's *Spectator* on May 16, 2020, as of around that date the virus had taken 290,000 lives versus 58 million global deaths in 2019 alone. In Shriver's words, "Covid deaths will barely register in the big picture even if their total multiplies by several times."[8]

Which means that what was the "grim reaper" for businesses and jobs wasn't the virus; rather, it was the political reaction to it. As Shriver put it, the economic tragedy that hit the world in sickeningly rapid fashion was "manmade." This book refuses to spend too much time on the virus itself simply because doing so furthers the shameful notion that a mass killer of mankind brought about brutal economic contraction, as opposed to panicked politicians.

To be clear, panicked politicians goaded by experts in rapid-fire fashion stripped the people of their ability to work. This came in the form of shelter-in-place orders around the U.S. and around the world that devastated businesses of all kinds, along with those in the employ of businesses.

At the same time, it should be stressed that even if the virus had been a major killer, or even if projections like those of Imperial College had been real, the view here wouldn't have changed one iota. Politicians should never, ever have forced lockdowns on their people to pursue decadent notions like "flattening the curve," or even to allegedly save lives.

That's the case because the biggest killer the world has ever known, by far, has been poverty and economic malaise more broadly. That poverty has such a tragic death count, the very notion of enforced lockdowns brought new meaning to non sequitur. And an incredibly cruel, *inhumane* non sequitur at that. The answer to a virus that potentially kills is mass economic desperation? Did politicians lose their minds?

If the challenge is health related, the only answer is economic growth.

Chapter Two

CAPTAIN OF MEN'S DEATH

"When you have exhausted all possibilities,
remember this—you haven't."

—Thomas Edison

Political commentator George Will was born in 1941. The year of his birth is relevant in consideration of the kind of hospital he was born into. Americans of today wouldn't recognize what was incredibly primitive.

In his 2019 book, *The Conservative Sensibility*, Will commented that at the time of his birth, "the principal expense of most hospitals was clean linen." As he goes on to write, this "was before MRIs, CAT scans, electron microscopes, laser surgery, and many other costly technologies."[9] How terrible it would have been to have fallen ill in the mid-twentieth century.

In that case, imagine coming into the world in 1860, in the United States. Though it wasn't the world's richest country yet, it was on the way toward that status. In this country that was a magnet for the world's strivers, life was still incredibly brutal by modern standards.

If you were lucky enough to be born, you had just as good of a chance of dying as living. Doctors didn't even know what cancer was in the 1860s since most people didn't live long enough to get it.[10]

With infections, there was no answer. Pneumonia was the number one killer and remained that way through the first decade of the twentieth century. It was "Captain of Men's Death."[11] In fact, World War I would be the first war in which disease wasn't the primary killer. Going back to the Spanish-American War, thirteen men died from disease (typhoid mostly) for every soldier killed by guns and bombs.[12]

Back to the 1860s, men in battle with broken limbs often waited overnight for attention. Shots of whiskey were what nurses offered as pain medicine for those who might live.

The reality of medical care in the 1860s was pretty grim. According to doctor and novelist Lawrence Dorr, one of the world's most prominent orthopedic surgeons, during the Civil War those "with gunshot wounds to the abdomen or chest were left to die." A fractured hip "was always fatal," and then a fractured femur carried with it odds of dying that were "three to one." Amputation was the "operation" for a broken leg.[13]

For the young people with 50-50 odds of living, diphtheria was one of many maladies that they faced. It was "the winter-time murderer of children." According to Dorr, it "started with a sore throat and fever, progressed to nausea, vomiting, chills, and often, finally, the lethal membrane in the throat or nose."[14] Inoculation for it wasn't discovered until 1891 in Europe, only for the less-than-certain fix to finally reach the U.S. in 1895. It was the first vaccine antitoxin. At long last doctors were in the position to save lives.[15]

It was at Johns Hopkins Medical School in 1897 that the first surgical operation that cured a disease—appendicitis—was performed.[16] The first breast cancer surgery took place there, too, a few years earlier. The medical school in Baltimore was a consequence of the philanthropy of

Johns Hopkins, one of the early investors in the Baltimore and Ohio Railroad. When he died in 1873, Hopkins left behind $7 million for a university that would be named after him and that would include a medical school. According to Dorr, for its time it was "the largest gift ever made to an American educational institution."[17]

Hopkins's generosity requires deep thought in consideration of the desire among some to tax away great wealth at the time of its creation or upon death. Either way, society loses. As evidenced by the myriad museums, universities, and hospitals around the U.S. with famous commercial names of the past and present affixed to them, when wealth is kept in the hands of its creators or inheritors, we all benefit. Better yet, we all inherit remarkable things—including medical advances.

Tragic with the above in mind is that society's losses are unseen in a sense. Indeed, we don't know what the superrich would have done with wealth that had been untaxed.

The simple truth is that the first breast cancer surgery didn't save a life. Just the same, penicillin in its earliest forms actually worsened patients, according to Dorr.[18] Progress is a consequence of relentless experimentation, but an obvious reason why some don't exhaust the possibilities is that they lack the means to do so. For there to be progress, there must be wealth left over. "Unspent wealth," let's call it.

No individual embodies the importance of unspent wealth more than John D. Rockefeller. Keep in mind that when the great creator of Standard Oil began thinking more ambitiously about philanthropic endeavors in the mid-1890s, medicine was still extraordinarily basic as the discussion of Johns Hopkins Medical School attests. That it was speaks to how important it was that Rockefeller's wealth was matched with the expansive mind of his main philanthropy advisor, Frederick T. Gates.

Gates saw the possibilities as it were. He could see the chance for remarkable advances if talented scientific and medical minds could be matched with abundant capital. As Rockefeller biographer Ron Chernow assessed it in *Titan*, Gates "had a sudden, vivid sense of what could be done by a medical-research institution devoted to infectious diseases."[19]

Chernow goes on to write that with fighting infectious diseases top of mind, Gates "drafted a strongly worded memo to Rockefeller" that sought the establishment of a medical institution in the vein of the Paris-based Pasteur Institute (1888) and the Berlin-based Koch Institute for infectious diseases (1891). The funding of such an institute would be commonplace now, and is, but at the time it was pretty revolutionary. Quite unlike today, medical schools were, in the words of Chernow, still "commercial operations" taught by doctors who "picked up spare money by lecturing on the side" in schools that often didn't "require a college degree for entry." Medicine at the time "hovered in a twilight area between science and guesswork."[20]

The Rockefeller Institute for Medical Research (RIMR) was founded in New York City in 1901 as a biomedical research center. Rockefeller told son John Jr., "We have *money*, but it will have value for mankind only as we can find able men with ideas, imagination and courage to put it to productive use." The RIMR did just that while putting scientists in charge of finding great minds, at which point the institute would, in the words of Chernow, "liberate them from petty cares, and let them chase intellectual chimeras without pressure or creativity."[21] Translated, Rockefeller would be the ultimate patron by virtue of freeing the greatest of scientific minds to exhaust possibilities in the pursuit of what was seen as impossible, only to continue to push boundaries in pursuit of new possibilities to exhaust.

William Welch, the first dean of Johns Hopkins Medical School, was appointed president of the RIMR board. He recruited as RIMR's first director one of his top students, Simon Flexner. Flexner quickly made plain that Rockefeller's medical philanthropy would be much more than a vanity project. When three thousand New Yorkers died from the cerebrospinal meningitis epidemic during the 1904–1905 winter, Flexner created a serum to treat it. Chernow asserts that "Flexner's serum mercifully spared hundreds, perhaps thousands, of lives."[22] In terms of death rates, Flexner's serum reduced the disease's mortality rate from 75 to 25 percent.[23]

Flexner's achievements cheered Rockefeller, who soon produced $2.6 million for an endowment. He then added more millions to his earlier contribution in order to create a hospital that treated, for free, patients with polio, lobar pneumonia, syphilis, heart disease, and intestinal infantilism. What had begun somewhat modestly of mission and finances was by 1910 the richest institute of its kind on earth, and according to one medical journal, RIMR was "probably the best equipped institution for the study of the causes and cure of disease to be found in the world."[24]

While curing diseases was a miracle in the nineteenth century, and really not part of the medical lexicon, by the early twentieth great wealth matched with great men freed from "petty cares" was making it possible for the sick, in the words of Dorr, to "Die Once, Live Twice." Medicine was rising as it were, and in the process lifting people from diseases that used to kill.

In subsequent years Rockefeller's wealth was directed at fighting other diseases, for instance, hookworm. Believed by some to foster indolence in those afflicted, a $1 million Rockefeller donation made possible a major effort to eradicate the disease in the American south. This initiative was later described as "the most effective campaign against a widespread disease which medical science and philanthropy have ever combined to conduct." Even better, the Rockefeller Foundation took the fight against hookworm global, extending it to "fifty-two countries on six continents and freeing millions of people from this worldwide scourge."[25]

Wickliffe Rose was the visionary behind the above campaign in his role as head of the Rockefeller-funded International Health Commission (IHC). Under Rose's leadership, the IHC operated around the world to fight malaria, tuberculosis, and scarlet fever, along with yellow fever, "the terror of the Western Hemisphere." Rose hired a Colonel Gorgas to lead the campaign against this health terror, and according to Chernow, "The disease was nearly wiped out in South and Central America by the late 1920s." The Rockefeller Foundation ultimately footed the bill for a group of scientists (six of whom died from exposure to the fever) to create a vaccine. The project was completed by 1937, and as Chernow wrote, "Millions of doses of the vaccine were distributed worldwide and saved innumerable American soldiers during World War II."[26]

As the 1910s turned into the 1920s, what began as dabbling (by Rockefeller standards) had morphed into something major that dominated John D. Rockefeller's philanthropy. Chernow calculates that Rockefeller gave away $530 million during his lifetime, and $450 million went directly or indirectly into medicine. The crucial point when it comes to understanding this chapter's message is that Rockefeller's wealth, wealth that was both a creator of economic growth and also a consequence of it, "dealt a mortal blow to the primitive world of nineteenth-century medicine."[27]

Stop and think about this for a second. In particular, please stop and contemplate that as of 1910, pneumonia and tuberculosis were still the biggest killers of Americans. According to Dorr, cancer was still "a distant eighth."[28]

Cancer was a distant eighth mainly because few people lived long enough to get it. "Living long enough" is on its own something to consider. According to Tuck School of Business (Dartmouth) senior fellow Matthew Rees, "Death from old age is a relatively recent phenomenon." Rees confirms what Dorr already asserted, that as of the late nineteenth and early twentieth centuries TB and pneumonia were still the main killers.

Rees goes on to write that "Americans began living longer in the 20th century, thanks to better sanitation and more effective vaccines and medicines. But growing old meant an increased vulnerability to other ailments, from *heart disease to cancer*. Progress in treating those conditions, in turn, has led to a higher incidence of *Alzheimer's*."[29] The emphasis in each instance in the previous sentence is your author's. That's the case because strange as it sounds, reaching the point when cancer and heart disease were the main killers paradoxically amounted to *progress*. And then as Rees notes, progress in the treatment of cancer and heart disease has brought on more instances of Alzheimer's.

The great Austrian School thinker Ludwig von Mises observed in *Liberalism* that luxury is historical,[30] and that's certainly true. Think back to how those alive in the 1980s would look at someone with a mobile phone with awe.

Luxury is historical, and so in a sense is disease. Assuming progress continues to be made in the medical sciences, cancer and heart disease will in time fall back as major killers, so will Alzheimer's presumably be dealt with, only for new diseases to be discovered as our time and quality time on earth grows. Let's once again call the discovery of new maladies *progress*—progress born of intense experimentation that helps erase or partially erase past killers.

Extraordinarily important about all this is that progress described is a consequence of wealth-creating capitalist endeavor that makes it possible for the very few to amass stupendous amounts of wealth. While Rockefeller gave away $450 million just in his lifetime to advance medicine, his modern equivalent in Bill Gates is spending billions of his own wealth on coronavirus vaccines alone.[31]

This is all a long way of saying that if disease or a virus is the problem, wealth creation is the answer. Indeed, it's not that people one hundred, two hundred, and three hundred years ago were stupid. But thanks to limited amounts of disposable income that could be directed toward those searching to craft all manner of advances, knowledge was a fraction of what exists now. As a result people died early and often given a primitive medical system that was cruelly unequal to what killed.

Wealth creation has made living longer and healthier a possibility. More and more of us will *live with cancer*, rather than die of it. All thanks to wealth.

Which raises a basic question: Why, when the coronavirus presented itself, was the response from the political class economic contraction born of lockdowns and other criminally stupid "shelter-in-place" orders? Had they lost their collective minds?

A virus reveals itself that some scientists viewed as lethal, so the answer was forced economic desperation? Forced economic desperation despite a century of medical progress against disease that was most certainly an effect of wealth creation? The panicked response from politicians was staggeringly obtuse and one that future historians will surely marvel at. Responding to a virus with contraction. Wow!

Which brings us to chapter's end. Fascinating and sad about what politicians did in response to a virus is that before politicians panicked, the possibility of another virus harming the U.S. had some spooked. The difference with this one is that it had nothing to do with health and everything do with ideology. In short, the initial "coronavirus" threat had nothing to do with the coronavirus.

Chapter Three

THE INITIAL "CORONAVIRUS" WAS A SOCIALIST POLITICIAN

"Stocks always look ahead, often fairly far."

—Ken Fisher[32]

On October 29, 1929, the stock market crashed in the U.S. The Dow Jones Industrial Average fell over 12 percent.

Crucial about what happened is that stocks never just *crash*. They don't owing to the basic truth that stock markets are relentlessly processing information, all day, every day, at nights, on weekends, and even on holidays. Such is the world we live in that if there's news about a corporation, or the economy more broadly, it's near instantaneously reflected in stock prices. Markets don't wait.

The fact that stock markets are relentless processors of information is very telling when it comes to trying to understand big market corrections. Those corrections and crashes are invariably a consequence of new information. Better yet, they're an effect of *surprise*. It's only when entirely novel information reaches markets that share prices can make huge lurches upward or downward.

Looking back to 1929, the surprising news was word that President Hoover would indeed sign the Smoot-Hawley Tariff in 1930. The expectation up until October 1929 was that Hoover wouldn't commit such a grave error. Figure that the wise in the world of commerce had his ear.

Wall Street eminence Thomas Lamont recalled, "I almost went down on my knees to beg Herbert Hoover to veto the asinine Smoot-Hawley tariff." General Motors (GM) was the Apple, Amazon, or Alphabet (Google's parent company) of its time, or realistically all three combined in terms of its U.S. economic prominence, and according to economic historian Amity Shlaes, "Washington received 106 wires from forty-nine General Motors overseas offices in fifteen countries" warning against the tariff. GM's European head, Graeme K. Howard, was particularly blunt in his telegram. It said about Smoot-Hawley that "PASSAGE BILL WOULD SPELL ECONOMIC ISOLATION UNITED STATES AND MOST SEVERE DEPRESSION EVER EXPERIENCED."[33] In short, Hoover knew.

Yet he once again indicated in October 1929 that he would sign the hideous tariff bill in 1930. Stocks quickly corrected in gruesome fashion to reflect this sad truth. Markets once again don't wait, or, as billionaire investor Ken Fisher puts it in the quote that begins this chapter, "Stocks always look ahead, often fairly far." They certainly weren't going to wait until 1930 to process news that would most certainly affect stock prices over the long term.

So why was Smoot-Hawley so harmful, such that stock markets priced its horrors so quickly and so gruesomely? The answer could fill many books, but this one will be relatively brief.

To begin, if you're a worker, you're an *importer*. Simple as that. If you're working, what you produce represents your demand for all the

goods and services you want to exchange the fruits of your labor for. Whether you're importing from next door, across the street, or the other side of the world is of really no consequence. What matters is that in working, you are in the process of expressing your desire to *get things* in return for your toil.

Taking this basic truth further, imports are the *reward* for your work. That's why it really doesn't matter to you, the individual, whether the markets for your production (whether next door, across the street, or the other side of the world) are open. What you care about as the importer is that you have as many producers as possible competing to meet *your* needs. The more competition to serve you, the better for you. The more competition to serve you, the greater your daily *raises*.

Indeed, while you're working for money, you're in a very real sense working for what money can be exchanged for, as in goods and services. The fewer the barriers placed in the path of producers eager to serve you, the greater the amount of goods and services you can get in exchange for the money you earn for your work.

So while it would be great for you if there were no barriers put in your way as you're trying to produce for others, the biggest harm done to you is when politicians place barriers in the way of producers trying to meet *your* needs. It means your work is exchangeable for fewer goods and services.

Considering tariffs, think of them as a cruel tax on your work. A principal aim of work is to get things, and tariffs raise the cost of getting. Suddenly there's a tax paid on much of what you trade the fruits of your labor for, which means you get less.

To which some will reply that to take in money is not the sole purpose of their effort on the job. Some will describe work as something they can't not do. Future chapters will make exactly this case—that work gives our lives wondrous meaning. No doubt it does, which speaks volumes about how injurious were the actions of panicked politicians in response to the coronavirus.

But for now, it's worth asking why work is increasingly so fulfilling, so giving of meaning to so many. A major driver of work's appeal is openness to foreign production. Think about it. So long as producers of all stripes around the world are free to meet your needs, you have the greatest odds of doing the work that most uniquely elevates your talents. If you can import from others the goods and services you either can't create or can create only in lieu of doing what lifts you up the most, you have the best odds of doing the work that most amplifies your talents.

Is it any wonder then that word of Smoot-Hawley's eventual passage so thoroughly spooked investors? There shouldn't be.

In its final, economy-sapping form, Smoot-Hawley amounted to the imposition of record-level tariffs on twenty thousand-plus foreign goods bound for the United States.[34] Not only would the work of every American be taxed at record levels through the barriers put up to imports, those same barriers would slow the process whereby work in the U.S. would increasingly animate the skills of every American. Smoot-Hawley meant the daily raises for American workers would cease thanks to taxes, plus more expensive imports would slow the process whereby Americans left certain tasks to others so they could focus on the work that would elevate their brilliance the most. Tariffs slow cooperation among people that enables specialization by people.

Smoot-Hawley was a surprise in the sense that investors didn't realize until late October 1929 that President Hoover would do something so injurious to every American, and by extension, so damaging to the U.S. economy. Economies are just individuals, and individuals most certainly benefit the more that they're able to do the work that most amplifies their skills, all the while importing the most thanks to no barriers being erected to those eager to produce for them.

After that, competition is good. Competition doesn't injure businesses; rather, it lifts them. "Only the paranoid survive" is a line from the late Intel legend Andy Grove, and implicit in Grove's statement is that a lack of competition ultimately suffocates businesses. Competition

induces paranoia that someone, somewhere is in the process of stealing your business's market share. The paranoia drives immense creativity among business leaders, which sets them up for long-term survival.

Basically tariffs injure individuals three ways. They get less for their work, reduced division of labor with workers around the world means their daily toil isn't as specialized, and then businesses are just a collection of individuals. Without paranoia-inducing competition from around the world, there exists the greater possibility of business stagnation.

Smoot-Hawley was an unexpected development that, if signed into law, would plainly bring great harm to the U.S. economy that some naively presumed it would protect. Once what was unlikely was confirmed as highly likely on October 29, investors didn't wait for the signing ceremony. That which is billed to "protect" individuals by shielding them from discounts, specialization, and the reality of the marketplace has to be priced right away. And so it was. On October 29, 1929, U.S. stock markets crashed.

Bringing what happened close to a century ago back to the present, Ken Fisher routinely makes a crucial point in speeches given to rapt audiences: your bad news is already priced in the stock market. Whatever you think you know or whatever you think looms as a huge catalyst for a stock-market correction or surge is, if real information, already priced into stocks. So don't let what you know, or what you think you know, inform your investment decisions.

Fisher's sage thinking unsurprisingly didn't inform the thinking of market commentators the last week of February 2020. Stocks were plunging, and the headlines were nearly uniform about "coronavirus fears" being the cause of those plunges. The headlines didn't make sense.

They didn't because, per Fisher, the coronavirus was already a known. And in a very big way. It had been in the news since January 2020. Better yet, some of the bluest of U.S. blue chip companies like FedEx had, as Chapter One of this book makes plain, fairly substantial operations in the epicenter of this new virus. Equity markets are yet again relentless processors of information, and as FedEx is a public company, in concert with it being a bellwether for global economic growth (think shipping), if the virus had revealed itself as a major or even minor destroyer of life, this truth would have already been known. And priced into U.S. shares.

After which readers might consider Apple Computer. Apple rates strong consideration when it comes to understanding the market correction in the last week of February 2020, along with Amazon, Alphabet, Facebook, and Microsoft. Those five companies were the main driver—by far—of the bull market in shares that took place between March 2009 and February 2020. Take those five companies out of the S&P, and there really wasn't much of a bull market to speak of.[35]

Important here is that Apple announced in the third week of February 2020 that the coronavirus development might limit manufacture and sales of its products.[36] Better yet, Apple's most successful product, the iPhone, is hugely popular in China. Indeed, one-fifth of iPhones are sold there.[37] In short, Apple's news had already been digested as stocks in the U.S. touched all-time highs. If China had been experiencing crushing death from the virus, this would have reflected in the prices of Apple shares. That it didn't was instructive. It should be added that it was already in the news at the same time that Amazon, fearful of supply disruptions, would be increasing its near-term purchases of inventory with coronavirus-related disruptions in mind.

Despite all this news in the marketplace, there wasn't a major correction in shares. While readers are hopefully bringing all manner of different opinions about the coronavirus to their read of this book, it's undeniable that investors had been pricing its impact on the U.S. economy long before the last week of February. By then, the virus was going to be an American reality one way or the other given how open of a country the United States is. Yet stocks were bouncing around their all-time highs amid rapid processing of news about a virus with Chinese origins. This tells us that the headlines the last week of February were errant, to say the least. Markets lurch in either direction once again based on surprise, and coronavirus was no longer that.

Still, stocks declined a fair amount on February 20 and 21, and then share declines picked up speed on the 24th and 25th. Something new jolted investors that seemingly wasn't apparent to them midway through the previous week. What was it?

In aiming to answer the question, it should be said that doing so is a fool's errand for anyone. That's why headlines about what caused stocks to go up or down are so ridiculous in real time and often preposterous when looked at in hindsight. If headline writers possessed a clue about what moves stocks, or even if they possessed a clue about whom to ask about what moves stocks, they wouldn't be headline writers.

That's a long way of saying that the assertion you're about to read is a speculation. At the same time, it cannot be stressed enough that surprise moves markets. In that case, what was the surprising new information in the second to last week of February 2020, and what was the surprise that further spooked investors over the weekend?

For a clue on the presumed surprise, readers should first look back in time to 2015 and 2016. At the time, Donald Trump was making a big, and rather unexpected, political splash. Odd about his polling strength was that he was doing well among Republicans even though his rhetoric was anti-immigration and anti-trade—plus it was in all too many ways pro–big government. Markets corrected at varying times amid news about Trump's strength, and one investor explained to your author what was happening rather succinctly: "Market's probability of Trump as president in June? Zero percent. Today, say what you will, maybe 10 percent. At least that is what various prediction markets are saying. So, I need to discount 10 percent."

Early on Trump's candidacy was viewed by the wisest of the wise as a joke until it was no longer a joke. Needless to say, Trump's electoral strength was real, it became progressively more real, and investors had to price this unexpected development.

Considering the second to last week in February, for quite some time media members had been marveling at the hundreds of millions spent by Michael Bloomberg, a wildly successful and economically moderate Democratic candidate for president of the United States. Though Bloomberg hadn't participated in the Iowa and New Hampshire primaries, it was broadly assumed that he was a major contender for the Democratic nomination, and precisely because he's worth tens of billions, Bloomberg was seen as a much more than reasonable opponent of Trump. Capitalist versus capitalist, though in Bloomberg's case he could buy and sell Trump many, many times over. Better yet, success for Bloomberg in the Democratic primaries would signal that the Democrats had seen semi-socialists in Bernie Sanders and Elizabeth Warren, only to reject their rather expansive vision of government, in concert with Sanders's particular disdain for business and businessmen. In choosing a billionaire businessman, Democratic voters would be saying that while progressive, they recognize the importance of capitalistic achievement to progress, and that they recognize the need to limit government somewhat.

Yet in the February 19, 2020, Democratic presidential debates in Nevada, Bloomberg was thoroughly attacked by his opponents precisely because his opponents sensed he was ascending to front-runner status. The big problem was that Bloomberg allowed himself to be throttled. And he was throttled despite it being known that he had the best, most seasoned advisors preparing him for the attacks that everyone knew were coming. Bloomberg's performance was roundly panned, and in the estimation of more than a few pundits, Bloomberg's candidacy was rendered a past tense concept. In short, the lone capitalist on the Democratic side was pushed aside during the Democratic debates—debates from which a rising semi-socialist in Sanders emerged largely unscathed. Keep in mind that Sanders emerged unscathed even though he basically tied Pete Buttigieg in Iowa and beat the former South Bend mayor in New Hampshire.

Oh well, the crushing of Bloomberg in concert with continued strength for a semi-socialist had to be priced by investors. Some felt at the time that Sanders had no chance of winning the White House, but the wise said the same about Trump. Sanders's success had to be accounted for, and markets went south on February 20 and 21. And then on Saturday the 22nd, investors were confronted with an even bigger surprise: not only was Sanders the front-runner in the Democratic presidential primary, he was the front-runner in *dominant fashion.*

Readers must understand Sanders's dominant Nevada win in the context of national elections. While presidents aren't dictators, and while they must invariably govern from the center, Sanders would have been a big departure from Trump in an economic sense. Trump, despite his frequent departure from market-oriented orthodoxy, was ultimately more market-friendly in his actions than his rhetoric indicated. Sanders? Who knew, particularly at the time? The only thing investors knew as February came to a close was that Sanders's long-shot status was no longer as long-shot as was once assumed. And since it wasn't, investors always looking into the future had to price in the possibility of major change in Washington—major change that would have a global impact. This very credibly explains a global rout for shares. Sanders was a big surprise that investors had to price.

If readers are still skeptical, consider what happened next. As news about the coronavirus continued to be priced by investors, the Democrats held their South Carolina primary on Saturday, February 29. Joe Biden won and did so in dominant fashion. Seen as moderate relative to Sanders's socialist-leaning radicalism, Biden's victory was seen as a sign that Sanders's candidacy wasn't nearly as inevitable as was once assumed.

On Monday, March 2, the Dow Jones Industrial Average surged 1,290 points—its largest ever one-day point gain.[38] Investors had looked into the future, and they'd deduced (correctly as Biden's ongoing strength among Democrats revealed) that the next president of the United States would not be a socialist. In closing, the initial coronavirus scare that wasn't was a senator from Vermont.

The true coronavirus scare was yet to come, but as readers are likely starting to see, the coronavirus scare quite simply wasn't. Politicians panicked.

Chapter Four

THEY WOULDN'T SHUT DOWN THE ECONOMY, WOULD THEY?

"There's so much to say but my mind keeps going back to New Year's Eve, when we watched the ball come down and knew the story of 2020 was the presidential election and whatever stray harassments history throws our way. No one that night guessed—no one could have guessed—that in the next few months we'd have a world-wide pandemic, an economic catastrophe, and fighting in the streets."

—Peggy Noonan, *Wall Street Journal*, June 6–7, 2020[39]

On October 19, 1987, the U.S. stock market crashed. The Dow Jones Industrial Average fell 508 points.

Hopefully by now readers are immediately wondering what surprise entered the picture to alter the sentiment about U.S. shares so substantially in such short order. Keep in mind that the DJIA's decline was *22.6 percent*.[40] The crash in 1929 was small by comparison at 12 percent.

So again, what was the surprise?

For one, on October 13, 1987, the House Ways and Means Committee floated a plan to essentially stop corporate takeovers by making the tax treatment of them intensely onerous.[41] This rates mention simply because U.S. shares had already reacted negatively earlier in the month to this still existent possibility.

Corporate takeovers are essential for economic progress for those moving precious assets into the hands of individuals with more expansive ideas for them. Ridding the U.S. of takeovers would shrink the ways that innovative thinkers could vivify great ideas through the accession of precious resources.

Added to fears about the tax treatment of takeovers, there was growing fear of "trade deficits." About these so-called deficits, there's really no such thing. An economy is just individuals, as has previously been discussed, and with trade our individual "imports" mirror our individual "exports" in dollar terms. For you the reader, you run a trade "surplus" with your employer or employers, and your employers run a trade "deficit" with you. This doesn't harm your employer; presumably you receive a paycheck because your value to the business you work for exceeds your compensation.

At the same time, you the worker are an "importer," as the previous chapter explains. Your imports are the *rewards* for your work. You once again run a trade surplus with your employer, but you run trade "deficits" with your favorite restaurants, clothiers, television manufacturers, carmakers, and the like. You work diligently to expand the "deficits" you run with the myriad individuals and businesses around the U.S. and around the world who work to meet your needs.

As for country trade "deficits," Americans can import more than they export solely because the U.S. export of shares in its world-leading corporations is so abundant. Translated, the most valuable companies in the world are mostly U.S.-based. Investors around the world line up to purchase shares in U.S. companies. This "export" of shares in the world's greatest companies doesn't count in a trade balance that shouldn't be calculated as is, but American import of shoes, socks, T-shirts, and televisions from around the world *does* count in the trade balance. In short, the trade "deficits" that excited some in the 1980s were of no consequence other than as a signal of just how attractive the U.S. was as an investment destination. Export of shares resulted, and still results, in the import of abundance from around the world. Our trade "deficits" are the wondrous result of massive investment in the U.S. Yes, *they're healthy*. There are no companies and no jobs without investment first, so the deficits signaled soaring economic strength in the U.S.

The shame then, and the shame now, is that some politicians didn't see what was undeniably good in a good light. In 1987 this revealed itself in growing political fear of Japan. This increasingly prosperous country, which had grown prosperous by meeting the consumptive desires of acquisitive Americans, had some politicians fearful. By 1987 there was growing talk of tariffs to be levied on Japan. Readers can hopefully sense where this is going based on the previous chapter.

Tariffs penalize work, and worse, they penalize workers for the tax on imports slowing the process whereby those "protected" by tariffs divide up labor with the global labor force. The slow-footing of labor's division acts as a weight on the ability of the worker to specialize his work, which means it acts as a negative barrier to increased productivity. After that, paranoia is healthy. Extraordinarily so. Tariffs neuter the corporate competition from around the world that induces paranoia, which means tariffs weaken the corporations they're falsely billed to protect. Investors understand this well as evidenced by the 12 percent correction in 1929 in response to confirmation that the Smoot-Hawley tariffs would soon be signed into law.

Fast forward to 1987, powerful congressman Richard Gephardt was energetically promoting Super 301 legislation in Washington that would require countries with "trade surpluses" vis-à-vis the United States to shrink them. Oh well, countries don't trade. Furthermore, we already know that trade "surpluses" are of no real consequence. Trade "deficits" yet again signal massive investment inflows into a country, which is a certain sign of economic health. Gephardt's saber-rattling necessarily spooked investors fearful that tariffs would be used to shrink the economy-enhancing "deficits."[42]

And then there was U.S. Treasury Secretary James Baker. Though it's common in modern times for pundits to suggest that the Federal Reserve manages the dollar as part of its policy portfolio, the central bank has never had exchange rate oversight—often to its frustration. Presidents largely get the dollar they want through their oversight of the dollar's market mouthpiece, the U.S. Treasury.

In 1987, U.S. equity markets were already on edge owing to fear of corporate takeover curbs and tariffs. Then as now, some believed that imports were hurting the U.S. economy. The very notion was, and is, an impossibility. To "import" is the purpose of our work, and the more competition to meet our needs the better. It doesn't matter where the products come from. Figure that most of us don't live in Cupertino, CA (where Apple is based), or Seattle, WA (where Amazon is based), but we're not harmed because we don't live where each company headquarters. Just the same, we're not harmed because some companies headquarter outside the United States. We work to get things, period.

This rates mention yet again because the view among some who incorrectly felt imports (from Japan in particular) were harmful was that dollar devaluation would limit imports into the U.S. while boosting exports out of the U.S. A "cheap dollar" would supposedly make the U.S. economy more competitive. Such a view quickly collapses under its own myriad contradictions.

For one, Americans earn dollars. How would it improve the individuals who make up the economy for the fruits of their work to be shrunken so that they buy fewer goods and services? To which some will reply that a weak dollar would make U.S. goods and services cheaper for foreign buyers, but that, too, contradicts logic. Every good and service is a consequence of inputs from around the world, so the wholly illusory competitive gains from devaluation would be erased by increased costs of production. And then there's investment.

Investment is the driver of increased productivity. Think of the smartphone you own. Does it enable greater productivity on the job and in life than the brick-size phone from the 1980s and 1990s—a phone that was out of reach for most as it was? The question answers itself. Why is today's smartphone so much more advanced than those brick phones? Investment.

All this must be said early on in *When Politicians Panicked* to make a simple case for what is blindingly simple: investment is what drives economic growth. Without savings directed toward the improvement of existing goods and services, along with the creation of new goods and services, all progress stops.

What are investors buying when they invest? They're buying investment returns denominated in currencies. Most often they're buying dollar returns in the future. Since they are, it's no reach to point out that dollar devaluation is frequently harmful to the U.S. economy simply because it puts a bull's-eye on the very investors whose capital commitments make progress possible.

Looked at in terms of 1987, there was much brinksmanship among monetary authorities about currency values, interest rates, and the currency values sometimes affected by the level of interest rates. Amid this conflict, Treasury Secretary Baker was interviewed on the Sunday morning political talk show, *Meet the Press*. The date was October 18, 1987. Baker announced that "we will not sit back in this country and watch surplus countries jack up interest rates and squeeze growth worldwide on the expectation that the United States somehow will follow by raising its interest rates."[43]

So while there isn't any kind of consistent correlation between currency valuations and interest rates targeted by central banks, Baker's statement was seen at the time as a strong statement that Treasury wanted a weaker dollar, and better yet, if the dollar declined that Treasury wouldn't intervene in that decline via Treasury's Exchange Stabilization Fund. The next day, and as previously mentioned, the Dow Jones Industrial Average plunged 508 points to 1,738.

Baker's statement was quite something. And a bit of a surprise. Devalue the dollar? From a Reagan official? Ronald Reagan had run for president in 1980 while routinely making plain at campaign stops that "no nation in history has ever survived fiat money, money that did not have precious metal backing."[44] Reagan's presidency was arguably a major consequence of electoral frustration with a falling dollar in the 1970s that had eviscerated the earnings and savings of every American, and that had logically correlated in flat nominal returns for equity investors.

As venture capitalist Peter Thiel so pithily explained it in his classic 2014 book, *Zero to One*, "The value of a business today is the sum of all the money it will make in the future."[45] A corporation's value is an effect of investor speculation about all the dollars that corporation will earn. Devaluation shrinks the value of those earnings and, by extension, a corporation's valuation. Baker's statement, one surely vetted in the White House, was a departure from Reaganite rhetoric, plus it was a surprise. Combined with fears of tariffs and anti-takeover legislation, worried investors seemingly had no choice but to price perilous information into equity prices.

Notable is that by 1987's end, more than half of what the Dow gave up on October 19 had been retrieved. Investors had been surprised by some negative information coming from Washington, but it hadn't come to pass. Anti-takeover legislation never took shape, Gephardt didn't get his tariffs, and the dollar didn't collapse. Investors caught their breath.

All of this rates as a backdrop for the spring of 2020 as a way of showing that the bad and good are constantly being priced. It's frequently been said that the coronavirus or COVID-19 stock market correction was nearly a month in length stretching from February 19 to March 23. Except that's not what happened.

As the previous chapter makes plain, there were two different corrections. The new coronavirus had long been in the news by late February, which makes it unrealistic to tie market corrections from February 19 on to the virus. As noted at the end of Chapter Three, the Dow Jones Industrial Average had its biggest nominal point gain in history (1,290) after Joe Biden halted the inevitability of a socialist Democratic candidate by the name of Bernie Sanders.

Still, stocks certainly corrected in sick-inducing fashion after the March 2 "Biden rally." So what was the surprise?

To understand what it was, consider what the world knew as of March 2. For one, there was no longer fear that there would be an electoral surprise of the socialist variety on November 3, 2020. As for the coronavirus, there was no powerful evidence of any kind coming from Wuhan, or China more broadly, that the virus was a major exterminator of life. Going back to Chapter One, the nature of technology as of 2020 would have made it impossible for the Chinese government to hide news like this.

Crucial here is that what the Chinese government might have wanted to hide would have been revealed by market realities in the United States. The previous truth cannot be stressed enough. As of 2019, China was Apple's third largest market, representing $52 billion in sales for the U.S. technology giant. For Qualcomm, 65 percent of its sales come from China, 24 percent for Intel, and 44 percent for Texas Instruments.[46]

Considering cars, General Motors sells more of them in China than it does in North America. And while U.S. consumers represent $12 billion in annual box office for Hollywood studios, China is not far behind at $9 billion.[47]

Shoe and apparel company Nike has a massive presence in China. Not only are more Nike shoes produced there than in any other country, the once desperately poor nation is now the second largest market for Nike products.[48] As of February 2020, Starbucks could claim 4,290 stores in China.[49] Notable about both Nike's and Starbucks's major presence in China is that in January and February, when the virus was most prevalent in the rising country, the share prices of both companies were firmly at fifty-two-week highs. This would not have been true if the virus had proved a major or even moderate killer.

U.S. market calm despite enormous exposure among U.S. companies to China paired well with calm from U.S. authorities, both political and medical. In late January, Anthony Fauci, director of the National Institute of Allergy and Infectious Diseases, told a radio host that the coronavirus represented "very, very low risk to the United States."[50] The World Health Organization (WHO) similarly observed that the virus's threat to health was meek.[51]

President Donald Trump had described the virus as "not a big deal," but he wasn't alone in the matter.[52] Hard left *New York Times* columnist Farhad Manjoo, boosted by information gleaned from WHO, asserted that his real concern wasn't sickness from the virus, "but the amped-up, ill-considered way our frightened world might respond to it." Manjoo expressed worry about "unnecessarily severe limits on movement and on civil liberties," and that politicians might "begin pushing for travel bans, overbroad quarantines, or other measures that might not be supported by the science."[53] Translating for readers, Manjoo, like Trump, feared overreaction.

Jonathan Tobin, a contributor to conservative publication *National Review*, noted that after Manjoo's late January column, the *Times'* editorial board didn't mention the virus again for another month, on February 29, when the board still displayed a lack of alarm as evidenced by the assertion that "there is still a chance that COVID-19 will be more fire drill than actual fire." Tobin reported that on the same day, *Times* columnist Nicholas Kristof was still hedging himself with reasoning all-too-often attributed to the right about how "thousands routinely die annually from the seasonal flu," and that the virus "may still fizzle."[54]

Just as Trump was skeptical about any kind of substantial death toll from the virus, so was New York City Mayor Bill de Blasio, even though New York state could claim as of June 11, 7 percent of the world's presumed death toll from the virus and 27 percent of the U.S. total. Presumed is used here given the frequency that those who passed with the virus could also claim other major health maladies. About this, it should be repeated right here that this book's argument, whether the virus was intensely lethal of the walked-back Imperial College kind, or not so lethal per skeptics, would have been the same. Particularly if a virus is lethal, there's no need for forced lockdowns of any kind. People once again don't need a law to protect their health.

Back to de Blasio, on March 2, 2020, he tweeted that "people should go see a movie."[55] The *New York Times* reported in May 2020 that de Blasio was still "resisting calls in March to cancel large gatherings," and that until the middle of March de Blasio "did not order major closures, including of schools and restaurants."[56] To be clear, none of what's been reported here is meant as an indictment of the mayor, Trump, Manjoo, Kristof, and all manner of conservatives who expressed skepticism or a lack of major concern about the coronavirus. That there was no news of major death out of the virus's epicenter as of March, that a substantial employer in Wuhan could thankfully claim no deaths from the virus as of March 18 (and plainly much sooner), was a fairly strong signal that the virus thankfully wasn't a major killer. To believe otherwise is to believe equity markets aggressively process all known information but chose to take a powder on what was happening inside a country that could claim the world's second largest economy, China—whose economy is a major driver of economic vitality and equity market vitality stateside.

The reason for reporting all of what's been reported about reactions to the virus is to make a case that as February 2020 came to a close, there was little investor worry about the impact of the coronavirus on the U.S. economy. We know this because as the month closed, there was little alarm in the media, among doctors, or from politicians. The Dow Jones Industrial Average yet again rallied 1,290 points on March 2, the Monday after Biden's resounding victory over Sanders in the South Carolina primary.

But then politicians panicked. On March 6 South by Southwest was canceled in Austin, TX, by Mayor Steve Adler, thus devastating all manner of businesses and workers in the city and state.[57] Equity markets look into the future, and in a sense the cancellation of South by Southwest heralded more of the same around the country. By March 19 a stay-at-home order was imposed in California, Texas's was imposed on March 31, and Florida's came a day later.[58] New York ordered shelter-in-place on March 20, only for Connecticut, Illinois, and New Jersey to quickly follow suit.[59] Crucial is that the lockdowns were strict. For instance, on March 19 Pennsylvania Governor Tom Wolf ordered that all "non-life-sustaining businesses" be closed, plus threatened "enforcement actions" against businesses that stayed open."[60] Perhaps impressed by Wolf's flexing of government muscle, on March 24 Los Angeles Mayor Eric Garcetti announced that water and power would be shut off for "nonessential" businesses in the City of Angels.[61]

Some will point out that all manner of voluntary closures happened too. Major League Baseball postponed its season, the NBA interrupted its season, NCAA college basketball conference championships were interrupted before completion, ahead of cancellation of March Madness. Disney amusement parks, among others, closed. It's all true, and this truth will be addressed in a future chapter. For now, it's worth simply asking if, absent panic among politicians and scientists, the response from the sports and entertainment world might have been more muted.

The main thing, however, is that a formerly dynamic U.S. economy that had been soaring just a month before was suddenly reduced to limited economic activity, in most instances *by force*. Readers should try to contemplate this in terms of stock markets. Is it any wonder that they corrected so fast? While doctors, politicians, and pundits had just weeks before expressed varying degrees of insouciance about the virus, out of nowhere the world's most prosperous nation went into lockdown. There's your correction.

Unknown is why the panic. Again, by March there was no news evidence of major lethality where the virus had begun, thus raising a question of why the lapse of reason stateside? Furthermore, how odd for politicians to fight potential illness and death with unemployment, bankruptcy, and mass desperation. Historically economic growth had been the greatest foe of disease, yet in a panic that future historians will marvel at, politicians on the local, state, and national levels chose to express their hysteria in the form of forced contraction.

Which is where this chapter will end. *Forced contraction.* This was not a recession. As the next chapter will make plain, the lockdowns born of panic had nothing to do with recession.

Chapter Five

PLEASE DO NOT INSULT RECESSIONS BY REFERRING TO THIS AS A RECESSION

"Thus I like to say success carries within itself the seeds of failure, and failure the seeds of success."

—Howard Marks, *Mastering the Market Cycle*[62]

In 1980 the supergroup Fleetwood Mac was on yet another one of its extravagant world tours. Band patriarch Mick Fleetwood was dating Sara Recor at the time, and this was problematic simply because Fleetwood had taken up with Recor while seeing bandmate (and close Recor friend) Stevie Nicks on the relative quiet. Nicks said she wouldn't go on tour if her ex-friend were traveling with Fleetwood.

Nicks's ultimatum ultimately proved expensive (in a relative sense, of course) for the band during its tour stop in Japan. One night Fleetwood, having another row with a frustrated-to-be-left-at-home Recor, stayed up all night arguing with her and presumably placating her. Keep in mind that this was the 1980s. The call cost *$2,000.* [63]

The $2,000 call wasn't the only extravagance for a band that had seemingly lost its way. Trite as it may sound, extravagance had consumed the music. As Stevie Nicks biographer Stephen Davis described it in his 2017 book, *Gold Dust Woman*, the 1980 Fleetwood Mac tour was a monument to waste. The band had "some of the most expensive hotels in the world repaint their presidential suites and install grand pianos for Stevie and Christine. Stevie's concert wardrobe—six costume changes per show—cost well into the fix figures. The tour's contractual refreshment rider stipulated gargantuan backstage buffets that no one hardly ever touched because they were running on the priciest Peruvian cocaine and could hardly look at food, let alone eat. The backstage bar bill at each show could have sent someone to college for a year. Their flights were met by so many black stretch limos—one for each band member and even some of the support people—that their hotel convoys looked like funeral corteges."[64]

Fleetwood Mac in 1980 brought new, descriptive meaning to decadence. The band's tour was one of the most expensive ever for its time. Sadly, at the end of the extravaganza, the finance whizzes couldn't report any profits for all the effort. This is what happens when no mind is paid to expense. Traveling by private chartered jet, it was noted by Davis that sometimes "the empty jet had been sent to LA to fetch a cocaine dealer on the band's payroll to renew supplies in Midwestern cities."[65]

The architect of this disaster was band patriarch Fleetwood. Nicks and other bandmates maneuvered his ouster as manager of the band at tour's conclusion when it became apparent that there were no profits to distribute. Everything would be done by committee going forward. Fleetwood was so financially wrecked by his own mismanagement and an inability to say no to Nicks et al. that he had to sell his Bel-Air Mansion. After the meeting during which Fleetwood was relieved of his duties, he went out to the back garden of his soon-to-be-sold house and cried.[66]

Fleetwood Mac the band and Mick Fleetwood the individual were in the midst of a recession. Call it an extraordinarily extravagant recession, but a recession nonetheless. At the same time, it rates stress that the recession was *healthy*. Thank goodness for it. Unhealthy was what happened before the band realized its incredibly wasteful tour had lost money.

The band had once again lost its way. It wasn't just the hotel rooms, the drugs, and the total cluelessness about costs. Figure that the tour was in support of the band's double album, *Tusk*. It was released amid a recession for the United States itself. The double album that was beyond the reach of many consumers in some ways symbolized a band that was plainly out of touch.

This little anecdote about Fleetwood Mac will ideally cause readers to rethink recessions. Painful as they are, they're a sign of *recovery*. Recessions signal rebirth, a fixing of errors previously made. When Mick Fleetwood went to his back garden to cry, it was a realization of mistakes made. The recession was the cure. Fleetwood was relieved of responsibilities, he lost his main house, addictions had to be dealt with. The agonies the band endured based on mistakes made in the good times set the stage for the bad times. At the same time, the bad times, the times of tears, were necessary so that the band could remake itself.

Considering Pixar, arguably the most successful film studio ever (*Toy Story, Finding Nemo, The Incredibles*, and so on), the mantra inside this Northern California personification of creativity is that "people need to be wrong as fast as they can." Those are the words of writer/director Andrew Stanton. Stanton's explanation of how things work at Pixar amounts to a succinct explanation for why recessions are frequently so short when they pass *untouched*. If mistakes are rushed to, then fixes are quickly made.

Pixar founder Ed Catmull writes in his autobiography, *Creativity, Inc.*, that "there is nothing like a crisis" to "bring what ails a company to the surface." One reason Catmull has achieved so much has to do with the fact that he and his senior colleagues are constantly self-evaluating, evaluating one another, and encouraging the company's employees to evaluate them. Catmull acknowledges throughout his business memoir that he's almost uncomfortable when a film production is going very well given his belief that success can obscure the errors that will turn today's blue chip into tomorrow's forgotten company. Rather than seek political cover from their mistakes, Catmull and his colleagues choose to profit from the inevitable production crises by virtue of embracing the correctable mistakes that they unearth.

Though Catmull and colleagues are not "economists," it's reasonable to suggest that they understand economics much better than do those with PhDs next to their names. Real economists routinely call for intervention, for government fixes of all kinds to lift up an economy that's listing. Years ago at a Hoover Institution session hosted by senior fellow Kevin Warsh, an audience that included your author was told by Warsh that amid the most worrisome times of 2008, Fed Chairman Ben Bernanke instructed Warsh et al. to essentially "try everything." Is it a surprise that the U.S. economy was so slow to revive amid all this intervention from the Fed, Congress, President Bush, President Obama, and everyone else with access to the money and swagger created by "others" in the private sector? Certainly not.

Though Catmull is likely too modest to presume to comment on economic matters, it seems he would intuitively understand why the 1930s was a difficult economic decade by American standards, as were the years after 2008. Mistakes are crucial for progress. When we learn what we're doing wrong and fix what we're doing wrong, we improve.

On the other hand, when we have the means to just throw money at our mistakes, or if government throws money at our mistakes, we're potentially robbed of the learning that will propel us to a better place.

Economies gain strength from periods of weakness precisely because so much forced improvement takes place during periods of weakness.

Looking back a hundred years, the U.S. economy recessed in a major way in 1920–21. Unemployment soared all the way to 11.3 percent. But this recession is rarely mentioned in history books, and it isn't because it was so short. That it was short was a consequence of Congress and President Warren Harding's "do nothing" response.

Contrary to popular opinion today that says governments must spend with abandon during times of hardship, back then federal spending was slashed from $6.4 billion in 1920 all the way to $3.3 billion in 1923.[67] As will be discussed frequently in future chapters, government spending amounts to government planning the allocation of resources (trucks, tractors, computers, desks, chairs, buildings, labor most importantly, and so on) always and everywhere produced in the private sector. In short, the response from politicians to a deep recession one hundred years ago was correct. With the economy weak, the federal government wisely shrank its economic footprint, thus allowing the market economy to expand its own.

Also contrary to popular opinion today that says governments must devalue the currency during times of hardship, back then the dollar's integrity was maintained.[68] With the previous chapter in mind, the decision of the Treasury and President Harding to not debase the dollar was instrumental in the 1920s recovery. Investment powers economic growth, and investors are buying future returns in dollars when they commit capital, so efforts taken to reduce the value of those future returns through devaluation amount to a tax or penalty placed on investment. The protection of the dollar in the 1920s was a signal to the investors who make economic progress possible that they didn't need to add devaluation to their list of worries.

This do-nothing response whereby less-than-nothing was realistically done proved very wise. By 1923 unemployment had fallen to 1.7 percent, and the "Roaring Twenties" took flight.[69] That the economy soared shouldn't surprise readers. Economies are just people. People do best when, in the midst of slow times, they're forced to fix what's wrong, as opposed to being shielded from it. Governmental responses to recessions meant to soften the blow of contraction enable individuals and corporations to be somewhat blind to what they're doing wrong. The oblivion doesn't erase the pain as much as it softens it enough only to extend it.

Which brings us to billionaire investor Howard Marks, one of the founders of Oaktree Capital Management. A quote by him begins this chapter. Marks has long made the point that we make our biggest blunders during the good times only for those blunders to be corrected during the more desperate periods. Marks's correct vision of recession and recovery requires discussion in light of what happened in the spring of 2020. *It wasn't a recession.*

What happened was that by March 22, 2020, over one-fifth of the U.S. economy was on lockdown. By then, more than 20 percent of Americans had been told to cease activity outside their place of residence. The individuals decreeing the inability of tens of millions to work, produce, and provide were politicians on the local, state, and national level.

On March 22, Governor Jay Pritzker of Illinois joined California and New York governors Gavin Newsom and Andrew Cuomo in telling residents to stay at home altogether.[70] Let's please keep in mind that California alone, if a country, would rank as the world's fifth largest economy.[71] On March 31 Texas joined the lockdown club, followed by Florida the next day.[72] Remember that if Texas were a country, it would claim the world's tenth largest economy. [73]

This wasn't a recession. What happened was an imposition of command-and-control that has always suffocated economic growth. Recessions are healthy and force the change that leads to better economic times. Command-and-control just asphyxiates. It's not as though the Iron Curtain countries that endured command-and-control in the twentieth century enjoyed periods of boom followed by bust. When government is suffocating economic activity, or disallowing it, there's no boom/bust to speak of. There's just bust.

Coming back to recessions, during good or booming economic times it's not unreasonable to suggest that the individuals who compose any economy sometimes develop bad personal and work habits. At the same time, companies are willing to take bigger risks in terms of how they expand and the individuals they hire, along with how many they hire. Banks and investment banks similarly are forced to reach somewhat. Precisely because there's more competition to make loans and to finance new and existing companies, capital allocators reach too. So do they with investments. That they do is somewhat logical. Money flows and lending may be denominated in dollars, but they signal the movement of goods, services, and labor. During good times production of goods and services grows, as frequently do labor forces, and all of this is revealed through credit expansion.

Recessions, far from a terrifying sign, actually just signal a broad realization of errors by individuals and corporations. Recessions signal recovery precisely because they signal the correction of the mistakes made during the good times.

That they do explains the corollary to Marks's point: during troubled times we lay the groundwork for better. Yet again errors are corrected of the expansion, hiring, investment, and lending variety; bad personal habits are nipped; bad hires that don't fit for companies and individuals alike are released into the market economy in search of better matches; plus individuals and businesses shore up their personal financial situations. The Keynesian (John Maynard Keynes) thinkers who dominate the economics profession believe consumption powers economic growth, but as the mildly sentient among us know well, investment is yet again the true driver of growth, consumption the consequence. Measures like GDP that are popular among economists are monuments to double counting. Crucial about investment is that it's a logical consequence of savings, which explains why good times emerge from the bad. As individuals and corporations shrink their outgoings, capital formation grows, thus setting the stage for growing amounts of investment that puts an economy once again on a growth path.

All this rates mention in consideration of the enormous amount of ink that was spilled by economists and pundits about the coronavirus "recession." They knew not of what they spoke, nor do they to this day when they describe what happened as a recession. Recessions are a flashing sign of a boom on the way born of feverish correction of work habits, while lockdowns signal cessation of production or forced limitation of production. Stated simply, the U.S. economy of March 22 (when Illinois joined the lockdown trend) was very different from the one of, say, February 22. That one was largely free, while the "coronavirus economy," if we can insult the word economy with what happened, was defined by government planning of economic activity.

Basically, in March 2020 matchlessly foolish politicians were to varying degrees not allowing individuals and businesses to work and produce. Good times didn't bring on the needless horror show we were forced to endure; rather, this contraction was a consequence of way-too-powerful politicians decreeing the work of all too many illegal.

To be clear, what reared its brutally ugly head was contraction born of monumental political error. Good history, necessary history, will make this screamingly apparent. There was never in 2020 an economic crisis born of a spreading virus; rather, a spreading virus proved oxygen for politicians on all levels on the way to them forcing contraction on an economy that, if large and growing larger, would have been best positioned to slay the virus.

Fascinating and sad about the crack-up overseen by politicians on the city, state, and national level was the response of normally market-friendly conservatives. Despite the contraction plainly resulting from a massive governmental boot being placed on the proverbial neck of the U.S. economy, left and right got to work on creating governmental responses to what was already a problem of too much government.

Government was suffocating the economy, at which point left and right were oddly calling for government solutions. The very central planning that conservatives decry in normal times oddly made sense to them in a crisis that was a creation of central planning. This shockingly obtuse thinking quickly revealed itself through someone already mentioned in this chapter, former Fed Vice Chairman Kevin Warsh. He called for empowering the very federal government that helped create the hideous contraction. Members of the left, like Andrew Ross Sorkin of the *New York Times* and Harvard professor Jason Furman—formerly chair of Barack Obama's Council of Economic Advisers (CEA)—didn't surprise anyone in their call for a massive governmental response.

The joke was on Warsh, Sorkin, Furman, and countless others in high places who called for all manner of central bank and government "stimulus." It seems they missed the simple truth that government spending is a consequence of private sector economic activity, yet the private sector was being suffocated by the very politicians that economic types on the left and right sought to empower. To witness the policy hysterics was to wish it were a bad dream. Except that bad dreams are never this awful. Various proposals from both sides will be addressed in future chapters.

Most important as this chapter closes is that there was no recession. Let's please not insult what happened with a word that has everything to do with recovery. Recessions signal something better on the way. Command-and-control economies designed by hapless politicians and central bankers signal agonizing economic decline without endpoint. Worse was that politicians goaded by policy elites aimed to pile on their imposition of command-and-control by making the federal government the primary allocator of wealth always and everywhere created in the private sector.

Chapter Six

THERE'S NO SUCH THING
AS "GOVERNMENT
SPENDING"

"The state is that great fiction by which everyone tries to live at the expense of everyone else."

—Frédéric Bastiat, *The Law*

66 **I**'ve joked about the fact that I want to build a wall around West Virginia and keep all the kids here. A state can't flourish that can't keep its young people there." So said West Virginia University president Gordon Gee in June 2020 to the *New York Times*.[74] The state's politicians would have benefited from his wise counsel long before his quip.

For background on why, West Virginia Senator Robert Byrd died in 2010 as the longest serving senator in U.S. history. While in office, Byrd amassed enormous power such that he was able to shower West Virginia's citizenry with all manner of government largesse. You see, Byrd was a powerful member of a prominent branch of the federal government, and that same federal government arrogates to itself trillions worth of private sector production annually through its taxing power. Byrd had long played a major role in the spending decisions of a federal government that is backed by the world's most economically productive people.

As former American Enterprise Institute president Arthur Brooks reported in his 2006 book, *Who Really Cares*, evidence of Byrd's generosity with the money of others is all over the state. There's the Robert C. Byrd Highway System, the Robert C. Byrd Bridge, the Robert C. Byrd Expressway, the Robert C. Byrd Federal Building, the Robert C. Byrd Health and Wellness Center, the Robert C. Byrd Institute for Advanced Flexible Manufacturing, along with countless schools, service centers, rest stops on West Virginia highways, and so on.[75] Byrd delivered copious amounts of federal spending to the state but did not deliver prosperity. West Virginia remains one of the U.S.'s poorest states and is a monument to the flawed thinking popular among pundits, economists, and politicians that says government spending boosts economic growth. No, it doesn't. Wealth and capital goods follow talent, which means tens of billions were consumed in West Virginia only for the proceeds to exit the state as its best and brightest people have been doing for decades.

As this book will repeat with at times tiring frequency, investment is what drives economic growth. Consumption is a consequence of investment. Investment follows people, which neatly explains why some cities and states prosper, yet others stagnate or regress. The closing of a factory or a business could never destroy a city or state despite what we hear from emotional members of the pundit class, but the departure of human capital decidedly will bring on decline. Talented people are magnets for the very investment that drives progress. Cleveland, Detroit, Flint, and Pittsburgh suffer in a relative sense economically because so many Americans are *from* those cities but no longer live in them. West Virginia is just an extreme example of the cities mentioned. Though it's showered with federal spending, the money quickly departs a state that has been leaking talented citizenry for decades and perhaps longer.

So while government consumption cannot create prosperity that is most certainly a consequence of people, the economics profession has designed for itself a measure of economic growth that suggests government actually *can* decree happy times through its consumption of wealth taxed away from the private sector. In 2014, economist Diane Coyle published a small book explaining how the economics profession designed this statistical sleight of hand. It's titled *GDP: A Brief but Affectionate History.*

Though attempts to measure country economic growth go back to at least the seventeenth century, Coyle explained to readers that what we know as GDP today "is one of the many inventions of World War II."[76] To this day, economists horrifyingly assert—with GDP as their evidence—that WWII was economically fruitful for the U.S. A tragically backwards number indeed.

Where it gets interesting is that prewar measures of economic growth explicitly showed "the economy shrinking if private output available for consumption declined, even if government spending required for the war effort was expanding output elsewhere in the economy."[77] Well, *of course* those numbers declined. Though it would be folly on the best day for number crunchers to divine economic growth, there was at least some honesty in pre-GDP measures of output: government spending correctly subtracted from growth.

If the reason why government spending weighed on prosperity isn't apparent, it's important to make plain to readers that governments are only able to spend what they tax or borrow from the private economy first. It's not that politicians in Haiti and Peru are different from the public servants in the U.S. and Japan such that they spend trillions less. More realistically, Haitian and Peruvian politicians spend less because there's very little economic growth to tax in those countries relative to the U.S. and Japan, and there's very little expected future growth to borrow against.

In that case, for government spending to be counted as economic growth would be for those attempting to measure economic activity to engage in fraudulent double counting. The growth already took place and is expected to take place; that's the *why* behind rising government revenues and similarly the *why* behind easy borrowing. Government spending and borrowing doesn't boost economic growth, but it's most definitely a consequence of it.

Coyle's acknowledges that for the longest time "'the economy' was the *private sector*" (my emphasis).[78] This is essential when it comes to understanding this chapter. Government couldn't add to economic growth through spending simply because government spending very definitely was the process whereby government shrank the real economy through political consumption of capital extracted from the private sector. The money that politicians spend must come from somewhere, so for every dollar spent by politicians, that's one less dollar for the private sector to allocate toward consumption, investment, or both.

To state the obvious, GDP was, and is, perfect for the political class simply because the false accounting that has defined it from day one promotes the obvious fiction that government spending adds to our overall well-being. Coyle is clear about the latter, that there was substantial resistance to what GDP became precisely because it was so blatantly false in its accounting, but her book is also clear about what informs its modern definition: "GDP was constructed around Keynes's model of how the economy works," and the John Maynard Keynes model was one that said government could use "both fiscal policy (the level of tax and spending) and monetary policy (the level of interest rates and availability of credit) to target a higher and less volatile rate of growth for the economy."[79]

In short, Keynesianism is the ultimate economic fantasy, which helps explain why it's so popular with the deluded types who enter politics, not to mention academic economists shielded from the real-world implications of their policy ideas. Wouldn't it be nice if government spending could boost growth during troubled times, but by definition it can only reduce it. If readers feel otherwise, they must explain how it is that Mitch McConnell, Chuck Schumer, Nancy Pelosi, and Kevin McCarthy can allocate capital better than you, Amazon's Jeff Bezos, FedEx founder Fred Smith, Paul Tudor Jones, Warren Buffett, and Ken Fisher. This isn't about ideology. Politicians simply can't allocate capital more skillfully first because they're arguably not suited to it, but most important because they lack the market signals that happily starve the bad ideas of Bezos, Smith, Jones, Buffett, and Fisher.

Some will reply that government must consume when the citizenry is not consuming, but this form of thinking is every bit as silly as the thought process that says political allocation of capital is the path to the next Amazon. Lest we forget, short of stuffing money under a mattress, money saved does not lie idle. Banks don't take in deposits in order to stare lovingly at the cash; rather, they pay for deposits (liabilities) by immediately turning those liabilities into assets. They would be quickly rendered insolvent if they paid for savings only to hoard them. Money saved is immediately lent to those with near-term consumptive needs, or it's lent to entrepreneurs and businesses eager to grow. Keynesianism presumes a world that has never existed in which banks warehouse deposits, and that is defined by politicians who are more expert than the private sector at investing funds extracted from the private sector.

Taking the absurdity of this most delusional of ideologies even further, Keynesianism presumes that just as politicians can consume limited private capital on the way to growth, they can similarly make credit cheap by decree. The latter is the equivalent of New York City Mayor de Blasio signing into law a ceiling on Manhattan apartment rents of $1,000 a month. There would be lots of demand for "cheap" Manhattan apartments under such a scenario, but very little—if any—supply. Lost on the Keynesians is that just as no politician spends dollars, neither do we. The spending of money speaks to the movement of precious market goods, services, and labor. When money is borrowed, what's being borrowed is access to those same market goods. Politicians can't decree cheap what is by definition limited in amount any more than de Blasio can declare rent cheap.

Considering the calculation of GDP, expenditure is the most common approach, and it's one that reveals the Enron-fiction that is GDP in living color. Once again, government spending adds to growth despite it plainly subtracting from it. That GDP rises thanks to consumption is all you the reader need to know about its faulty nature. Consumption is a consequence of production, which explains why consumers in Manhattan enjoy so much buying power relative to consumers in the Bronx. We produce something of market value first, and consumption is our reward. In measuring consumption, GDP measures the consequences of growth as opposed to it measuring actual growth. Government spending is most certainly a consequence of taxable private production, yet its growth adds to the main measure of economic growth used by economists.

With GDP's fraudulent, consequence-of-growth nature properly expressed, it's useful to now pivot to the accepted wisdom that prevailed in the spring of 2020. With the U.S. economy collapsed due to political panic, the call among politicians and those up high who advise them was to spend with abandon. The very politicians who had created so much misery in incredibly short order would be empowered to throw the money of others at the problems they had created.

Especially odd was the acceptance of a massive governmental response from conservatives. The *Wall Street Journal's* editorial page is the most important of its kind in the world and easily the most influential among conservatives, libertarians, neocons, Trump lovers, Never Trumpers, and seemingly anyone else on the right, but with the U.S. economy wrecked by mid-March, a *Journal* editorial endorsed the creation of a federal loan program that "could lend to companies hit by the economic shutdown."[80]

Arguably one reason equity markets were so shaken in the middle of March had to do with the sad fact that by midmonth there was a growing sense that "we're all Keynesians now." As evidenced by the *Journal* editorial board's embrace of a muscular federal "lending facility" for businesses, there was little evidence that any source of actual influence in Washington was willing to state the obvious: any and all government aid brought new meaning to non sequitur.

That was so when it was remembered how, just one month before March 16 (the date of the *Journal* editorial endorsing a federal response to economic collapse), no one was calling for federal aid of any kind, certainly not on the right. Goodness, U.S. equities would reach all-time highs the following day. This basic truth existed as a subtle hint that federal aid in March was the equivalent of a doctor putting a plaster cast on the arm of a patient with a clearly broken leg. Looked at in terms of businesses and individuals, they didn't need money as much as they needed politicians on the city, state, and national level to quickly end the lockdowns that had so quickly wrecked the U.S. economy.

That nail-biting politicians had done so much damage in such short order plainly raised another question, one that will be asked throughout *When Politicians Panicked*: Why would the very politicians and government bureaucrats who'd created so much needless wreckage be handed the chance to fix what they so cruelly broke? In the private sector, the creators of stupendous misery generally don't get second chances, but politicians vivify *self-unaware* in a way that few do.

At which point it was seemingly missed by conservatives calling for a federal response that government spending is just another word for private sector spending *orchestrated by politicians*. All wealth is created in the private sector only for government to politicize spending of this private sector wealth creation to the tune of $4 to $5 trillion per year. The growth once again *already happened*, hence the ability of Nancy Pelosi, Mitch McConnell et al. to spend.

Implicit in the call from conservatives for substantial amounts of lending to private businesses was that the federal government and the Fed it created had resources all their own, waiting patiently to be mobilized in times of trouble. Such a view wasn't serious. Government spending is yet again the politicized allocation of wealth that's been produced and *will be* produced in the private sector. Production first, then government spending. In their haste to help politicians and central banks craft a federal response, it seems conservatives forgot Say's Law, which is merely the commonsense truth that all consumption is a consequence of production. In order to consume market goods, we must produce market goods first.

Taking the bad dream further, the previously referenced *Journal* editorial acknowledged what was true, that the federal government was approaching the coronavirus "health crisis" with "command-and-control emergency powers." Translated, city, state, and federal politicians were shutting down the economy, presumably for our own good. Or at least what they presumed to be our own good.

But even if some wanted to accept what vandalized common sense, that politicians were wrecking the economy in order to save our lives, had the very conservatives who correctly diagnosed the role of "command-and-control" in the economy's demise stopped to contemplate the track record of past "command-and-control" economies? That they were thoroughly downtrodden is one of those blinding glimpses of the obvious, which then raised a question of which investors of the private sector variety would lend or invest in size fashion into an economy that's in the process of being taken over by hysterical politicians on all levels? The question answers itself, at which point it was not unreasonable to ask why taxpayers were being forced to lend toward an economy that a private sector investor wouldn't then touch.

The March 2020 response from market-friendly conservatives like those at the *Journal* was essentially "this time is different." As the oft-referenced *Journal* editorial put it, there was a "liquidity panic" that could only be solved by government beneficence. The response was inadequate. Lest anyone forget, tight liquidity is a market signal like any other; in a mid-March 2020 sense it was one logically signaling horror on the part of investors that politicians on all levels were in the process of forcing a centrally planned economic reversal on the most dynamic economy in the world. Conservatives claim to revere market signals; market signals were telling politicians to stop the economic asphyxiation they were imposing on the economy, but conservatives wanted taxpayers to blunt the signal?

One would think conservatives would have learned their lesson from 2008 when, amid their clamor for bailouts, markets spoke anyway. Logically they spoke quite a bit more harshly thanks to the interventions. Yet conservatives wanted government to intervene again? You couldn't make this up. Capital was already scarce thanks to political ineptitude, so the conservative solution was for government to oversee the waste of even more on loans that no private investor would ever issue?

Readers can rest assured that members of the reliably hysterical left will have their hysteria featured in the coming pages. *When Politicians Panicked* isn't solely a story of Republicans. Not by a long shot. This was a crack-up overseen by both sides. At the same time, it's not unreasonable to expect of those most rhetorically friendly to markets to be friendly to markets when it's most needed. That's the case because the central planning that fails in impressive fashion during good times fails even more flamboyantly during bad times. Yet the ideology most rhetorically associated with free markets and free minds was calling for politicians to plan resource allocation for an economy that was in the process of being shut down by politicians. You really, *really* can't make this up.

All of which brought us to the justification for this mass handover of power to government. The economic shutdown that the *Journal* editorial suggested could be measured in months (the horrifying prediction proved correct) was explained away by those editorialists as "prudent" and as "a health measure to 'flatten the curve' of infections."[81] This was surprising considering the source. And discouraging. Indeed, let's please unpack what was implicitly said: the very humans who had created awe-inspiring prosperity, who had lifted billions out of the most desperate of living conditions, and who had created all manner of cures for diseases that used to kill and maim, were now a *danger* to one another.

Dear reader, this was what the world looked like in March 2020. It wasn't just that politicians on both sides panicked. So had the most reliable sources of market-oriented thought. Care of politicians, economists, alarmist scientists, and their editorialist enablers on the left and right: we the people had become a lethal menace to one another, and since we were, the expectation was that we were to give our liberty and prosperity away to politicians until such a time that they deemed it OK for us to have it back. This *political* tragedy that was wrecking the economy was real, and it was *heartbreaking*. And it was dense, as the next chapter about Kevin Warsh's call for a Federal Reserve "lending facility" will make plain.

Chapter Seven

CORPORATIONS NEVER, EVER RUN OUT OF MONEY

"Businesses, like people, seldom if ever fail solely because of a lack of money."

—Warren Brookes, *The Economy in Mind*[82]

Looking back to March and April of 2020, it's hard to convey the 1 + 1 = 1,000 atmosphere that alarmist politicians, doctors, and medical experts foisted on us. On March 15 Anthony Fauci, told *Meet the Press* host Chuck Todd that in response to the new coronavirus "we should really be overly aggressive and get criticized for overreacting."[83] Fauci, whose income was a sure thing, was rather explicitly saying that he would gladly risk the livelihoods of *millions of others,* all based on some kind of gauzy notion that people getting too close to other people would lead to illness, death, or both. Maddening about all this is that back in 1983, Fauci wrote a paper for the medical journal *JAMA* in which he said AIDS might infect others via "routine close contact, as within a family household."[84] How little he knew then. Worse was how little Fauci learned from how little he knew about AIDS. Had he, he might not have been so adamant about pushing politicians to wreck the economy over a supposition.

Politicians more than overreacted. In their extreme panic, they lurched toward ridiculous, comically so. Except that their actions brought extraordinary misery to tens of millions in the U.S. alone. Tragic then and now was how all the hysteria manifested itself. Illinois state senator Dan McConchie perhaps vivified the stupidity most effectively in an opinion piece for the *Wall Street Journal*. As he put it about Governor Jay Pritzker's Executive Order:

> I can visit Target to buy furniture, Walmart to buy clothing or my grocery store to buy flowers. But I can't go inside a furniture store, a clothing store or a florist, even though those stores could easily adopt the same safety measures required of the retail outlets permitted to stay open.[85]

To be clear, the lockdowns were never justified. *Ever.* If the virus were modeled to kill ten thousand Americans, lockdowns in response would have opened up theoretical calls to ban automobile driving, too, in consideration of the multiple of Americans annually killed in car accidents. In 2020 alone, the prediction for the latter was thirty-eight thousand deaths.[86]

But what if the models predicted three million, five million, or ten million American deaths? If so, any forced lockdowns would have been superfluous. It cannot be stressed enough that people don't need a law to avoid that which might kill them. The answer to any virus is logically always freedom. Freedom produces economic growth and the subsequent resources to fight what's lethal, plus freedom produces crucial information about what's potentially lethal. So again, the lockdowns were never justified.

At the same time, it's useful to contemplate state senator McConchie's correctly sarcastic analysis. No furniture, clothing, or flower shopping so long as it doesn't take place in furniture, clothing, or flower shops. But if in general stores, shop away so long as you have a mask, or don't have a mask. Figure that the World Health Organization's stance on the matter was a moving target.[87]

Okay, but wait a second. Wasn't the most prominent theme of this whole lapse of reason "social distancing"? If so, wouldn't the answer have been to protect property rights and allow business owners to choose how little (if at all) to keep their businesses open? After all, some businesses closed on their own well before the shelter-in-place orders were instituted. Some did so out of fear for employees, some out of fear of brand risk related to being branded as a virus "hot zone," some no doubt did so for publicity purposes, and some out of fear that alarm among customers rated shutting down for a time. Just as people don't need a law, neither do the people who run businesses.

Whatever the answer, if "social distancing" was the goal, it read as odd then and reads as *incredibly* odd now that the response was to limit the kinds of businesses consumers could patronize. Why not, if the goal was limiting contact, once again protect property rights *and* allow business owners to decide on the way to customers populating more businesses in less dense fashion? Why recommend that colleges and universities close so that the young people (as of 2020) least vulnerable to the coronavirus wouldn't be forced to crowd into homes with older parents presumably more vulnerable to the coronavirus?

Of course, clear thinking was in tragically short supply, particularly in March 2020. Politicians' answer to the new coronavirus was mass economic desperation that revealed itself in tens of millions of jobs lost, a national unemployment rate that reached 14.7 percent,[88] and a wave of corporate bankruptcies. What was thankfully not terribly lethal from a human life standpoint proved brutally lethal for businesses. As a *New York Times* report explained it, 2020 would bring on "a record for so-called mega bankruptcies" and also a record number of "merely large" corporate bankruptcies.[89] The names of those taken out included popular brands like Hertz, J.Crew, and Neiman Marcus. Just as humans need oxygen to breathe, businesses require freedom to meet the needs of customers in order to remain in business.

Which brings us to the Warren Brookes quote that opens this chapter. Brookes's observation about corporations was plainly forgotten amid a panic caused by the coronavirus. As unemployment and bankruptcy exploded to reflect the suffocation of businesses and workers by clueless politicians, policy types feverishly spilled ink in pursuit of policy solutions that would erase, or at least reduce, all the desperation.

None of the solutions offered by the pundit class bothered to state the obvious: that witless politicians had wrecked the economy in short order with shutdowns, so end the shutdowns. Policy types never offered common sense as a fix. How very low rent! Really, how could elite policy types justify their pay and their fancy titles if they merely called for an end to the shutdowns?

In Kevin Warsh's case, it was seemingly never about the money in consideration of his marriage to a Lauder heiress. At the same time, Warsh is a Distinguished Visiting Fellow at Stanford's Hoover Institution, a right-of-center think tank populated by a who's who of boldfaced policy names. Many of the major names can claim high former positions in government, including Warsh. Warsh had of course been a vice chairman at the Federal Reserve. Unsurprisingly, his solution wasn't the obvious one of ending lockdowns that served no purpose. Warsh had bigger ideas. It seems he never read Brookes, or if he did, Brookes's common sense wouldn't fit an opinion piece by a *Hoover scholar*.

Needless to say, it should be stressed before pivoting to Warsh's proposal that no companies ever run out of money. *Ever*. The most obvious example of this basic truth is Amazon, which is presently one of the most valuable corporations in the world. That's what we know now. What's perhaps less known, and what perhaps never occurred to Warsh, was that for the longest time the internet retailer was incredibly unprofitable, so much so that its nickname was "Amazon.org."

Yet Amazon survived. Even though the Seattle-based company lost money for years, there were enough investors who trusted the fledgling company's long-term prospects. So they continued to provide capital, and as the company's market-cap makes plain, the true believers were amply rewarded.

Amazon's long path to profitability rates prominent mention given the popular view among conservatives (including Warsh) that the answer to an economic contraction of government's own making was—you guessed it—more government. Warsh prominently called for a Federal Reserve/Treasury created "lending facility" to boost liquidity within businesses rapidly descending on illiquidity.

The problem with such a plan was that it clearly glossed over why businesses were illiquid, or more realistically, it ignored what changes would have to take place so that businesses could be liquid again. This unwillingness to address the policy source of illiquidity meant that Warsh's "liquidity facility" meant to shower asphyxiated businesses with funds was going to achieve much less than nothing.

Stock markets, the objective truth tellers now and then, agreed that Warsh's plan wouldn't. Indeed, the always forward-looking market's correction continued for over a week after Warsh published "Let the Fed Administer an Antiviral Shot" in the *Wall Street Journal* on March 15, 2020. No surprise there. A normally market-friendly right wing that had tentacles inside the Trump administration was aggressively embracing a big-government solution that mystifyingly mistook the proverbial smothering of U.S. businesses by government for a liquidity problem that could be solved by government.

No. Not even close. Illiquidity doesn't just happen; rather, it's a *consequence* of something else, almost always policy error. The *Journal* editorial board hit on the policy error. Per the editors, politicians on the local, state, and national level had out of nowhere imposed "command-and-control" on the U.S. economy. Translated, they rapidly engineered a shutdown of what was only a month before the most dynamic and easily one of the freest economies in the world.

It was a screaming reminder that to focus on "liquidity" in March 2020, as Warsh and countless right-of-center deep thinkers were, was for policy types to miss the point. Businesses once again never run out of money. What they run out of is trust on the part of investors that they'll be able to operate profitably in the future. Clarifying all this for readers, if investors trusted in mid-March 2020 that politicians at all levels would soon take their booted feet off the U.S. economy, the illiquidity troubling businesses would have vanished in whiplash fashion.

Amazon was yet again instructive. For the longest time it was bleeding money much as suffocated businesses were amid the COVID-19 panic, but investors saw a better future such that they chose to liquefy an ugly present.

Looked at through the prism of March 2020, the outlook for businesses was hideous. Worse, the future wasn't looking much better. The shutdowns arguably had no precedent, and no endpoint. How do you price such decadence? A virus is said to threaten, so the answer was a cessation of economic activity?

So while there was arguably fear related to the shutdown's unprecedented qualities, along with uncertainty about when the shutdowns would end, there was clearly no mystery as to what would arrest the uncertainty and a lot of the fear. End that which had in short order taken an economy and equity markets down in gruesome fashion. The lockdowns were destroying businesses and jobs, so end them. End of story.

Some, including Warsh, argued then and will argue now (presumably to justify their incomprehensible stance) that there wasn't time to wait for an end to the shutdowns, that businesses needed the money right *now*. Of course, the obvious problem with such a stance was that "money" would once again prove meaningless absent a cessation of what had caused a shortage of money within businesses to begin with.

Worse, the call for the state to blunt the message of the markets would at best achieve nothing, and at worst obscure the truth behind business illiquidity: political error. Which would be a shame. Markets were rapidly exposing political malpractice, so let them. Let markets noisily expose the asphyxiation so that it will hopefully stop. Ultimately markets are going to speak loudly either way, and they did speak loudly, which means there was no sane reason to give politicians any kind of cover.

After that, it couldn't be stressed enough that what was being proposed by Warsh (and other conservatives comfortable with state solutions) was going to be economically harmful. It would be for two main reasons beyond the one explained in the previous paragraph. For one, businesses die all the time in a dynamic, market economy. Failure is a crucial source of economic vitality as the enormously high failure rate in superrich Silicon Valley attests. Along these lines, *Journal* editorial page columnist Andy Kessler has long made a variation of the point that the "dirty little secret of Silicon Valley is that nine out of 10 funded investments fail, often spectacularly so."[90] This in mind, a blanket attempt by a Fed/Treasury "lending facility" to keep businesses afloat would, assuming a "successful" facility, keep in operation all sorts of businesses that market forces would have put out to pasture on their own, and to the economy's betterment.

To which intervention apologists might reply that they were calling for a lending facility to provide liquidity to "otherwise healthy businesses jeopardized by the pandemic shutdown." OK, but imagine if COVID-19 had reared its ugly head in the summer of 1997 or in the fall of 2001. Would Apple have rated Fed/Treasury finance, or Amazon, based on the desire among conservatives to "only" prop up the healthy? The question answers itself, and the answer explains why it's so economically harmful to have government play the role of capital allocator. It can't. Period.

It's been said before in this book, and it will be said again: central planning fails. *Always.* And if it always fails during the good times, which it does, it most certainly fails during the bad times. For an obvious reason: during the bad times capital availability is going to be scarce, and as future chapters will make plain, no amount of Federal Reserve fiddling can overcome this basic truth. That being the case, the idea that government should arrogate to itself even more control over the allocation of always precious capital beggars belief.

Yet awful as Warsh's solution was, members of the left came up with even dopier answers, which is where we'll turn to in the next chapter.

Chapter Eight

THERE'S NO SUCH THING AS GOVERNMENT INVESTMENT EITHER

*"Capitals are increased by parsimony, and
diminished by prodigality and misconduct."*

—Adam Smith, *The Wealth of Nations*

It bears repeating again in a book that will be defined by lots of repetition, but investment powers economic growth. It's that simple. This basic truth may well trigger certain readers who "know" from their economics textbooks that consumption is what drives growth, and that 70 percent of GDP is consumption, but the simple truth is that economic models divined by credentialed economists are wrong. As we know from Chapter Six, backwards numbers like GDP are monuments to double counting, to growth *that already occurred.*

For those not offended by the obvious, it should be said that we all have endless consumptive desires. But as individuals we all know that those desires can't be fulfilled absent production first. Consumption is a consequence of production, and investment powers production. The more investment in our capacity to produce, the more resources boosting our ability to produce, at which point our ability to consume soars. Consumption comes *after* growth.

Looked at more broadly, the innovative, life-altering, growth-boosting businesses in the economy are almost invariably a consequence of wildly courageous, risk-ignoring investment. Very occasionally these bold capital allocations lead to wondrous surprises. General Electric was once just that. GE came to be because an oddball inventor by the name of Thomas Edison found a rich banking heir by the name of J. P. Morgan who rather uniquely thought the light bulb had promise.[91] Morgan was rich; hence, he had money *to lose* on something that thoroughly transformed living standards for the better but that few believed would.

Looked at in a twenty-first century sense, Edison's highly fruitful combination with Morgan helps explain why a dollar in Michael Bloomberg's pocket is exponentially more growth-stimulative than a dollar in yours or mine. Bloomberg has money to *lose*. He can take huge investment risks. Goodness, he lost $570 million on a presidential campaign that was dying just as the new coronavirus was set to eclipse retail politics for a time. The wealth of the staggeringly rich is the most important wealth of all. *Period.* That is so precisely because the wealth of the rich can be directed to the riskiest of ventures that frequently never bear fruit but that boost productivity and living standards remarkably when they do. And even when they fail, they produce crucial knowledge that lays the groundwork for future advances.

Which brings us to Jason Furman. Just as the right has its elite policymakers for whom simple common sense gives off the odor of low brow, so does the left. Interesting about Furman is that while he's a card-carrying and very senior member of the American left wing, he's a regular contributor to the *Wall Street Journal's* right-leaning editorial page. In a March 5, 2020, essay for the *Journal*, Furman offered up what passes for policy sophistication on the left. It was titled, "The Case for a Big Coronavirus Stimulus." No, it was Furman's case. Surely not *the* case. The half awake among us always rejected the notion that there was *any* case for government to respond. Never considered by the policy high-brow was that precisely because the virus had some unknown qualities, the role of government should have been minimal—an early 1920s approach as discussed in Chapter Five.

When times are the most unsettled, that's when government should pull back so that precious resources can be directed by market-disciplined players to their highest use. Needless to say, such a viewpoint was never aired in the proverbial corridors of power in the spring of 2020. The coronavirus scare gave life to a policy crowd ever eager to centrally plan good outcomes. In short, the policy theorists on the left and right *were* the crisis. They were substituting their limited knowledge for that of the marketplace. Readers may have an idea by now where this is going…

In Furman's case, one supposes that the Harvard professor, because he's a *Harvard professor*, could afford to be ridiculous. Tenure is cushy. Furman's solutions, like those of Warsh, would bring on the opposite of growth, which arguably helps explain why markets went haywire in the first few weeks of March. Each side was revealing how it had nary a clue about why economies grow and how crucial actual economic growth is to medical advance. Government can't create growth, but it certainly can consume the fruits of it. Warsh and Furman's solutions were and are monuments to this truth.

So while the actual coronavirus had been priced in rather sanguine fashion (see equity markets in January and February), what the governing class would do in response *hadn't been.* How could it? Humans are wild cards—politicians in particular. They've got power over taxpayer-funded entities that consume trillions every year and that have the capacity to borrow trillions more. Political action is all a speculation.

Though Furman was Barack Obama's former CEA head, thus unable to craft policy for the GOP, his approach was telling as to where policy was headed, irrespective of political party. Indeed, once it became apparent that hysteria from the political class would rule the day, investors had little reason by March 2020 to believe that Republicans would be much different from Democrats in response to the virus. Also, government was divided. Assuming Republicans hadn't panicked in the way Democrats frequently do, the policy response was going to reflect panic since Democrats had a say. Divided government is most often a good thing for limiting policy but dangerous when opposing ideologies find themselves agreeing that there's a crisis brewing. Both sides want to fix things, which meant that investors had a pretty good idea that "do something" would reveal itself in expensive, growth-sapping fashion.

Translated, Republicans fearful of appearing indifferent to the suffering of the American people at the hands of politicians would hoover up trillions to indiscriminately throw at the suffering, along with many who weren't. If war is the health of the state per Randolph Bourne, then "crises" invariably created by politicians are the state's *oxygen*. Looked at in stock market terms, they were logically selling off to reflect certainty that any solution achieved by eager-to-solve-things politicians would have nothing to do with economic revitalization. How could it? Barring solutions that would include a cessation of the lockdowns, no policy fixes would make sense. Republicans will say in retrospect that they wanted tax cuts, which is just a reminder of how clueless both sides were. Nothing against real tax cuts, they're certainly great, but their incentive effects are pretty limited when your business is no longer "essential." To be clear, policy responses were a monumental non sequitur.

In Furman's case, it's almost comical to look back and see that he wasn't even offering a shrinkage of government's wallet share. He was just offering more government. So typical.

First off, Furman observed that "the lower interest rates [from the Fed] and depreciated dollar will provide only modest relief after a substantial lag."[92] Though he considered the Fed's March 3 emergency rate cut (pushing the Fed's target rate down 50 basis points 1-1.25 percent[93]) "bold," he feared a lag. Furman missed the point. Credit is a consequence of production. *Always.* We borrow money for what the money can be exchanged for. Assuming slower growth, meaning less production, there was going to be less credit available. The Fed couldn't alter this truth, thus raising a question of what Furman meant by "modest relief" from the Fed. Try none. One of the saddest comments on the modern economics profession is how many of the credentialed believe the Fed can boost credit. The naivete that informs such a view is quite something.

As for a "depreciated dollar," the obvious truth covered in Chapter Four that investors denominate their returns in dollars was seemingly lost on Furman. A depreciated dollar is an investment deterrent; it's a tax on the very investment that powers economic growth. Fear not, Furman's insights hardly improved as his opinion piece dragged on.

The professor then argued that "Congress should pass a simple one-time payment of $1,000 to every adult who is a U.S. citizen or a taxpaying U.S. resident, and $500 to every child who meets the same criteria." Amazing is that he was serious.

Let's not forget that the vast majority of federal revenues come from the richest taxpayers. Put numerically, the top 1 percent of earners account for 39 percent of federal taxes collected.[94] What this meant was that Furman was calling for a massive transfer of wealth of the hundreds of billions variety from the rich to the middle class and poor. His expressed innocence about what causes capital to form, corporations to sprout, and jobs to be created was impressive. Furman was ignoring the economic truism that unspent wealth in the hands of the rich is the most economically stimulative, company- and job-creating wealth of all, and it is because the rich will *invest* it as opposed to spending it. Once again, investment drives growth. Spending is a consequence of growth.

Is it any wonder investors were a little bit worried about the future? Right when investment was needed, many policy types were looking to stimulate consumption through the extraction of wealth from those most capable of investing. They can do no such thing as is. They can merely shift wealth from the hands of investors into the hands of consumers. The big loser in the Furman scenario would be the economy given the alarmist economist's professed policy meant to shrink the availability of always essential growth capital. Yet bad as Furman's theorizing was, he came off as moderate relative to others in his world. To see why, we'll shift to Andrew Ross Sorkin, *DealBook* columnist at the *New York Times*.

About Sorkin's highly emotional plea for the federal government to essentially nationalize U.S.-based investment, every so often it's worth restating the empirical truth that just about every business ever founded in Silicon Valley has gone bankrupt. As Peter Thiel described it in *Zero to One*, "Most venture-backed companies don't IPO or get acquired; most fail, usually soon after they start."[95]

This factoid rates prominent mention ahead of Sorkin's panicked response to the economy's sickening decline. Sorkin famously wrote *Too Big to Fail* about troubles in the financial sector in in 2008. The book was a very engrossing read despite the author's mistaken analysis whereby he associated bank failure with crisis, as opposed to *intervention in bank failure* leading to crisis. Despite that, it was a great read.

Funny is that Sorkin billed his solution to the 2020 economic contraction as so obvious and timely that it could avert a "depression." Actually, Sorkin's solution was of the kind that would have made the 1930s feel like the 1920s by comparison. It was laughably obtuse. To read it was to see that the *Times* columnist mistook what causes economic progress and what doesn't. Most notably, he misunderstood that governments only have resources to throw at economic contractions of their own making insofar as economic growth has already occurred or will occur. For governments to act, they must shrink resource availability in the real economy. This stubborn bit of common sense remains elusive to *Times* columnists like Sorkin and those who read the *Times*. Sorkin's solution was that:

"The government could offer every American business, large and small, and every self-employed—and gig—worker a no-interest 'bridge loan' guaranteed for the duration of the crisis to be paid back over a five year period." He added that the "only condition of the loan to businesses would be that companies continue to employ at least 90 percent of their work force at the same wage that they did before the crisis."[96]

To see why such a solution would have made the awful spring of 2020 even worse, readers need only imagine if back in 2001 politicians applied the Sorkin solution to the technology sector as internet companies and share prices collapsed everywhere. If so, eToys, Webvan, and theglobe.com (to name a few) would have gotten new, highly lucrative leases on life. Though it came later, Friendster might still be consuming precious capital of the human and financial kind, and then imagine the myriad search companies that aimed to be Google before Google became *Google*. Figure that the latter was founded in 1998. How unfortunate if, in the clutter of 2001, hundreds and perhaps thousands of Google-style businesses had been propped up care of the federal government. Imagine the massively shrunken dynamism in the Valley if the bad and unequal were routinely saved.

Looking at this in bigger picture fashion, let's think about GE some more. It was the world's most valuable company when the twenty-first century began. Tyco was seen as the next GE, Lucent was cutting-edge communications, AOL and Yahoo were the thoroughly dominant players in the internet space, and by all-too-many accounts Enron was the best managed company in the world. At the same time the aforementioned were at the top of the corporate heap, Microsoft was on the verge of fifteen years of flat share-price returns after the horrid treatment of it by the DOJ; Apple was just limping out of near-bankruptcy care of a business-saving investment from Bill Gates; Amazon peddled books, CDs, and DVDs rather unprofitably; Google was unknown; and Facebook didn't exist on account of founder Mark Zuckerberg still being in high school! Today the five previously mentioned are the most valuable companies in the world, while GE is less than a fifth of its old value, AOL is a monument to a distant internet past, and Enron is…

Seemingly missed by Sorkin was that economies gain strength from periods of weakness precisely because the bad are starved of precious capital so that the good can get more of it. Imagine if this natural, economy-enhancing process were blunted by the federal government? Think of all the great businesses along with all the great concepts that would never be able to attain funding thanks to the federal government siphoning enormous amounts of wealth out of the economy, only to give it back to individuals and businesses without regard to the worth of their work or business model.

What read as economic suffocation got worse in consideration of the price tag Sorkin blithely offered up to his gullible readers. He acknowledged that his vision would cost "a lot," but in casually suggesting "as much as $10 trillion," Sorkin vastly understated how economically expensive his inept vision for revival was. One guesses his understatement was rooted in a misunderstanding that trips up all-too-many economists and pundits: they assume money is a separate entity to real resources. More realistically, money is the natural consequence of resources. Money is just a measure that only exists and is only useful insofar as real resources of the product, service, and labor variety are being created and exchanged. In short, Sorkin was calling for a plan that would empower the federal government to play the biggest lender in the world by many miles, its lending dictating the direction of up to $10 trillion worth of products, services, and labor. Imagine then, the horrid economic impact this would bring about as federal officials operating sans market discipline basically commandeer resources amounting to something quite substantial as a portion of the overall U.S. economy. The harm to existing and future economic growth would have been incalculable but surely disastrous.

To which Sorkin might respond that the coronavirus represented a health crisis of major scope that neither businesses nor individuals could have prepared for. In his perch at CNBC, Sorkin wasn't immune to breakdowns on air, so fearful was he that the new virus was the modern equivalent of the bubonic plague.[97]

Sorkin's nail-biting blinded him to a rather costless economic answer: for politicians on the local, state, and national levels to end their shutdown of the U.S. economy. Such a move would have quickly ended talk from either side about federal loans simply because the U.S. economy was fine before the lockdowns. About the previous statement of the obvious, Sorkin surely knew that almost exactly a month before he penned his overwrought plea for government to play banker, capital for businesses was plentiful. With equities at all-time highs, capital for private and public businesses was logically abundant. Then command-and-control happened. For Sorkin to then call for the nationalization of capital allocation on top of government force brought new meaning to the concept of economic illiteracy.

Of course, the losers in economically bankrupt responses from left and right were the people in the less protected parts of the economy who saw prosperity vanish in tragically rapid fashion. Growth is yet again a consequence of market-driven investment, but policy types were goading policy makers into making an awful situation worse with their naive pleas for a huge shift of wealth from investors to consumers, alongside the *politicization* of investment. It wasn't serious. Indeed, it cannot be repeated enough that the central planning that never works in boom times certainly doesn't in trying times.

But central planning was where things were headed.

Chapter Nine

LET'S NOT INSULT "STIMULUS" BY CALLING THIS A STIMULUS

"Here's my strategy on the Cold War: We win; they lose."

—Ronald Reagan[98]

On June 18, 2020, rocket scientist Sergei N. Khrushchev died at the age of eighty-four of a self-inflicted gunshot wound to the head. His wife, Valentina Golenko, reported the apparent suicide to Cranston, RI, police.[99]

Khrushchev was the son of Nikita Khrushchev, soviet premier from 1958 to 1964. The father looked like what people imagined communists looked like. Worse, his rhetoric brought to mind evil. As he famously told Western officials in 1956, "We will bury you!"[100]

Khrushchev père died in obscurity in the thankfully former Soviet Union in 1971, but his son died in the U.S.? Despite his father's bold declaration that didn't come true, son Sergei interestingly became a U.S. citizen in 1999 along with his wife. Khrushchev explained his decision in 2001: "I'm not a traitor. I did not commit any treason. I work here and I like this country." Khrushchev was a senior fellow at Brown University and a lecturer on matters related to the Cold War.

Where it becomes a little bit fascinating is when Nikita and family visited the U.S. in 1959. Katharine Q. Seelye of the *New York Times* reports that the Khrushchevs felt as though they'd "landed on Mars, seeing things they have never imagined."[101] As Sergei recalled it for the *Providence Journal*, the prosperity was pretty awe-inspiring: "It was palms, cars, highways, everything."[102]

At the same time, at least one aspect of the trip proved disappointing. Disneyland had been open four years by the time they visited. The family was highly eager to visit but was refused based on safety concerns. According to Seelye, Nikita "exploded in anger: 'What is it? Is there an epidemic of cholera or something?'"[103]

It's almost trite to state that which is so obvious, but the Khrushchev family was plainly blown away by the sad fact that the U.S. was everything that the Soviet Union wasn't. In the latter, the economy was the epitome of command-and-control, right up the Five Year Plans created by alleged economic "experts" in the Soviet Union. When an economy is planned, there's little to enjoy.

That's the case because the entrepreneurs who bring the future into the present generally do so by going against the grain and creating for consumers what they didn't know they wanted. Disneyland is instructive in this regard.

In his 2019 history of the amusement park's creation, *Disney's Land*, historian Richard Snow made plain to readers that no one wanted the amusement park that Walt Disney had imagined. Not Roy Disney, Walt's brother; not the bankers whom he approached about financing; not his wife. Walt ultimately secured dollars for the financing of his wholly rejected idea by borrowing against a life insurance policy.[104]

Entrepreneurs are just that because they generally believe what no one else does.

Disney's vision was crucially only brought to life through the accession of capital. This blinding glimpse of the obvious rates mention as a way of reminding readers of a theme that will continue to reveal itself throughout this book: politicians cannot play investor. Period. There's no way. It's not an ideology thing. It's in truth a conservative thing in the nonideological sense. Governments are by their nature conservative. They're limited by the known. Entrepreneurs want to take us to the unknown. The latter first explains why so many fail. They're yet again rushing us to a future that only they can conceptualize. Change is incredibly difficult, which helps explain why entrepreneurs fail so much. It's hard to alter existing habits. Yet they persist against very high odds of failure. Which also explains why governments cannot play investor: politicians can't risk putting taxpayer money to work on ideas that will nearly always go belly-up and realistically go belly-up in scandalous fashion.

To be clear, good ideas only seem good after the fact—and in the rarest of instances. Disney was seeking capital to build an amusement park on 240 acres of land in Anaheim, CA. In the early 1950s. Wait a second, what? Keep in mind that Anaheim back then was farmland in many ways. Build an amusement park? You can't be serious. Thank goodness for the different thinkers who see what we don't see. Imagine our living standards and enjoyment of life without them. Think of any remarkable, life-enhancing business today, and rest assured that exponentially more venture capitalists and investors passed on the business than leaped at the chance to fund it.

When politicians control the resources, the audacious ideas naturally suffer the most. In good times, this merely results in stasis. In bad times, it results in mass desperation. Those living in the Soviet Union were desperate. With Khrushchev et al. overseeing allocation of limited resources, what was produced in the former Soviet Union was of intensely low quality. Assuming there was something to purchase.

This rates particular mention in consideration of what underlay the economic contraction engineered by witless politicians in 2020. It can't be repeated enough that in response to a spreading virus, they chose to crush the world's most dynamic economy. To think about what they did is to always be mystified. Why?

"Why" is easy to ask because it's once again incomprehensible that politicians would choose to fight a virus with economic decline. Where was the outrage? Economic growth is the biggest foe of ill health.

This mention of the screamingly obvious comes up in consideration of cancer. In a 2015 opinion piece for the *Wall Street Journal*, the late Thomas Stossel, a Harvard medical professor, informed readers that of "the 78 potential treatments for brain cancer that underwent clinical trials from 1998–2014, three proved safe and effective enough to win Food and Drug Administration approval."[105] Stossel's observation was a reminder of just how few attempts at medical progress succeed but also an implicit comment about expense. These attempts at advance don't come cheap. But are they ever meaningful.

As a 2015 *Wall Street Journal* editorial noted, "Two-thirds of Americans now survive at least five years after a cancer diagnosis, up from half in 1990."[106] While cancer of varying kinds remains a killer, it's increasingly the case that those who get it can attain medical care and advanced drugs that enable them to *live with* cancer, as opposed to dying of it. Per Dr. Lawrence Dorr in Chapter Two, "Die once, live twice." But maybe three times.

Indeed, the more that wealth is created, the more funds directed to those trying to rush the future into the present. Looked at in terms of medical science, it doesn't take a doctor or a scientist to conclude that if the U.S. economy continues to grow, the odds of cancer in its various forms being pushed from the top of the lists of the biggest killers seems perfectly reasonable. What a wonderful world that will be.

But it takes aggressive investment in the opposite thinkers. Per Stossel, it takes aggressive investment in ideas that will most likely result in the proverbial "dry hole."

How maddening then, that after engineering an economic collapse, politicians proceeded to extract $2.9 trillion more from an economy they helped wreck in order to wastefully throw precious resources at their own wreckage.[107] Hopefully readers know by now that this economy-sapping tribute to double counting had nothing to do with growth. Again, governments can only spend insofar as they arrogate to themselves a portion of present and future growth from the private sector. The growth already occurred, or would occur. There would be no stimulus from this massive extraction of wealth from the real economy. It wasn't at all "supply side" when it's remembered that "supply side" is about a reduction of barriers to production. In this case, growing government expenditure would expand barriers to production. To call what the Trump administration crafted with the House and Senate a "stimulus" bill was to insult the very word.

This was obvious because the bill merely shifted wealth from one set of hands to another. The federal government extracts enormous wealth annually from the economy through taxation and borrowing, only to redistribute it. There's no growth in those checks going out or alleged "liquidity" provided to corporations suffocated by politicians on the local, state, and national level; there's just a shift of consumptive ability. Consumption doesn't power growth as much as it's a consequence of it. Again, the growth already happened.

And while conservatives arguably overstate the need for incentives when it comes to getting up and going to work, it's worth pointing out that the faux stimulus bill provided those rendered unemployed by the contraction $600 extra per week over four months. This number came in addition to the $400 weekly that the unemployed would have normally received.[108] Basically Congress was going to pay all-too-many Americans more to be unemployed than if they went back to work. Business owners were going to potentially face a difficult challenge related to luring work-ers back into production. The entity bidding for them to remain idle to the detriment of the production side of the economy (meaning the only side): the federal government.

All of which leads us to the most economy-crippling aspect of the laughable stimulus bill that logically slowed recovery: it was anti-invest-ment. Though it's previously been said that the federal government's access to trillions worth of American production on an annual basis is a consequence of it legally arrogating to itself a substantial piece of that production, it should also be made clear yet again that not all producers are equal producers of funds for the federal government to redistrib-ute. Most of those funds come from a tiny part of the U.S. population: the rich and superrich. Thirty-nine percent from the top 1 percent was the number from the previous chapter. This matters a great deal when it's remembered that the rich, precisely because they are, have really no choice but to invest the copious wealth they don't spend, and there are no companies and no jobs without investment first. Yet in its infinite wisdom, the political class was redistributing wealth from the well-to-do most capable of investing and directing it toward those most capable of consuming.

In short, the nearly $3 trillion would be consumed when, if not extracted by the political class, it might have been invested. Conservatives should have been aghast, but the economic discussion of the time wasn't a very good one.

Where was Sergei Khrushchev during all this? The question is rhe-torical. Not only was he months from his death, he was obscure. The former rocket scientist and lecturer on matters of the Cold War wasn't on the speed dial of economic tinkerers short on common sense. Still, he could have provided the planners in Congress and the White House with quite a lot of homespun wisdom care of a thankfully defunct nation. Khrushchev saw up close the disaster of command-and-control and was lucky enough to see the opposite with his 1959 visit to the U.S. He could have told the planners in Washington that you don't overcome command-and-control with more command-and-control, but that's exactly what happened.

The contraction of the economy and markets was *political*. What threatened health but plainly wasn't a big killer could never have brought the world's biggest economy to its knees. The U.S. economy was strangled, only for it to be blinded by a massive increase in government spending—which is where we will go next: the blinding of an economy that was already gasping for air.

Chapter Ten

WAIT A MINUTE, THE ECONOMY WAS ALREADY CONTRACTING, WASN'T IT?

"Capitalism is not chiefly an incentive system, but an information system."

—George Gilder, *Knowledge and Power*[109]

"Yeah, and there's 6 billion things left to name." So said Peter Griffin in a biblical-era *Family Guy* episode, which unspooled on the Fox Network on May 10, 2020. The episode was titled "Holly Bibble."

Two days later *CNN.com* led with a headline about a "New threat to the economy. Americans are saving like it's the 1980s."[110] Griffin's quip about "6 billion things" and the title for reporter Matt Egan's piece were both economic in nature, but which one conveyed good insights about economics, and which one sadly misinformed readers? The answer is easy. *CNN* was the source of the faulty information.

Egan's misguided thinking was rooted in the fallacious notion that a "so-called V-shaped recovery can't happen if consumers are sitting on the sidelines." Egan was writing about a collapsed U.S. economy that had Americans far more careful with the money they had in their pockets. They weren't buying things in the way they had two and a half months before, which explained Egan's expressed fears. In his defense, economists believe consumption powers growth. No, it's yet again a consequence of growth. Egan's worries were grounded in the delusion embraced by economists that consumption authors progress. No, it doesn't.

We all have endless needs, wants, and long-term yearnings. All three are limited by our ability to produce first. The more we produce, the more we're able to consume. Consumption comes after economic growth, as opposed to stimulating it as Egan errantly assumed. But for now, we're getting ahead of ourselves.

It should be stressed first that an economy isn't some living, breathing blob, or a tangible machine that can be goosed by politicians or central bankers. An economy is just people. It's individuals. And individuals are surely not harmed by savings. No doubt many individuals wished they had more savings when the hideous lockdowns began, particularly those who lost their jobs.

Individuals are enhanced by their savings, and so by extension is the "economy" enhanced. That the economy benefits is one of those statements of the supremely obvious, and it's explained by what powers our individual ability to produce.

To be clear, savings massively boost our productive ability. Back in the biblical era, human productive capacity was brutally limited, and it was as a consequence of there being very little savings for the entrepreneurial to draw on in order to innovate. Since most were living the most deprived of existences, savings were a luxury few could afford or imagine. One imagines "savings" wasn't much of a word or even used by many back then. It was one of the "six billion" that would eventually be invented or made better known by progress. Really, who could save? Life was a daily struggle just to survive. What little anyone had they consumed, thus explaining how little economic growth there was to speak of.

Since there was so little unconsumed wealth, there weren't savings for innovators to access in order to create tractors or fertilizer or other technological advances necessary to make it possible for exponentially more food to be made with exponentially fewer hands. Cal Berkeley professor Enrico Moretti noted in his 2012 book, *The New Geography of Jobs*, that as recently as 150 years ago, every other person had a job related to farming.[111] *In prosperous America.* So imagine what life was like in biblical times. A lack of savings meant that nearly everyone had to unproductively work as a farmer to produce very limited amounts of food. That clothes amounted to rags back then wasn't a fashion statement as much as it was a consequence of nearly all human endeavor being directed toward mere survival. Clothes were covering. Nothing more. Nothing less.

Crucial is that words were surely few in biblical times simply because there was little to describe or little variance in life. Without savings enabling the creation of new products and services and new ways of doing things, words were very few. Conversely, the massive growth of words signals *progress*.

The reason for the increase in words by the billions over the millennia is a clear result of savings. The use of unspent wealth to create new ways to farm like the wheat thresher (18th century), the tractor (late 19th), and the back hoe (mid 20th) thankfully meant that there could be fewer farmers and more people doing work commensurate with their talents. And when we do what reinforces our talents, we're much more productive.

Looked at in terms of *CNN's* perception in the spring of 2020 that savings were a "threat" to recovery, such a view couldn't have been more backwards. Savings quite simply *are* recovery since they set the stage for the creative to be matched with capital on the way to gargantuan productivity advances. It's crucial to point out that innovations are expensive in consideration of how few bear fruit. But when they do…as Jeff Bezos has put it, "If you can increase the number of experiments you try from a hundred to a thousand, you dramatically increase the number of innovations you produce."[112]

CNN and Egan were focused on consumption as the answer to a wrecked economy, and they were because the economists they get their information from have long mistaken consumption for growth. So were Jim Tankersley and Ben Casselman at the *New York Times*. In writing about the $600 weekly unemployment "bonus" first discussed in the previous chapter, the eternally confused Tankersley and Casselman enthused about research that "has found that unemployment benefits are an unusually potent form of fiscal stimulus because the money goes to the people who are most likely to spend it."[113] Hopeless…and wrong. Back to reality, consumption is the easy part. It's the production that's the challenge, which is why savings are so essential. They make production on a massive scale much more likely, which is always and everywhere what precedes consumption.

And which tells us why *Family Guy* provided an answer to the growth question far more expertly than did CNN. Word expansion is yet again a consequence of progress, and progress is a creation of savings that enable entrepreneurs to rewrite the future in amazing ways. Future generations will know that consumption won out over savings if word usage in 2030, 2050, and 2100 resembles that of 2020. A lack of savings would be the catalyst for this kind of depressed outcome.

A discussion of savings provides a good backdrop for this chapter. No doubt some readers have been asking what would be a reasonable question: Wouldn't the U.S. economy have collapsed anyway? Figure that the NCAA canceled "March Madness," the lucrative annual collegiate basketball tournament on March 12, 2020.[114] Major League Baseball canceled spring training and delayed the start of its regular season on the same day.[115] World-renowned chef José Andrés closed his restaurants on March 15,[116] which put him ahead of Washington, DC's closures, and then Disney officially shut down its U.S. amusement parks on March 16,[117] which put it in line with the earliest politician-ordered closures.

Some of the economically focused have keyed on anecdotes like those above, along with evidence that people began taking major precautions long before the lockdowns, to make a case that the U.S. economy was already in rapid decline before mid-March. In an analytical piece for the *New York Times* on May 8, 2020, Emily Badger and Alicia Parlapiano pointed out to readers that "in the weeks before states around the country issued lockdown orders this spring, Americans were already hunkering down. They were spending less, traveling less, dining out less. Small businesses were already cutting employment. Some were even closing shop."[118]

Badger and Parlapiano went on to write that,

"Even in states that imposed stay-at-home orders or closed nonessential businesses relatively early, households and businesses had begun to shift their behavior about 10 days before those orders. In states that closed later, that shift had come about 20 days earlier." Crucial for those making a case that politicians weren't at fault, that they were responding to panic rather than fomenting it, the *Times* scribes noted that "even states that never put in a statewide stay-at-home order, like Iowa, South Dakota and Utah, saw significant drops in consumer spending and employment, as well as in the shares of small businesses open."[119]

To believe Badger and Parlapiano, the panic predated political panic, thus rendering the political reaction to the virus moot from an economic perspective. It all seemingly makes sense if looked at through conventional economic eyes. Consumption is the fuel for economic expansion; it began to vanish in early March only for the U.S. economy to nosedive. Politicians exonerated. Okay, but not so fast.

Though Badger and Parlapiano thought they were explaining the onset of a recession, what they unwittingly conveyed to their readers is why what economists, politicians, and pundits describe as recession is actually a sign of the recovery on the way. Savings don't stunt growth; rather, savings *fuel* growth.

Almost uniformly missed by economists, along with the reporters who hang on their every word, is the nearly always glossed-over truth that businesses and entrepreneurs are in a constant battle for precious savings. The battle is very real when it's remembered just how much fun it is to consume. It's more than joyous to splurge on the plenty that American shops are filled with, along with shops around the world in an increasingly prosperous world. Governments needn't ever work to stimulate consumption. Consumption stimulants are all around us in the form of voluptuous shopping locales, restaurants, travel brochures, cars with the latest technology, and the like.

Businesses and entrepreneurs must overcome our urge to live in the present so that they can create a different future for us—one we're often not demanding. Indeed, of the readers who were teens or adults by the 1990s, how many of you were demanding the internet, Amazon, or both? For those of you who came of age in the early 2000s, how many of you were demanding Uber or the touchscreen smartphones that made Uber possible? Rest assured that as you're reading this very page, entrepreneurs backed by savings are feverishly at work creating goods and services that you'll soon enough marvel at how you ever lived without them.

Fascinating about those creating the future in the present is that those who make it will eventually recall in interviews and inevitable memoirs how many times their now *obvious* innovations nearly went belly-up, how many venture capitalists turned them down, how often those closest to them shifted uncomfortably as they were learning about what would ultimately prove essential to millions and perhaps billions...

For the doubters out there, consider something as ubiquitous as the GPS. When an entrepreneur by the name of Ed Tuck set out in search of investors for consumer versions of a device formerly thought to solely have military applications, he was turned down no less than *eighty-six times* by investors.[120] Though Pixar is now the most prolific producer of blockbuster hits in all of filmdom, when owner George Lucas put it up for sale in 1984, the twenty prospective investors that looked at the still unknown animation company passed on an opportunity that eventually made Steve Jobs a billionaire.[121] About the early days of Nike (originally Blue Ribbon), cofounder Phil Knight recalls spending "most of every day thinking about liquidity, talking about liquidity, looking to the heavens and pleading for liquidity. My kingdom for liquidity."[122] What Knight would have given for an excess of savings back before Nike became a prominent brand.

Looked at in terms of what was happening before March 15, 2020, people became nervous about a virus that had originated in China. Though this book makes what is hopefully a compelling case that the virus's presumed lethality was already a dead letter in January and February (see Chapter One), markets are markets. The market was plainly saying in early March that customers of various businesses were going to exercise a bit more caution than before. Businesses were going to exercise caution too.

Where the analysis goes off the rails is in the presumption that a slowdown in buying represented an economic correction. No. Implicit in such a view is that what's not spent just sits idle, as though unspent funds are hidden under a mattress or in a coffee can. No once again. The act of not spending hardly signals a lack of spending. It merely signals a shift of spending power to entrepreneurs and businesses that need capital in order to give life to an idea, or to grow. Banks can't pay for deposits only to sit on them. The latter would quickly invite insolvency. Unspent wealth is fuel, not contraction.

Which brings us to Sweden. Sweden famously limited its lockdowns while putting "stock in the sensibility of its people." Rather than force the economy into lockdown, Swedish leaders properly understood that people generally don't need to be forced to protect themselves.

Naturally the left in the U.S. directed a lot of venom at Sweden. Really, isn't the point of government to force all manner of outcomes?

Notable here is that in July 2020, Peter Goodman of the *New York Times* reported on a study conducted by Sweden's central bank that indicated the economy there would "contract by 4.5 percent" in 2020, a decline similar to that of neighboring Denmark, where the response to the virus was quite a bit more muscular in the governmental sense. Goodman concluded from Sweden that it "is simplistic to portray government actions such as quarantines as the cause of economic damage. The real culprit is the virus itself." And with 5,420 deaths in Sweden related to the virus, Goodman concluded that "Sweden suffered a vastly higher death rate [than neighboring countries] while failing to collect on expected economic gains."[123] There's so much errant about what Goodman concluded.

For one, GDP as a measure of growth is rather faulty as readers know from Chapter Six. What measures consumption would naturally decline during a pandemic, with or without lockdowns. Indeed, explicit in the Swedish government's not forcing behavior was that people wouldn't need to be forced to be more cautious. What was true in Sweden was also true per Badger and Parlapiano in U.S. states that didn't lock down right away. Much as the left wants to imagine people to be truly clueless sans the guiding hand of politicians, they broadly get it. Because they do, consumption was going to decline in the face of a virus, thus bringing down GDP. What's not spent doesn't hide; rather, it's shifted, frequently to those who need growth capital.

For two, it doesn't insult Goodman to say what's true but that was lost on him: the only closed economy is the world economy. Every good and service is a consequence of global cooperation and production that takes place globally. And as a future chapter will reveal through El Salvador, much of country GDP in some countries is a consequence almost entirely of production in other countries. In short, it's only natural that Sweden's economy would contract amid a worldwide panic among politicians. Just as the "world catches a cold" when the U.S. economy contracts, so would Sweden naturally see its economy shrink substantially amid a global rush toward lockdown.

Imagine if the U.S. had gone the route of Sweden—as in if politicians on the local, state, and national levels recognized that Americans were already taking precautions related to the virus such that they didn't need their hands held. Imagine the latter happening at the same time that the rest of the world was locking down. Could Goodman possibly believe that such a scenario wouldn't result in a major decline in U.S. growth? As we know from Chapter One, China alone represents an enormous market for the U.S.'s greatest companies. So assuming politicians hadn't panicked stateside, the U.S. economy would still have contracted, just not as much.

Reducing this to a more unlikely scenario, imagine if China suddenly reverted to the collectivist policies that prevailed in the once desperate country. Rest assured that the U.S. economy would contract substantially. As the previous paragraph makes plain, China is a huge market for U.S. companies, but more importantly hundreds of millions of Chinese working productively enable much greater productivity in the U.S. When work is divided up, workers get to specialize.

Just the same, the U.S. is a huge market for any corporation anywhere in the world with global ambitions. It's not just that the U.S. is a huge market for the world's best businesses; rather it's also the case that U.S. labor and innovation render the rest of the world exponentially more productive. Take the U.S. out of the economic equation, or even take California out (the world's fifth largest economy), and it's going to be felt globally. That the U.S. shut down a quarter of its economy signaled contraction elsewhere even if every other country had largely followed Sweden's model.

Funny about Sweden's model is that while the *New York Times* and Goodman were gloating in July 2008 about the country's alleged failures related to too much freedom, by September the tune of the newspaper had changed. *Times* reporter Thomas Erdbrink pointed out that as a consequence of the country's "current low caseload" amid "sharp increases" in COVID cases elsewhere, that "many European countries" were "trying to preserve a degree of normalcy, with schools, shops, restaurants and even bars open." In other words per Erdbrink, other countries "were quietly adopting the Swedish approach."[124]

As for deaths from the virus, Goodman left out that Tokyo didn't lock down in repressive fashion, yet according to the *Wall Street Journal's* Alastair Gale, "deaths attributed to the virus" as of late May in 2020 were 777.[125] Sweden suffered deaths per 100,000 of 54, but heavily locked down New York experienced a death rate per 100,000 of 161. Sweden is less densely populated than New York in parts, but then Tokyo is very densely populated. Arguably more telling, *Times* reporter Peter Goodman later acknowledged in an October report that the "vastly higher death rate" in Sweden that he'd reported on in July had nuanced qualities. As Goodman and Erik Augustin Palm noted in October 2020, "Among the nearly 6,000 people whose deaths have been linked to the coronavirus in Sweden, 2, 694, or more than 45 percent, had been among the country's most vulnerable citizens—those living in nursing homes."[126] Was Sweden's "vastly higher death rate" a consequence of the coronavirus, or were many in nursing homes already near the end? This is not a health care book by any stretch, but it's somewhat reasonable to conclude that there's less correlation about the death and the coronavirus than has sometimes been assumed.

Which reminds us again of the tragedy that panicked politicians engineered. Having forced an unnatural contraction on the economy via lockdown orders, they then compounded their error with an extraction of $2.9 trillion more from an already crashing economy as witless politicians set to work on fixing command-and-control problems of their own making with even more government. Capitalism, per the George Gilder quote that begins this chapter, is an information system. It's about leaps born of intrepid investment that enable intrepid experimentation. But when it was needed most, when matching talented innovators with growth capital was most needed, politicians blinded an economy seeking to create a future made more uncertain by a virus with a massive extraction of capital from that economy.

With their lockdowns politicians forced an outcome that would have been profoundly different and had a profoundly different impact on growth if private individuals and businesses had been free to work around customer, employee, and *business owner* fear of a virus. Panicked politicians needlessly wrecked the economy, period. This isn't to say that economies in southern U.S. states didn't contract despite locking down less strictly than the rest of the U.S. Contract they did. The only "closed U.S. economy" is the U.S. economy, so if California purposely gets sick, it's going to be felt throughout the U.S. and around the world. At the same time, it cannot be denied that the U.S.'s southern states didn't contract as much thanks to the lighter touch of their politicians. According to a *Wall Street Journal* report from October 2020, the number of people employed in the U.S. south was "6% lower in August than in February," compared with "declines of 10.6% in the Northeast, 8.2% in the West and 7% in the Midwest."[127] The lockdowns were significant.

After that, if the lockdowns weren't the source of economic contraction, as in if scared-out-of-their-wits Americans were going to shelter in place no matter what such that the economy would collapse, then what was the point of the lockdowns? If some think Badger and Parlapiano were right about the citizenry sheltering without coercion, then they're rather explicitly saying that the lockdowns served no purpose. Pick a side.

Which leads us to the next chapter. What if, in response to the virus, politicians had done nothing? It's something worth thinking about before we return to the policies that were a creation of panic.

Chapter Eleven

WHAT IF THEY'D JUST DONE NOTHING?

"There would be nothing more tragic than if, in our efforts to preserve our health, we were to lose our freedom."

—Malcolm Turnbull, former prime minister of Australia[128]

"John Delgado has slept in a tent in his backyard for 57 nights and counting." *New York Times* reporter Frances Robles wrote the latter about the inventory manager at Farm Share, which Robles described as "an immense South Florida food bank."

So why was Delgado sleeping in a tent? Robles reported that he was going to great lengths to "avoid contaminating his wife, aging mother-in-law, three sons and a grandson." He was even practicing "socially-distanced yard work with his sons." While on the job at Farm Share, Delgado found himself "holding his breath under his face-covering" while speaking "to the many clients who came in without masks, for fear

– 90 –

that coronavirus particles" would make their way through the fabric of his mask.[129]

Important about Delgado's precautionary ways is that no one forced them on him. Florida was not only late to lockdowns (April 1), it was also quick to begin the process of reopening. Had Delgado wanted to, and had his family members approved, he could have slept in his own bed in his own house each night. He could have conducted yard work without regard to distancing, and he could have served his customers without a mask, on the unlikely assumption that his employer would have allowed him to work sans face protection.

It's a reminder of something plainly forgotten by politicians who so aggressively forced their solutions on the citizenry in the spring of 2020: most of us don't need to be told to protect ourselves from illness or, in extreme cases, death. "Extreme" is the operative word here simply because Florida never experienced enormous numbers of deaths related to the virus despite locking down well after states like New York and despite reopening well before New York. As of the end of June 2020, the Empire State had suffered deaths per 100,000 people of 161, while Florida's deaths per 100,000 was a paltry (in relative terms) 15.[130]

Despite this, Delgado was very careful. He *exceeded* the State of Florida's requirements. Considering businesses, it was near impossible to enter one in which employees weren't wearing masks. That businesses required their employees to wear masks regardless of local or state decrees was an *economic* decision. Why risk offending or turning away even one customer?

All of which sets the stage for the next question: What if politicians on all levels had quite simply done nothing? Lest readers forget, politicians and those in government's employ used to not be part of government. That they are, or were in the spring of 2020, hardly puts a halo on their heads. It's not as though being in government altered their IQs.

Some will say politicians provide crucial information during times of peril, but that's not a serious view. Even if they do provide information, it's not as though we would be blind to the world around us without them. Thinking back to the middle of the nineteenth century, it's said that three hundred thousand fortune hunters from around the world made their way to northern California in search of what was said to be abundant gold. Somehow word about opportunity in California made it around the world then despite the fact that transatlantic cable communications of the most primitive kind were still over seventeen years away with telephones, internet, and Wi-Fi, respectively, much more distant.

It's a massive cliché, but in 2020 the supercomputers also known as smartphones produced for most of us information instantaneously. Looked at through the prism of a coronavirus that some thought very deadly, it's not as though we weren't going to know sans politicians. More than most would ever admit, the information age rendered them superfluous from an information standpoint.

Didn't we need politicians to set boundaries for us? That's what Andrew Cuomo, governor of New York, seemed to indicate. The darling of major media during the craziest days of virus hysteria accused the states that locked down less aggressively than New York did of playing politics. In Cuomo's words, "You told the people of your state and you told the people of this country, White House, 'Don't worry about it. Just open up, go about your business, this is all Democratic hyperbole.'"[131]

The easy, shooting-fish-in-a-barrel response to Cuomo would be that the governor of the state that suffered the most coronavirus-related deaths (by far) wasn't in a position to be critiquing any other city or state. But such a stance would achieve nothing. This is once again not a medical book. It's instead one that aims to tell an economic story that was a consequence of panic by politicians. Stop and think about the previous sentence for a second. Then think back to the chapter that precedes this one.

In Chapter Ten, the argument offered by the *New York Times* was that politicians were not at fault for the economic meltdown. Quoting *Times* reporters Emily Badger and Alicia Parlapiano directly, "Even in states that imposed stay-at-home orders or closed nonessential businesses relatively early, *households and businesses had begun to shift their behavior about 10 days before those orders. In states that closed later, that shift had come about 20 days earlier.*" It should be clearly noted that the italicized words represent your author's emphasis as a way of making plain that the lockdown-at-all-costs crowd that made a saint out of Andrew Cuomo can't have it both ways. They can't say out of one side of the mouth that the unsophisticated masses would have ignored medical science absent the wise guidance of politicians, only to say out of the other side that those same individuals of limited sophistication (you know, the people in states that were slow to shut down or didn't altogether) were aggressively shifting their behavior ahead of any political decrees.

Notable about the decrees is that Badger and Parlapiano confirm that in the states that closed later, the shift began sooner—as in *free people* decided on their own to protect themselves against an unknown. The very excellent Holman Jenkins of the *Wall Street Journal* noted that "masks and hand sanitizer disappeared from store shelves even as Berlin was still downplaying the [coronavirus] threat and warning about anti-foreigner bigotry."[132] Force wasn't required. Not in the U.S., and not overseas. Frustrating about the previous point is that we know, and knew, that force isn't required.

For background, we can start with culture. Culture is a window into society itself. In consideration of it, it's useful to consider a great episode from the near-uniformly great television show, *Seinfeld*. "The Pothole" is the title of episode 16, season 8. In this one Jerry accidentally knocks girlfriend Jenna's toothbrush into the toilet, only for Jenna to use it before Jerry can tell her about his accident. This rated a plotline given Seinfeld's known aversion to germs. Readers can imagine where the story went. *Seinfeld* was surely a comedy defined by manufactured situations "about nothing," but one reason the show was so popular (and still is) is that people could relate.

Certainly they could relate to Seinfeld's obsessive aversion to germs. We all know people like this, or we are those people. These individuals never open doors by the door handle, obsessively wipe down tray tables and armrests on airplanes, and particularly if they have young kids they require all visitors to wash or disinfect their hands upon entering their house or apartment.

In a work sense, most readers can probably remember their first job or jobs. They paid hourly. If so, no doubt some can remember how holiday work paid double the hourly wage or sometimes more. Eager to remain open for customers whose wants and needs don't cease on holidays, businesses pay workers extra to make sure they'll serve their customers on days when most aren't working.

These anecdotes gained extra relevance as the mass shutdown of "non-essential" businesses picked up speed. How very unnecessary it all was. It was unnecessary simply because free people were already shifting to new ways of working, of operating their businesses. Despite free people deciding for themselves how to brace for an unknown, panicked politicians decided they knew better.

As previously mentioned, California's forty million residents were put on lockdown per the order of Governor Gavin Newsom. The mayor of Hoboken (NJ) banned restaurants and bars from serving food, plus instituted a 10 p.m. to 5 a.m. curfew.[133] Austin's mayor canceled South by Southwest, thus devastating local businesses. On the national level, President Trump ascribed to himself "wartime" powers that would enable the commandeering of the means of production in order to produce what he deemed essential for the fight against the virus.[134]

Seemingly stunned Americans, perhaps shocked by the swiftness of the political power grab, sat back and let it happen. In fairness to the American people, it's arguable they were too surprised to protest after seeing politicians on all levels so rapidly take away their ability to work and enjoy the fruits of that work. Some probably believed it would just be for two weeks in order to "bend" the infection curve downward. Naaah.

Americans were told the crushing of the economy by the political class was in so many words "for their own good," and that they should respect the "science" informing their decisions. Didn't the American people get it—politicians were fighting to save their lives! Since their actions were noble, Americans apparently had to forfeit their liberty and prosperity.

Seemingly lost in all this alleged governmental beneficence was that people broadly get it. See yet again the shifts that took place before politicians decided to aggrandize themselves. See once again *Seinfeld*. The episode was relatable because we yet again know all too many people who are exceedingly careful about being around the sick or those they presume to be germ carriers. This was true even in times free of virus scares. Translated, people are self-regulating when it comes to their health. *They don't need a law.*

Which brings us back to the counterfactual theme of this chapter: What if politicians had sat on their hands? If so, does anyone seriously think that the death rate would have been substantially higher and that information about this potentially lethal virus wouldn't have reached a population increasingly connected to the internet all day and every day? Some will say that shelter-in-place orders kept people distant and thus less likely to infect each other, but as of May 6, 2020, it was reported about New York that "two-thirds of patients recently hospitalized in the state were people who were sheltering at home."[135]

No doubt some readers will respond that the above stat is anecdote as opposed to statistic, to which the response will be *precisely*. The *New York* figure revealed shelter in place as not terribly effective, which well explains why uniformity in approach from politicians was such a mistaken way to fight the virus. This will be discussed more in a future chapter, but free people produce crucial information by doing as they wish. Applied to the coronavirus, some would have never left their homes for months, some would have left on occasion with gloves and masks, and some would have lived as though the virus were nonexistent. You need all three, and millions more variations in pursuit of information about why and how a virus spreads.

What about businesses? What if there had been no lockdowns? What a great question. It's safe to say that many would have operated short-staffed as is with germaphobes top of mind. Rather than forced furloughs, it's not unreasonable to suggest that a good percentage of workers on all levels of the economic food chain would have voluntarily opted out. Others fearful of contracting the virus would have "flattened" the alleged curve *voluntarily* by taking a well-needed and rather isolated vacation somewhere, including one of the "staycation" variety.

The main thing is that as opposed to businesses shutting down, it's not unreasonable to contend that in concert with certain workers opting out or vacationing during the period of greatest COVID uncertainty, patronage of bars, restaurants, movie theaters, amusement parks, stadiums, arenas, hotels, motels, casinos, and everything else would have similarly declined naturally, thus shrinking the need for fully staffed operations. Again, this was already happening before the lockdowns, *voluntarily*. Crucial is that none of what's been said was a speculation. See again the "shifts" from Chapter Ten.

And what if some businesses stayed packed no matter what? If so, high customer demand would have given businesses fearful of potentially morphing into contagion zones a reason to limit customer inflow by, yes, charging higher prices for said food or service. Assuming broad aversion on the part of the public to being in public, other businesses would have advertised their adherence to strict customer limits in order to bring in consumers who would have otherwise studiously avoided public places out of fear of big crowds.

Still other businesses, perhaps newly opened, would have used a period of uncertainty to stay open while gaining market share that would be harder to attain during periods of normalcy. And if the newer, suddenly busier businesses were to find it challenging to staff for relatively larger customer inflow, they might offer holiday style or hazardous duty pay to attract quality help, including quality help from established businesses that chose to stay closed with brand risk top of mind. The new businesses staying open would have provided essential clues to closed, more established businesses about how to eventually reopen.

The major point in all this is that as opposed to a one-size-fits-all shutdown of businesses that was wrecking the finances and dreams of tens of millions, market forces and market fears would have made it possible for many more businesses to stay open, albeit in a way that wouldn't have imperiled workers or customers. And if it had been true that simply being around others had proven lethal, this essential information would have reached us much sooner. About the previous sentence, it's fair to say we already knew the answer as evidenced by grocery stores and all-purpose stores like Walmart not morphing into "hot zones," not to mention that according to the *New York Times*, Disney World experienced no coronavirus outbreaks three months after reopening.[136] After which there's always China. If the virus had truly been a major killer, or even a mediocre killer, we would have known long before March. Information travels fast, and it travels really fast in a world thick with internet-enabled smartphones.

What of movie theaters, stadiums, and sports arenas? Unknown is the *why* behind the uniformity of shutdowns in certain parts of the U.S. Here, perhaps absent politics, those staging events and films might have used prices, and in particular *high prices*, to limit the size of crowds as opposed to canceling events altogether. If the game plan is distance, let price signals arrived at in the marketplace shrink crowd sizes not just in restaurants and bars, but in all manner of venues. Thinking about March Madness, what a slap for politicians and the NCAA to assume that absent cancellation, arenas would have been packed-to-the-gills hot zones. No, the shifts previously mentioned indicate that all too many would have opted out on their own.

A potential response is that a "business as usual" approach doesn't work in the face of what is potentially lethal. Such a view is insulting.

It implies that, absent the guiding hand of government, people would completely disregard their own well-being. That's not serious now, and it wasn't then. In fact it was obnoxious to presume that Americans needed to be forced to protect themselves.

Free people naturally prosper, and they do precisely because their individual well-being means so much to them. Had governments done nothing in response to the coronavirus, individuals and businesses would have done much more, and done so without going out of business. The Ruling Class that oversaw this crack-up deserves the mother of all come-uppances that goes well beyond being thrown out in the next several election cycles. The architects of this wholly avoidable debacle need to be publicly shamed and ridiculed.

The shame, of course, is that it wasn't just the lockdowns. In the next few chapters there will be a pivot back to the horrid policy responses to the economy-wrecking lockdowns. Politicians don't just break things. They break things, only to foist on us aftershocks in terms of policy responses.

Chapter Twelve

THE AUTHORS OF THE "STIMULUS" PROGRAM WANT TO PROTECT YOU FROM A VIRUS

"All capital, with a trifling exception, was originally the result of saving."[37]

—John Stuart Mill, *Principles of Political Economy*

I t was all so predictable. There's a saying about the perpetually inept that they never disappoint. For those who don't get the allusion, it needlessly flatters the incompetent to feign disappointment when they live up to their incompetence.

Politicians and the governments they're part of never disappoint. With the U.S. economy on its back, politicians were going to vacuum up precious wealth from the private economy only to misallocate the funds. *It's what they do.* Naturally they would use GDP to hide behind their economy-shrinking waste of precious private capital. As readers hopefully remember from Chapter Six, GDP is a monument to double counting. Politicians extract from the economy wealth that was already created, dole it out sans market discipline, then cheer on the GDP "growth" that is solely a consequence of growth that *already occurred*. No, politicians don't disappoint. Economists *really* don't. But that's a digression. Sort of.

It's a good jumping-off point to news that came out in late June 2020 to much fanfare and outrage. According to a Government Accountability Office (GAO) report from the time, over $1.4 billion worth of "stimulus" checks sent out by the federal government went to dead people.[138] Again, oh so typical.

Of the delusion that a struggling private sector could be goosed economically by the extraction of trillions from that same private sector, the federal government raced to push $270 billion worth of "stimulus" checks worth $1,200 each out the door as quickly as possible to allegedly get the economy moving again. Missed by those who never disappoint was that the checks were the equivalent of moving money from the left pocket to the right. Actually, that's not true. The checks were an economic depressant. In the words of John Stuart Mill, "The limit of wealth is never deficiency of consumers, but of producers and productive power."[139] The "stimulus" checks of $1,200 each were going to stimulate consumption at the expense of production.

To see why, it has to be remembered that not everyone received "stimulus" checks. Singles who earned $75,000 annually or less and couples who earned $150,000 annually or less received the full amount of either $1,200 (single) or $2,400 (couple). If income was above either $75,000 (single) or $150,000 (couple), the check from the federal government gradually shrank. Singles earning $99,000 or above and couples earning $198,000 or more received nothing.[140]

To consumption-obsessed economists, which is the vast majority of economists, the "stimulus" plan made sense. Extract savings from the real economy, then redistribute from savers to those most likely to spend. In extracting savings from the economy with an eye on enhancing consumption, the political class shrank a capital base for an economy that, as evidenced by its struggles, was desperate for more capital. Lest readers forget, businesses were short on cash due to the shutdowns, plus those shutdowns necessarily had investors gun-shy owing to uncertainty about when the shutdowns would end. Piling on, politicians extracted trillions worth of savings from the economy. All of which explains why the proverbial shift of dollars from one pocket to another was much less than benign.

Taking it all back to the million-plus checks sent by the feds to dead people, they were merely the beginning of the comedy of errors that was the $2.9 trillion "stimulus" program. The outrage on social media was noisy. The outraged missed the point, as will soon be made plain. Soon is operative mainly because there were other very real "outrages" that at the same time needlessly distracted those who were at least rhetorically for limited government. As though this will surprise anyone, it wasn't just checks to dead people that had some Americans on edge.

Sidwell Friends is one of the most prestigious private schools in all of Washington, DC. The name no doubt rings a bell for many readers simply because Sidwell is where Chelsea Clinton was educated, along with Barack and Michele Obama's two daughters, Malia and Sasha. Even though Sidwell has an endowment of $53.4 million, the school accepted $5.2 million in "federal" dollars from the corona-inspired Paycheck Protection Program (PPP) "in light of actual and anticipated shortfalls, mounting uncertainty," and "the importance of maintaining employment levels."[141]

John Burroughs School is generally viewed as one of the most exclusive in all of St. Louis. Its alums include (among others) actors Jon Hamm and Ellie Kemper, restaurant mogul Danny Meyer, and perhaps ironically *House of Cards* creator Beau Willimon, plus its endowment is similarly in the $50 million range. Yet the school accepted a $2.55 million federal loan "at this unprecedented time to ensure we can support our employees, and our ongoing operations in a manner that is not detrimental to the long-term financial health of the school."[142]

St. Andrew's Episcopal School in Potomac, MD, probably most famous for being where Baron Trump was a student, accepted PPP funds "to ensure retention of our full faculty and staff, including hourly employees and coaches during this very challenging and uncertain time."[143] The U.S. economy was to varying degrees smoldering, but the feds were commandeering precious savings in order to direct them to dead people, elite high schools, and… It didn't stop there as the mildly sapient among us can probably guess.

You see, Harvard University is arguably the most prestigious university in the world. It's hard to contemplate a degree that opens up more doors than one from Harvard. Still, wise minds can debate the "best of" or most prestigious. What's not debatable is that with a $40 billion endowment, Harvard has the largest university endowment in the world. This rates mention because the Cambridge, MA-based institution accepted $9 million in PPP funds with designs on spending them. The school ultimately refused the funds once it became apparent that the PR related to their acceptance would be more than unfortunate, but still.[144]

Looking back to Danny Meyer, his Shake Shack was awarded $10 million in PPP funds, only for the chain to refuse them.[145] Goodness, even the Los Angeles Lakers received $4.6 million in PPP funds that were ultimately returned.[146] The Lakers are worth many billions.

On its face, the indiscriminate throwing around of money speaks to the horrors of government. In the real economy, precious capital is allocated with returns top of mind. Government just hands out money. Other people's money. And precisely because there's no thought to how the money is being allocated, you have some of the most prestigious private schools, universities, and businesses receiving what is scarce. Government is incompetent but also populist. It's bad PR for the "rich" to get handouts, but invariably government incompetence results in stories like this. It's just what happens. Rest assured that the outrage related to all this was loud. A government this inept with precious funds aims to fight a virus? Can the political class be serious?

At the same time, it should be noted that the outrage that the political class unearthed with its mindless allocation of funds had a very hollow quality to it. Indeed, the anger, if looked at honestly, truly missed the point. So much did it miss the point that it almost raises the question if the politicians who never disappoint are smarter than they perhaps appear? The errant dispensation of funds arguably speaks to their wily ways. What a brilliant distraction they created! Think about it.

The problem wasn't the $9 million that Harvard received and almost spent. Goodness, *if only* politicians would solely feed their pet causes on occasion. The much bigger outrage was that a federal government with powers allegedly "few and defined" had a claim on so much of our existing and future production that it was able to instantly come up with trillions to throw at an economic disaster created by politicians on the city, state, and national level.

Which is why the Shake Shack freak-out was similarly mystifying. Yet it was everywhere. Shake Shack is a big corporation that can more easily access funds from banks and private investors! How dare it take $10 million from taxpayers! Small businesses are the "backbone" of the U.S. economy (more on this in the next chapter) and should get all the federal money. Let the big fend for themselves! Shame on "lobbyists" for using their power to boost the big at the expense of the small! The big chains don't need the money; they should leave it for the small that lack access to "high-priced lobbyists," connected banks, and the like.

As usual, the fury was misplaced. A much bigger problem than forgivable federal loans to businesses was the sad fact that the federal government had secured for itself a role in matters economic to begin with, and that it once again had the power to summon copious amounts of money to throw at the problems of the political class's own making. In short, the outrage was blind in its hatred.

Realistically the indignation should have been about the spending itself, not who got the money. Absent the lockdowns there wouldn't have been trillions extracted. And while the small business argument will once again be addressed in greater detail in the next chapter, the perpetually outraged were going to let "big," $1.6 billion Shake Shack take up sizable space in their heads?

About this critique of the anger and the subsequent venom spewed at Harvard and others back in spring 2020, this should in no way be construed as an endorsement of federal loans or handouts to Harvard, Shake Shack, the Lakers, and many others. Far from it. At the same time it is a call for proportionality. Government shouldn't be handing out money to businesses or universities *as a rule*, as opposed to handouts being OK depending on size of business or size of university endowment.

After that, the real outrage should yet again be centered on the federal government's extraction of $2.9 trillion from the economy. It was an economy-weakening non sequitur. It was the equivalent of a doctor walking in on a patient being smothered, only to blithely recommend a ventilator. The federal handouts made no sense. Repeat that over and over again. You don't reward the creators of misery with extra funds to throw at their mistakes, plus the spending missed the asphyxiation point. Businesses didn't have a money problem in the spring of 2020; rather, they had a problem of suffocation by politicians, two times over: first the lockdowns, then massive spending that exacerbated the latter. Government was growing at the expense of the real economy right when the real economy was dangerously low on capital.

The problem was the spending in 2020. Always the spending. That the spending was happening in pursuit of the impossible is where we'll pivot to in the next chapter.

Chapter Thirteen

THEY WOULD STOP YOU AT "JOB CREATION"

"When you walk through, we want you to be awed, jawdropped, inspired."

—Don Ghermezian, creator of the American Dream shopping mall in Meadowlands, NJ, October 2019[147]

In late February 2020, and just a few weeks before a political crack-up over the coronavirus that cruelly forced economic contraction on the American people in whiplash-inducing fashion, it was announced that the Glover Park (Washington, DC) Whole Foods would reopen later in the year. The location had closed in 2017 for a quick remodel, only for a landlord-tenant dispute to keep it shut down and idled altogether for nearly three years.[148]

Glover Park is a partially run-down, partially posh commercial and residential area just above Georgetown. Word of reopening was welcome news to the small businesses located in Glover that, in some instances, opened in the area specifically to be near a Whole Foods. As Justine Bernard, a small business owner in the area explained it to the *Glover Park Gazette* in 2018, "We've lost the habit of people coming here to shop at Whole Foods. That was maybe 300 to 500 people a day. It had become part of the weekly routine to be in Glover Park. We lost that foot traffic."[149]

The highly regarded grocery chain is a big lure for shoppers. Even better, Whole Foods attracts a rather well-heeled clientele. Since it does, the arrival of the grocery store in neighborhoods invariably heralds or foretells economic revitalization.

The great Canadian economist Reuven Brenner has long written about the "vital few." His useful descriptor is arguably easiest to understand through sports. Before the arrival of Larry Bird and Magic Johnson in the NBA, the league's playoff games were televised in tape-delayed fashion after 11:30 p.m. in markets across the U.S. Bird and Magic brought the NBA into prime time. The NFL's Dallas Cowboys frequently play in prime time given the viewership they near uniquely can generate. Looked at through the prism of Hollywood, certain actors and actresses—think Robert Downey and Jennifer Lawrence—can pretty much guarantee substantial opening-weekend box office. When they're "attached" to scripts, movies get made.

Business is no different. Consider malls. There's a reason they all have anchor tenants that can invariably claim national, and sometimes international, brand recognition. What's big and well known generates foot traffic for the small, almost invariably lesser-known brands that cluster around them. And while Apple Stores are rarely anchor tenants in the square foot sense, where they open ensures quite a lot of exposure for the businesses lucky enough to be near them.

It seems none of this was considered in the silly economic spring of 2020. The view among the credentialed in March and April was that businesses had a "liquidity" problem. No, they didn't. Figure that

Amazon's stock was soaring owing to its existing and presumed future ability to meet the needs of people who might be quite a bit less eager to leave home to purchase life's necessities. Amazon didn't have a liquidity problem. Neither did Zoom as its utility became increasingly apparent during the mass shutdown of offices. Peloton shares soared, too, as it became increasingly apparent that politicians desperate to protect our health weren't going to "allow" *health clubs* to reopen anytime soon. On the other hand, millions of businesses *did* suffer liquidity crunches, and they did because they were being suffocated. Those with funds to invest or loan don't go out of their way to lend to businesses that politicians deem "non-essential," or that can't operate on account of politicians decreeing lockdowns.

Contra the musings of policy theorists, former Fed officials, and existing Fed officials, liquidity cannot be decreed; rather, it's a consequence of the free movement of people and capital. In the spring of 2020 there was little freedom of movement in the commercial sense, hence a lack of liquidity. This simple truth eluded Milken Institute scholars Michael Klowden and Michael Piwowar. Writing in the *Wall Street Journal* on April 8, 2020, in a column titled, you guessed it, "To Boost Liquidity, Expand the Definition of Collateral," the scholars made the claim that "America's 30 million small businesses are the heart and soul of its economy. They are the engines of economic growth and the creators of the jobs that provide income and dignity for nearly half of the workforce." They, like seemingly everyone else deep in thought, were looking for government solutions to a problem of liquidity *caused by government.* Worse, they were promoting the falsehood that economic revitalization would be driven by small businesses resuscitated by government. No, it wasn't a serious view.

While it may well be true that small businesses provide tens of millions of jobs in aggregate, Klowden and Piwowar were putting the cart before the horse. Far from being the "engines of economic growth," small businesses and the jobs they create are most often a consequence of big business.

No doubt it's fun and comforting in some kind of American frontier way to imagine Main Street and the small as the drivers of the world's most dynamic economy, but that's the extent of it. It's fantasy thinking. It's saccharine-sweet, much-less-than-empty comfort food.

Rather explicit in the view that small businesses would power U.S. economic recovery in 2020 was the idea that the mediocre or average pull the excellent and well above average upward in a business sense. No, it's the reverse. Goodness, did large $40 billion endowment Harvard locate in Cambridge to benefit from the small businesses, or did the small businesses locate there to benefit from being around Harvard? Readers know the answer. It insults small businesses in no way to say they're largely a consequence of the big.

Which was why the commentary from spring 2020 was so troubling. Though the nobility of small business had always been an empty but rather popular rhetorical device for pundits and politicians, hundreds of billions were on the verge of being spent on the exceedingly easy-to-discredit view that recovery would come care of the average in the business world. A political class that should have been sidelined had dreamt up the Paycheck Protection Program (PPP) as the policy answer that would promote the debased view that economic vitality springs from the middle.

Notable about the PPP was that there wasn't much pretense to it. It was what it said it was. Since "business" seemingly isn't "evil" or "too powerful" if "small" is next to it, the PPP would fit the extreme stupidity of the times the U.S. found itself in like a glove. The PPP was in the words of the *New York Times* "a $660 billion relief effort intended to help struggling small companies retain or rehire their workers."[150] Which was the obvious problem with it, among many other things. That the PPP was all about job preservation was the surest sign of how pointless and wasteful it was.

Think about it. In the real world of finance, they would stop you at job creation. Who would? Venture capitalists and other capital allocators if, when presenting your new business idea, you led with how many jobs your venture would create or save.

No one starts a business to put people to work. No one could. Investors would run from such a concept with great gusto. It should more realistically be stated that every commercial and technological advance is all about *shrinking* the amount of labor required to achieve some kind of productive outcome. Technology is the process whereby machines and other advances produce exponentially more with fewer hands.

This is so often forgotten by economic types on the left and right as they obsess over "labor force participation" rates. How very backwards. If readers are looking for 100 percent labor force participation, just travel to the world's poorest countries. Everyone is realistically working all the time at jobs that those of us in the developed world would be revolted by. Life is defined by unrelenting drudgery.

In rich, economically advanced countries work is the norm, but more and more it's a *choice* as opposed to a necessity. There are dual-earner couples and people who work until their dying day not because doing so is a matter of survival, but because work itself brings its own rewards.

It's worth stressing with great regularity that work is most rewarding in the parts of the world where jobs are destroyed the most rapidly. Looking at it in terms of the United States, "what do you do?" in 2020 would elicit wildly different answers relative to 1920 when agriculture was still a major part of the U.S. economy, but so would the answer have been very different in 1990, 2000, and 2010. In "destroying" jobs, technology expands the range of ways we can specialize our work, as opposed to it putting us in breadlines. That's why the flow of humans is almost uniformly to the most technologically advanced locales and away from those that turn their noses up to advances that transform how we work.

In rich countries what we call work is constantly changing precisely because technological advances mothball the toil of the past. Contrast that with the poorest countries where "what do you do?" results in the same answer for all too many year after year and decade after decade.

Looked at through the prism of the PPP, what an obnoxious, intelligence-insulting non sequitur. No one was clamoring for a PPP in the first quarter of 2020 simply because politicians at that point hadn't happened on the shockingly dim idea whereby they would engineer mass unemployment, business bankruptcy, and desperation as the solution to a new virus.

About the U.S. economy pre-coronavirus, it's not as though businesses weren't failing then. In truth, they were going under with great regularity. Doesn't anyone remember the endless whining about how Amazon was going to make shopping malls and "big box" retailers the telephone booths of the 2020s? It didn't matter that Amazon itself was aggressively moving into so-called "brick and mortar" with Amazon Go and Amazon Books, not to mention its purchase of Whole Foods. It didn't matter that as of 2019, the internet could still only account for less than a fifth of total sales in the U.S.[151] The view before the coronavirus political crack-up was that Amazon was set to swallow much of the retail economy. So while the worry was well overdone, a changing team picture for commerce is the norm. Such is the way of a dynamic economy: endless experimentation conducted by entrepreneurs and, as a consequence, lots of businesses shuttering all the time only to be replaced by better ones.

Needless to say, a certain sign of economic sclerosis is a static business scenario whereby the ones populating malls and other shopping areas are unchanging. Conversely, somewhat rapid turnover signals *progress* as the present is constantly being replaced by the future. In short, with or without the coronavirus, the nature of work and the names of businesses meeting our needs was going to change markedly between 2020 and 2030, and just as reasonably, between 2020 and 2025. The year 2025 will be wholly unrecognizable relative to 2050. Thank goodness!

Yet even with the signs dotting the U.S. commercial landscape changing with great rapidity, there was once again no serious movement before March 2020 for something along the lines of the PPP even though the future for most businesses was far from certain. But with the forced lockdowns by politicians who wrecked the present and future of all manner of businesses indiscriminately, and for reasons that had nothing to do with "free markets," government stepped in to throw the money of others at what it broke. The PPP existed then and will forever exist as yet another reminder of why government cannot—*ever*—play investor, lender, or any kind of resource allocator.

Indeed, with politicians having cruelly put tens of millions out of work as a consequence of neutering and bankrupting businesses with their lockdowns, the PPP was created by government so that businesses could rehire some of the very people government had rendered unemployed. And in classic government fashion, this brain-dead program required that 75 percent of the PPP funds go toward employee pay.[152] Maintain jobs at all costs!

That's how people in government think. In state and national capitols, it's all about *doing less with more people*. Hiring to hire. Don't you get it: hiring without regard to the purpose of the job creates "economic growth"! Actually, productivity powers economic growth, which is why businesses routinely strive to do more with fewer hands. Technology enables all this.

In the spring of 2020, and at any time, for many businesses their biggest expenses are rent related and physical infrastructure. This is particularly true in prosperous cities. A business close to the well-to-do is in some instances going to pay quite a bit more just to be in that location than to employees working in, say, Beverly Hills, Greenwich, or River Oaks. Naturally the PPP didn't recognize this reality, among others. How could it? Government is one-size-fits-all, while private investment is bespoke. With PPP the federal government was simply offering to use the money of others to help businesses access debt, *if* they were going to keep on superfluous employees made superfluous by—you guessed it—government.

The main thing is that the PPP was in so many instances pointless under the best of circumstances and crippling under the worst. That was so because there was no way of knowing what the future would look like for companies in terms of human employees. Precisely because some consumers might prefer less human interaction in the future with virus-spreading top of mind, it was possible that businesses would devise all manner of ways to save on labor while meeting new or evolving needs of customers that they didn't express before the spread of the coronavirus. It's also worth pointing out that *workers* were in some instances quite a bit more cautious about the future. As a July 2020 report by *Investor's Business Daily's* Paul Katzeff indicated, factories and warehouses were themselves in a rush to automate away some aspects of human exertion simply because employees of companies like Amazon were demanding the evolution.[153]

After that, let's not forget that businesses would to some degree be impaired in the coronavirus aftermath simply because previously locked down consumers would be. Stating the obvious, you can't shut down an economy for months and expect all your customers to emerge from such a scenario as flush as they were amid soaring economic times just a few months prior. For government to demand near pre-virus levels of employment as a precondition of receiving PPP money was for government to set the stage for business failure just as soon as those hideous and unnecessary lockdowns had ended.

Which was why demand for PPP loans wasn't as brisk as politicians expected. While it's yet again the norm in government to hire for the sake of hiring, actual market-driven commerce is much different. It was asking a lot of businesses to take on more debt in order to maintain levels of staffing that arguably no longer made sense.

"Arguably" was operative here simply because the lockdowns themselves had logically blinded businesses to the future. Who could reasonably predict what was ahead when so many businesses were shuttered? On the other hand, and looking back to Chapter Eleven, what if politicians had done nothing? If so, some businesses would have stayed a lot or a little open amid rising caution among their customers, and the business-customer interactions would have produced valuable information for shuttered businesses about what was ahead.

But with lockdowns broad, the future was rendered quite a bit more opaque than it should have been by politicians who were more than clueless about the challenges their politically wrecked constituents faced. Take a PPP loan to keep unnecessary workers? Not a good deal. What about taking on debt in general if an inability to keep up staffing levels forces payback of the loan? What about the sheer rage inside the heads of all manner of proud business owners that a panic on the part of politicians needlessly placed them in the awful, pride-wrecking position of having to go to the only "lender" open to some businesses in the spring of 2020?

Everything about this program was impossible. The strings naturally attached to the loans made no sense, nor did the broad economics of the loans. As has already been said, and will be said in a book that promises lots of repetition along with lots of repetition about those promises of repetition, future chapters will vivify even more that the nature of work in a dynamic economy is ever-changing. So are the businesses changing. It's once again called progress.

The sad thing was that few, in or out of government, understood the simple point that government lending presumed government knowledge as to who—large or small—would be expertly meeting our needs tomorrow, or ten years from now. Except that this knowledge doesn't exist in government, and since it doesn't, the lending would restrain the arrival of a much better future, precisely because it would prop up the biggest and best, or maybe because it wouldn't. You can't know. The future is intensely blurry, which is the point. Today's giant isn't always tomorrow's. Just the same, today's small also-ran is sometimes tomorrow's giant. Those meeting our needs today will not necessarily be meeting them tomorrow, or ten years from now. Yet government was throwing money at the small of the present, just hoping for takers.

All of which brings us back to the venture capitalists, investors, and lenders who will decide whether cruelly impaired businesses will make it in the aftermath of this most political of crack-ups. About the future, it should be said yet again, "They would stop you at jobs." No business will attract funds if it presumes to operate at staffing levels that perhaps made sense before March 2020. A PPP that would support the past would not maintain it. Reality always intrudes. Again, the initial PPP restrictions were relaxed. They had to be because the program was an impossibility.

Unfortunately, it wasn't just the PPP that was created by politicians to fix what politicians had broken. You the reader *do* recall the Fed, don't you? Ever in search of relevance that never really existed for it as a lender of last resort, America's central bank tried to rewrite reality too—which is where we will pivot to next.

Chapter Fourteen

THE FED CAN'T CREATE THE FUTURE, BUT IT CAN PERHAPS DELAY IT

"If you had given my family an extra $1,000 a month, this would not have done anything to lift us out of poverty. This extra cash would not have moved us up the economic ladder or closed the income gap. It wouldn't have empowered us to buy a home, move into a neighborhood with better schools, or pay for college."

—Damon Dunn, *RealClearMarkets*,
July 2, 2020[154]

I n January 2009, the Pittsburgh Steelers were set to play the Baltimore Ravens in the AFC Championship game. The winner would go on to play in Super Bowl XLIII, which would take place at Raymond James Stadium in Tampa, FL.

Writing in the *Wall Street Journal* the day before the conference championships, economic commentator Jerry Bowyer pointed out an essential economic truth that all too often eludes politicians on the left and right, along with economists. Always focused on "bringing back jobs," they show rather expertly how to *repel* them. To promise the past, or even the maintenance of the present, is to promise economic decline.

In a sense, jobs are the easy part. Really, if endless work were the goal we could simply abolish tractors, computers, and cars in the U.S. Everyone would be working. Life would also be *remarkably dreadful,* but everyone would be working. Let's never forget that work is man's natural state. The true goal should be work that's rewarding, and that's rewarding because it showcases the worker's unique skills and intelligence. When we're doing what animates our talents, we tend to be much more productive. Productivity correlates well with better pay.

Good work that is good because the work options are incredibly varied is a consequence of *people*—talented people in particular. They're a magnet for the investment without which there is no work. Where they are is where abundant work opportunity is, which suggests the wise route for politicians eager to foster prosperity is the pursuit of people.

Think back to Chapter Six and West Virginia University president Gordon Gee. To refresh the memory of readers, Gee quipped that he wanted "to build a wall around West Virginia and keep all the kids here. A state can't flourish that can't keep its young people there." Gee gets it in the way that most politicians do not. Jobs come and go. *People* are always and everywhere the answer to any question about prosperity.

Reducing it to what some might deem absurd, imagine if Jeff Bezos were to announce plans to relocate to West Virginia ahead of starting an all-new business. The billions in investment that would flow Bezos's way, not to mention the amazingly talented *humans* that would follow Bezos into the Mountain State would be awe-inspiring. West Virginia's transformation from poor state to prosperous destination for the economically creative would take place with great speed.

Politicians promise jobs and money, but what they should really be promising are policies most appealing to human capital. That's the only way the "money" will stick around. We know from Chapter Six that the billions that came to West Virginia care of Sen. Robert Byrd departed as quickly as they arrived.

Bringing it all back to Bowyer, he wrote of how Pittsburgh Steelers bars could be found all over the country. As he put it, "Steelers bars are a visible cultural artifact of a kind of economic diaspora." The bars celebrating one of the NFL's greatest traditions could to some degree be found all over because Pittsburghers had "voted with their feet."[155] Pittsburgh had once been a prosperous city, but the people who made it so had left. Pittsburgh's jobs reflected the past. Think mills, factories, mines, or what some would call "dirty work." This was the cause of the diaspora referenced by Bowyer.

Notable here is that Pittsburgh played the Seattle Seahawks in Super Bowl XL three years before. The Steelers won, though some will say to this day that they were aided by some truly horrendous, outcome-altering calls. So what? Bowyer's broad point, one made years after the game took place, was that cities like Seattle were winning the economic battle because they had proven a magnet for *people*. Bezos was in Seattle. So was Bill Gates. So was Howard Schultz of Starbucks. The list was, and is, long. Seahawks bars are in *Seattle*. Jobs in Seattle, and that reward all manner of talent, are plentiful there as a consequence of all this remarkable talent.

People drive prosperity in ways that preservation can't. It's so common nowadays to hear about a city devastated by the loss of a factory or the closure of a business or a decline in government spending. Nonsense. Consider the manufacturing that so many politicians and pundits romanticize. As of 1927, manufacturing in Los Angeles trailed only New York, Flint, and Milwaukee.[156] Nowadays it's difficult to find factories in Los Angeles, and they're arguably nonexistent in New York City. Yet the two cities thrive. The manufacturing jobs that represented the past left, but *people* shaping the future kept arriving.

Many no doubt came from places like Pittsburgh, Flint, and Milwaukee. Though politicians yet again romanticize steel mills, factories, mines, and other commercial monuments to an allegedly better past, though Bruce Springsteen built a musical career with songs written about factory-worker types even though by his own admission he'd never set foot inside one,[157] those who actually know what factories and mills are like frequently have a less idealistic view of them. And so they run away from it. Think Pittsburgh. Think West Virginia. The best and brightest left. As Brice Shumate, a West Virginia University student and son of a coal mine worker explained it to the *New York Times* in 2020, "I've got a lot of respect for the work, but it wasn't what I wanted to do with my life. I didn't want to destroy my body to make a living."[158]

Shumate was one of the star students whom WVU president Gee managed to convince to stay in the state. Unknown is if he'll stick around after graduation. Will the kinds of jobs that he wants be there? The strivers don't want what used to be good work. They want what *will be*. So they migrate to where the brilliant are shaping the future.

Which brings us to the Federal Reserve. Somehow those who should know better have gotten it into their heads that the Fed has magical powers, that it can decree economic growth by virtue of it being able to expand or contract credit through its interest rate lever. It can do neither.

If the Fed could do what people naively think it can, East St. Louis, IL, would no longer be a slum. Neither would Cairo, IL. Missed by those who should know better is that credit is a *consequence*, not an instigator. It follows people. The resources that we call credit didn't remain in places like Pittsburgh when the best and brightest left. Unless the Fed controls the people whom credit follows, it can't do much of anything. It should be stressed that credit also follows people out of countries. The U.S. attracts enormous amounts of global investment simply because wealth is treated well in the United States. If ever this isn't true (surely the lockdowns in 2020 gave investors pause), the wealth will depart the U.S. And there will be nothing the Fed can do about it.

No one borrows money. They borrow what money can be exchanged for. They borrow access to real economic goods like computers, smartphones, and desks, and, most importantly, they "borrow" labor. *People.* The Fed can't expand the supply of market goods, it can't clone Bezos, and oh yes, it can't expand time. Probably the best way to look at the Fed is to look at it for what it is: just another federal government entity seeking relevance with the money of others. The Fed's way oversold swagger is not its own contrary to all the breathy, reverential, Jim-Nantz-at-the-Masters coverage of it by the business media.

The above in mind, no doubt economic fabulists of the Keynesian persuasion will tell you that government spending multiplies growth. Such a view isn't serious. Governments only have money to spend insofar as they have taxable access to economic activity that's already happened in the private sector. As always, this book promises to be repetitive.

Please think of Fed interest rates and so-called Fed "ease" in the same way. There's no such thing. The Fed is just another arm of a federal government that exists to redistribute wealth that's already been created. The Fed can at best influence the direction of some of the wealth created in the private sector, but even then its influence is questionable.

Whether the Fed or Congress or Fannie and Freddie, there are no private reserves within government. Governments just spend what they've taken. Nothing more, nothing less. The allocation is economically harmful when it's remembered per the previous chapter that government almost as a rule is funding stasis. Or worse. What ultimately propels us rarely looks attractive at the time, which is one of many reasons why government investment is an oxymoron. *It's not investment.* Investment is an agent of growth. Government ineptly funds what exists, or what is seen, at the expense of what could exist and what isn't seen.

Furthermore, markets are just that. They speak no matter what. This is important because the Fed projects its well overstated influence through banks, and it also projected its Main Street Lending Program (an attempt to boost "liquidity" within desperate companies amid the lockdowns) through banks. Yet banks were tightening credit. It didn't matter that the Fed took its funds rate to "zero" on March 15.[159] Credit was going to be more difficult to attain no matter what.

Remember, to borrow money is to borrow real market goods. Yet the U.S. economy was rushing toward lockdown as of mid-March. With production down, so logically would credit be. No one borrows just to borrow. And with the economy in a deep freeze, growth was logically going to slow, thus increasing the cost of borrowing on top of rising costs related to reduced supply. In early April JPMorgan Chase announced that it would raise mortgage borrowing standards as a response to an increasingly bleak economic outlook.[160] On April 30 Wells Fargo announced that it would no longer accept applications for home equity lines of credit.[161] In a CompareCards survey of credit card holders conducted in late April 2020, "almost 50 million people saw their credit limits decreased or cards closed involuntarily."[162] Oil companies, including pretty major ones like Chesapeake, were filing for bankruptcy amid a huge decline in credit availability for businesses reliant on a high price for crude.[163]

The Fed can't rewrite reality. See above. And then look around you. Most of all, consider yourself. Unless you the reader are Bezos (one can hope), it's unlikely you could have borrowed very much money or attracted much investment for your surely brilliant business idea in and around mid-March 2020. Those with funds were scared. They were parking wealth in sure things, not speculations. The Fed's zero rate represented "easy money" in the way that a $1,000 ceiling on apartment rentals in Manhattan would result in "easy." Not very likely. The low Fed funds rate was a sign that credit was paradoxically *tight*. Banks were lending at low rates, but only because they were limiting their loans to what was certain. No one lends in the hope of not being paid back, and in the spring of 2020 fear about borrower creditworthiness was substantial.

Amid this, the Fed as previously mentioned instituted a Main Street Lending Program that would "extend loans through banks to midsize businesses."[164] Really PPP all over again, with the same sappy sentimentality about small and midsize as the backbone of the U.S. economy. Ultimately the Fed expanded the meaning of "Main Street" to include companies "with annual revenue up to $5 billion in 2019 (from $2.5 billion) and up to 15,000 employees (from 10,000),"[165] but the problem remained one of wealth vacuumed up from the private sector only for it to be allocated in politicized fashion. This couldn't be growth.

And as always, it was a non sequitur. Before March 2020, there were no Main Street lending facilities of any substance simply because the U.S. already had the greatest Main Street lending facility in the world in 2020: the U.S. financial system. Some would call it Wall Street. Call it what you want. Finance has long been plentiful for U.S. businesses. It was plentiful in 2020 until it wasn't. Implicit in the PPP and Main Street was that an asteroid hit the U.S. economy out of nowhere. No, the lockdowns happened on the way to liquidity problems for businesses. Even if "Main Street" could liquefy businesses, they were still going to be insolvent so long as their ability to operate was impaired by—you guessed it—the lockdowns. Insolvency authors illiquidity, and vice versa.

Yet the problem with Main Street wasn't just that it was the equivalent of a doctor handing a Band-Aid to a patient writhing in pain from a broken leg. That Main Street ignored a problem born of lockdowns was shooting fish in a barrel.

The bigger problem was that businesses die all the time. And not just in Silicon Valley. Sixty percent of restaurants fail within their first year of operation, and 80 percent within five.[166] Where there's dynamism there're lots of openings and closings.

In mid-February 2020, when equity markets were at all-time highs, Pier 1, the home furnishings retailer, filed for bankruptcy.[167] In September 2019, clothing retailer Forever 21 filed. Seven months before, Payless did the same. All manner of energy and energy services (including global player Weatherford) went under in the year leading up to the coronavirus lockdowns. It's a reminder that the energy sector was troubled well before politicians oversaw a global panic in response to a virus. Pacific Gas and Electric, the massive California utility, filed for bankruptcy nearly a year before the coronavirus became news in the U.S.[168]

That bankruptcy is the norm in the U.S. has to be remembered when trying to understand what the Fed was expected to do in 2020. It wasn't just expected to lend to corporations asphyxiated by the unnecessary lockdowns. The expectation from former Council of Economic Advisers Chairman Glenn Hubbard (under George W. Bush)[169] was that the Fed should be providing *grants* to gasping businesses instead of loans. The view was that the Fed, backed by the U.S. Treasury, should be ready to *lose* money on the loans made. A *Wall Street Journal* editorial puzzlingly lamented that Fed loans "must have a 'pass' rating from financial regulators, which is the highest rating."[170]

All of which is a reminder of just how ridiculous the economic conversation had become in 2020. Companies that rated "pass" plainly didn't need the Fed in 2020 any more than they did in 2019, or for that matter in 1913 when the Fed opened its doors. This is important simply because contrary to odd pleas from the right (think Kevin Warsh and Hubbard, among many others) for the Fed to lend somewhat indiscriminately, Fed Chairman Jerome Powell was fighting back (presumably for the central bank's solvency) with, "We can't lend to insolvent companies. We can't make grants."[171] Treasury Secretary Steven Mnuchin somewhat parroted Powell, explaining the Treasury's reluctance to lose money through the Main Street Lending Program as, "I think it's pretty clear if Congress wanted me to lose all the money, that money would have been designed as subsidies and grants, as opposed to credit support."[172] Both sides missed the point.

Missed by seemingly all the policymakers was that today's solvent or "pass" company is potentially tomorrow's bankrupt one. And today's company in desperate straits is potentially tomorrow's superstar. The business landscape changes all the time. In 2005 Blockbuster Video was seen as so imposing by the federal government that its merger with Hollywood Video was blocked out of fear that the combined company would be too powerful. In 2010 Blockbuster filed for bankruptcy care of Netflix. Notable there is that in 2000 Blockbuster had the chance to purchase Netflix for *$50 million*, only to pass.[173] In the spring of 2020, Netflix's valuation soared past *$200 billion* as investors priced a future that would perhaps be defined by a great deal more home entertainment.

The slight Netflix digression is useful as a way of pointing out yet again what continues to be true: government can't play investor. Or lender. *Ever.* What would have been a "pass" in 2005, wasn't by 2010. Going back to Chapter Seven, it's debatable whether Apple or Amazon would have received Main Street Lending Program funding if a virus had caused a political crack-up in 2000; Netflix almost certainly wouldn't have, but by 2020 the giants didn't need one. Their share prices were soaring.

Which is why the Main Street Lending Program thankfully never took flight. As of July 16, 2020, a $454 billion program that the Fed was expected to expand to $4 trillion had only backed $13.6 billion worth of loans.[174] It's a reminder of the Fed's own superfluous nature vis-à-vis the banks that it normally deals with. The Fed is seen as a lender of last resort to solvent banks, but solvent banks don't need the Fed. Much the same revealed itself in 2020. As a *Wall Street Journal* report explained it, "Companies in dire need of cash aren't likely to be approved [by the Main Street Lending Program], while more creditworthy borrowers are likely to find similar or better terms on their own."[175]

Somehow this state of affairs bothered policymakers, but they were seemingly more troubled in 2008 when U.S. banks ran into trouble. Under the Main Street Lending Program banks were required to keep 5 to 15 percent of loans made to struggling corporations on their books,[176] which underscored why the loans couldn't be grants. Banks have little room for error. Loans must perform, which means Main Street was yet again superfluous but problematic just the same.

That's the case because the Lending Program was a $496 billion allocation to the Treasury from Congress that the Fed was supposed to expand the value of through banks. Basically Congress was trying to make the Fed and Treasury major allocators of precious capital at a time when the economy was on its back. This was plainly dangerous, and it was for reasons that readers might not expect. Main Street couldn't work *precisely because* the Fed and Treasury had such stringent, "pass" requirements.

Indeed, it cannot be stressed enough that the business landscape of today rarely reflects tomorrow's, yet armed with trillions, the Fed and Treasury were empowered with money not their own to maintain the look of today. About this, readers might once again ask the question: What if the coronavirus reached the U.S. in 2000 as opposed to 2020? Would Apple, Amazon, or Netflix have rated loans? Likely not. At the same time, AOL, Enron, and Tyco likely would have rated loans that they wouldn't have needed. In 2000, private investors were lined up trying to finance the doings of all three.

Saying what isn't said enough, investment powers economic growth precisely because it brings the future into the present. Though the Main Street Lending Program was to be overseen by the Fed and Treasury, the reality is that the Fed and Treasury are part of a much bigger Leviathan naively trying to improve the future by propping up the present and past. Translated, politicians wrecked the economy only to be handed trillions to further wreck it by funding stasis, which is yet again why you can't empower government as investor—*particularly during troubled times.*

During periods of difficulty, the all-important future is even more opaque. What's thriving won't always be, and what's sagging will be soaring down the line. With this uncertainty top of mind, the answer should never be to arm federal entities with trillions. The answer is to let the intrepid sort things out given the certainty they'll take chances on some of what looks awful in the present, and they'll pass on some of what looks pretty good. The Fed and Treasury could only lend to what looked good in 2020, which was a loud signal that it was the wrong capital allocator—one that would cruelly delay progress.

Thank goodness the Main Street Lending Program proved unworkable. As a July 2020 report in the *Wall Street Journal* indicated about it, interest in the lending program "has been sparse."[177] Well, of course. Like the PPP, the "MSLP" was impossible, which was to the economy's betterment. Anything that restrains the misallocation of what's precious is good, particularly when the allocators are feverishly trying to maintain the present over the future. Pittsburgh and West Virginia more broadly remind us how ill-advised such an approach is. And they also explain why assumptions about the Federal Reserve and stock market similarly don't stand up to scrutiny—which is where we'll head next.

Chapter Fifteen

THE FEDERAL RESERVE IS A LEGEND IN ITS OWN MIND

"America has been obtaining a disproportionate flow of skilled innovators by attracting these 'vital few' to its shores. Without their contribution, America may neither sustain the economic growth required to absorb the penurious many nor raise their standards of living."

—Reuven Brenner, *First Things*, 2010[178]

On April 14, 2019, Tiger Woods won his fifth Masters Championship and fifteenth "Grand Slam" tournament overall. His fellow professional golfers had to have been deflated. Woods was a shell of his former self thanks to relentless back problems, not to mention persistent snickering about the actual man behind the formerly carefully cultivated façade. Yet he still won the Masters? If Woods could win the big events when still injured, what might he do if healthy? Yes, they had to have been a bit downcast.

Actually, it's a safe bet that many of Woods' opponents were *thrilled.* When Woods wins, or even when he's playing well, so do they win.

So while Woods has a surly reputation, he's beloved.[179] Or at least appreciated. The simple truth is that fellow touring pros recognize that they earn more *losing* to Woods than they earn when *winning* on a PGA Tour that doesn't include him.

As legendary caddy Steve Williams explained it in his 2015 memoir, *Out of the Rough,* "When I started, the prize pools were quite small by today's standards but since Tiger Woods came along and prize money skyrocketed thanks to increased TV ratings, a professional can earn over $1 million for a win, which means the caddy can pick up $100,000 for a week's work, or a 10 per cent cut of a player's earnings."[180]

Williams and Woods won a lot together: eighty-four tournament wins to be exact. And with prize money way up, Williams the caddy made so much money that he was able to start an eponymous foundation that has donated in the seven figure range.[181]

Certain people elevate everyone around them. Tiger Woods is the personification of this truth. His achievements have not only enriched fellow players but also swing coaches, trainers, and everyone else associated with what is an increasingly lucrative sport.

The NFL is similar to professional golf. The stars drive television ratings, which lead to lucrative television deals for the league, only for those stars to be paid enormous sums. As evidenced by the $500 million-plus contract that Kansas City Chiefs quarterback Patrick Mahomes signed in July 2020, the best, most popular players command the lion's share of each NFL team's salary cap. But are the midrange and backup players angry? No way. Stars yet again drive ratings and all manner of lucrative deals. As a result, team salary caps that are a consequence of television revenues continue to rise. In 2013, the salary cap per NFL team was $123 million. By 2020, it was $198 million.[182] That's why some thought

Mahomes's contract was a bargain. *For the Chiefs.* With fan interest in a star-driven league continuing to grow, by the year 2031 (when Mahomes's contract is set to expire) team salary caps are expected to be quite a bit higher than $198 million, which means Mahomes will, if anything, be underpaid by then. Lower pay for him will flow to his teammates, who will get to enjoy ever-rising salaries—those salaries increased by the NFL's best and most popular players. It's better financially to be a backup in a league with Tom Brady, Pat Mahomes, and Aaron Rodgers than a star in a league with none of them.

So what does this have to do with the Federal Reserve and the stock market, which is what this chapter is about? Well, nothing and everything. The "everything" has to do with the basic truth that in all walks of life, the few pull the many upward. As Warren Brookes put it in his classic book *The Economy in Mind,* "We are all blessed by the genius of the relatively few." In pharmaceutical terms, one blockbuster drug pays for countless other drugs that will never make it to market. The same scenario applies to movies, books, and seemingly everything else.

In an appliance sense, Jeff Bezos notes that "I've made billions of dollars of failures at Amazon. Literally billions."[183] The vital few successes pay for endless experimentation and quite a few mistakes, which should have Amazon's huge customer base thrilled about the ubiquity of the Echo. That tens of millions are talking to Alexa nowadays means that Bezos will have even more funds at his disposal to figure out products and services to improve our lives in ways we never imagined. Amazon is the world's most valuable company because what began as a peddler of books has become a locale for us to get anything we want from anywhere, along with all manner of things we never knew we wanted. If you want to age yourself with those who've only known Alexa, tell them about how in "your day" (not too long ago—we're talking '80s and '90s, and realistically well into the 2000s) people would call into radio stations to make musical requests, only to wait by the "stereo" or "radio" for the song to be played. How things have changed.

Great individuals thinking and doing very differently have changed things for the much better. Imagine what life would be like without Bezos, the late Steve Jobs, or the founders of Google, Larry Page and Sergey Brin. One might say that the world would be quite a bit more equal in consideration of their enormous wealth, but life would by the same token be quite a bit less convenient. The unequal elevate us, *always*.

Where it grows increasingly exciting is when we remember how many the unequal can elevate in rapid fashion. Bezos is an interesting way to consider this. Indeed, imagine if he'd reached his business prime in 1970 versus 2020. If so, it's not unreasonable to speculate that someone possessing his remarkable genius would have listed among the world's richest then, just as he does now. If so, Bezos likely would have claimed a net worth of several hundred million or, at the very high and unlikely end, $1 billion.

Bezos's net worth would have been much smaller fifty years ago simply because technology was so primitive relative to today. And with it primitive, the ability of supremely talented people like Bezos to reach us with their genius was quite a bit more limited. Even if Bezos had imagined the Echo in 1970, it's not as though the technology existed to put one in a home, let alone in tens of millions of homes. Unable to meet the needs of anywhere close to the number of people in 1970 versus today, Bezos would have been poorer. And so would the world have been *quite a bit poorer*. Bezos is the richest man in the world because he's made the world a much better, much more convenient place.

The technological advances that minted centimillionaires and near billionaires in the Silicon Valley of the 1970s and 1980s set the stage for people like Bezos to reach exponentially more people with his innovations in the 1990s and beyond. Jeff Bezos stands on the shoulders of giants.

Notable about a technological evolution that made Amazon possible is what it's meant for earnings distribution among companies. While in 1975 the biggest one hundred public corporations could claim 49 percent of the earnings of all public companies, by 2015 the top one hundred companies accounted for 84 percent of all earnings.[184] Translated, as technology has brought the unequal closer to us all, the unequal have captured a bigger share of earnings. This is a good thing. If readers doubt it, imagine if technology limited Amazon's reach to Seattle. Would you be happy?

Understand that corporations not Amazon are happy with the above state of affairs too, or they should be. Think about it. It's Tiger Woods all over again. The vital few elevate us all. Even if we're not winning, our piece of the "loser's" pie is bigger than the piece would be of the winner's pie minus the unequal. Winners attract investors looking to shape the unequal businesses of the future. So while Amazon can claim a market cap well north of $1 trillion thanks to its growing dominance, the number of "unicorns" (companies valued at over $1 billion) in Silicon Valley grows by leaps and bounds each year to reflect investor interest in tomorrow's innovators who will, hard as it is to imagine, stand on Bezos's remarkable shoulders.

For now, Bezos is the giant alongside a few others. His ability to meet our needs is otherworldly. What men like John D. Rockefeller would have given for the kind of technology at Bezos's disposal that makes it possible for him to do so much for so many. This isn't to minimize Rockefeller's genius as much as it's to say that while Rockefeller greatly improved the lives of his customers, he could do quite a bit more today. Where it gets really exciting is to imagine what the entrepreneur who vanquishes Amazon will accomplish in order to fell today's giant. Rest assured that it will happen—probably in a matter of decades. The entrepreneur may not even be born yet, but this person will understand present and future technology in ways that even Bezos doesn't, only to knock him or his company off its lofty perch. And life will be grand. Not because Bezos is no longer on top, but because someone figured out a way to improve on his genius.

Such is life in a free society. The capacity for the unequal to improve the world around them on the way to enormous wealth is somewhat limitless.

For readers who are wondering, there's a very important Federal Reserve connection (though not what you've been taught to think) to the greats who elevate us all, but for context we must first take a step back in time to March 23, 2020. It was on that day that the S&P 500 bottomed. It had been a gruesome month for U.S. shares. First it was Bernie Sanders's ascendance that had investors spooked. Just as Donald Trump represented major surprise for investors back in 2015 and 2016, Sanders had them wondering in 2020. U.S. voters shocked the world with Trump in November of 2016; might they do so again with the socialist-leaning Sanders in 2020?

Of course, Sanders soon enough fell as quickly as he rose. This, as readers may remember, resulted in the biggest one-day point gain ever for the Dow Jones Industrial Average on March 2. Joe Biden's resounding win over Sanders reassured voters that a non-socialist known would beat a non-socialist known in November 2020.

But then came the lockdowns. Surprise, as discussed in detail in Chapters Two and Three, is always and everywhere behind any major market move. A 30 percent-plus decline was clearly related to something unexpected, and logic says it was surprise at how quickly the world's most dynamic economy was strangled by panicky politicians. No one expected this. Not politicians, not columnists, not people in fashion. Just as President Trump described the virus as "not a big deal," so did *Vogue*'s Anna Wintour tell her staff in late February that the virus was "not a big deal."[185] When Trump and Wintour agree on something, it's an anecdote more pregnant with information than the typical one involving two people. Furthermore, it wasn't just Trump and Wintour. Left and right, *New York Times* and *New York Post*, there was very little worry in February about the new coronavirus. Certainly no expectations of a forced cessation of economic activity.

Yet what had been booming was soon enough defined by tens of millions rendered unemployed, mass bankruptcy, and broad economic desperation. Investors had to price this shocking reversal of fortune for the world's richest country, along with an incredibly fast lurch from economic freedom to "non-essential" businesses literally being threatened with power shutoffs if they had the temerity to operate.

But as previously mentioned, U.S. market indices like the S&P 500 and the Dow Jones Industrial Average (DJIA) essentially bottomed on March 23. Notable here is that it's not that stocks didn't stop falling then as much as after the 23rd, U.S. shares began a brisk and largely uninterrupted move upward. At the close of June in 2020, stocks had just finished their strongest quarter in over two decades. After the fastest 30 percent decline in the history of U.S. share prices, stocks then had their fastest fifty-day increase in the annals of U.S. shares.[186]

So what drove the big rebound for stocks? While it's worth stressing yet again that it's always more than a reach to presume to understand the movements of equity markets that are relentlessly processing information produced around the world, it's not unreasonable to speculate. In doing so, this chapter will first a make a case that the conventional wisdom about the stock market's revival didn't stand up to the most basic of scrutiny.

So what was the conventional wisdom? It was that "the Fed did it." That was Steven Rattner's explanation. The longtime Democratic Party bigwig, Wall Street eminence, and counselor to the U.S. Treasury in the Obama administration put it this way:

> My vote for the most significant driver of stock prices is the huge amount of liquidity that the Federal Reserve has injected into the financial system, in an effort to counteract the depressive economic impact of the virus.
>
> That has pushed interest rates to record lows, turning money market funds, bonds and other fixed-income instruments into low-returning investments.[187]

Rattner was referring to all the bond buying and lending from the Fed that began in March. In February 2020 its "balance sheet" was $4.2 trillion, but by June it had reached $7 trillion. The central bank also reached in the sense that it was buying corporate bonds and loans to small businesses, along with the near-term debt of counties and states.[188] What Rattner mistakenly presumed to be the source of market ebullience had others up in arms. Without defending government intervention in the market for even a second, both sides well overstated the meaning of what the Fed did. We know this from the previous chapter. The Fed had refused to reach on loans or on any kind of allocation. Basically it was pursuing "sure things" in the near-term sense. The Fed's actions weren't nearly as meaningful as anyone wanted them to be, and they certainly didn't boost the stock market.

In short, Rattner's argument is easy to discredit. Though in his defense, his argument was hardly unique, or even a left-wing or Democratic argument. Eminent Austrian School economist Mark Thornton said much the same, that it's "generally the case in normal times" that a falling Fed funds rate correlates with rising stock prices.[189] Even libertarians like Cato Institute Vice President James Dorn have long promoted the notion that the U.S. stock market is somewhat rigged by the Fed. In his words, "A law of the market is that when interest rates fall, asset prices rise. As long as markets believe the Fed will support asset prices by keeping rates low, stocks will be the investment of choice, rather than conservative, low-yield saving accounts, money market funds, or highly-rated bonds."[190]

Funny is that there's very little evidence supporting the claims of Rattner, Thornton, and Dorn. Looked at in 2020 alone, the Fed cut rates fifty basis points on March 3,[191] but U.S. shares fell substantially. On March 15, 2020, the Fed reduced its funds rate to zero, only for the DJIA to plunge 13 percent the following day.[192] Looking back in time, the Fed aggressively reduced its funds rate in 2001 only for stocks to plunge throughout the year. In 2007 and 2008, the Fed similarly pushed down rates only for stocks to plunge yet again. Fast-forward to 2015, the Fed consistently raised rates through the end of 2018 as stocks soared.[193]

Never explained by the Fed-obsessed is why an attempt by the central bank to influence the cost of overnight borrowing between banks would somehow cause stock prices to move one way or the other. There's no sense to the thought process. Not only is it hard to find a correlation between the Fed's *artificial* rate machinations and stock prices, the very notion is a non sequitur. Think back to Chapter Four and how Peter Thiel described corporate valuations: "The value of a business today is the sum of all the money it will make in the future." Why would artificial Fed rate fiddling change the expectations of all the dollars a company will earn in the future?

Looked at internationally, the Bank of Japan pushed its funds rate to zero in 1999,[194] yet the Nikkei 225, at 22,614, is still *16,000* points off highs achieved in *1989*. But again, Japan's no different from here or Europe or the world for that matter. Figure that central banks around the world were aggressively cutting rates after 2008 alongside the Fed (the European Central Bank first took its overnight rate to zero in 2016[195]), but from 2009 to May of 2020, the S&P 500 returned 350 percent versus 89 percent for the MSCI All Country World Index.[196] If equity prices were about central banks and rates as so many deep thinkers assume, there would be uniformity in returns to reflect the reality that rate meddling, as opposed to company performance, was the driver of returns.

Back to reality, a stock price is a reflection of investor expectations about all the money the company will earn in the future. The previous truth stubbornly raises a question of why playing around with overnight lending rates would influence expectations about future earnings. The central bank–obsessed have answers, but they're not terribly compelling.

In Dorn's case, he claims that stocks will be "the investment of choice" so long as yields on highly rated bonds are low. That's why he tied the Fed's various "quantitative easing" programs from 2009 and beyond to the rally in U.S. shares. Dorn's analysis ignores that the Bank of Japan has conducted more than *eleven* QE programs over the last few decades with no subsequent stock market rally.[197] Funny is that the Fed's QE program amounted to it borrowing trillions from banks only to purchase U.S. Treasuries and mortgage securities, thus subsidizing government spending alongside subsidization of the very housing consumption that had concluded in rather teary fashion in 2008. It seemingly never occurred to the academic in Dorn that actions taken by the Fed like the previous ones would never cheer equity markets focused on the future. But then it's apparent Dorn wasn't really looking hard at what he aimed to analyze.

To see why, consider his main assertion about low yields on "highly-rated bonds" making equities the "investment of choice." If true, there would logically have been a massive rotation from 2009 to 2020 to reflect investor exit from low-yielding bonds to equities. Except that's not what happened. The average yield on the ten-year Treasury Note was 3.26 percent in 2009 versus *1.02* in 2020.[198] During that time, U.S. shares rallied 350 percent. Basically Dorn was talking well out of turn. Stocks rallied amid plummeting Treasury yields meaning there was no rotation out of them as his thesis suggested.

Others say the Fed's "easy money" had to find a home, so it sought out equities. Oh well, see Japan again. See the MSCI All World Index yet again. See Europe. If it were just central bank fiddling, stocks would once again rally in lockstep globally. After which, the intellectually lazy who made this argument ignored the basic truth that for a buyer to buy equities, a seller must *sell* equities. For every QE or central bank–duped buyer, there must be a wise seller. In a "market," bulls and bears duke it out. Get it?

That the Fed's QE program ended in 2014, only for stocks to continue their rally didn't then, nor does it now, deter those who always revert to "the Fed did it." Interesting is that while QE ended in 2014, it was a known quantity going back to 2012 and 2013 that it would end. Markets are a look into the future, which tells us that if QE had been the source of investor "exuberance," the correction in U.S. shares would have taken place—for good—seven to eight years before they briefly collapsed thanks to a political panic in 2020.

There's quite simply no evidence supporting the routine and impressively doltish claim that equity markets are essentially rigged by central banks. Despite this truth, readers can rest assured that what had the deep thinkers duped in 2020 will still have them tricked in 2030 and beyond. Economics is said to be a science, but it's generally a profession for the lazy and thoughtless. Almost to a man and woman, nearly every credentialed economist in existence believes that economic growth causes inflation (no, it's the surest sign prices are falling), that government spending boosts growth (no, the political allocation of precious resources weighs on progress), and that wars grow an economy. Actually, *people* are the drivers of economic progress, so the idea that you can expand an economy by exterminating the very humans who create the expansion is too horrifying for words.

The best that can be said for the PhD view that central banks author market rallies is that such a view is less offensive than most of the others embraced by those with PhD next to their name. The belief really is bothersome. As readers will soon see, it's insulting.

Still, there's one more way of looking at this that requires discussion. Think back to the previous chapter. What do the talented run away from with great gusto? The answer is that they rush from the past and present. They want to create the future as opposed to running in place. That's why towns and cities that cling to what used to be prosperous nearly always decline.

Looked at through the prism of the Fed, this notion that "the Fed did it" presumes that what props up the present cheers investors. No, that's not true. Think back to Chapter Eight.

In moving briefly in reverse, readers might imagine if the Fed had gone to "zero" for good in 2000, only to conduct endless QE programs.

To believe those focused on the Fed, such a scenario would have resulted in a booming stock market. If so, what a disaster for the U.S. economy.

Indeed, back in 2000 GE was the world's most valuable company with a market capitalization of over $500 billion. As of 2020 investors valued it at *$58 billion*. In 2000 Enron was the darling of investors, and AOL and Yahoo were the most innovative internet companies. While Amazon terrifies the witless with its alleged "market power" in 2020, in 2000 the tagline, "AOL Everywhere" had the nail-biters worried. The FTC delayed AOL's merger with Time Warner for one year[199] out of fear that the combined entity would be too powerful. Columnist Norman Solomon warned of the "servitude" customers would face if the two combined.[200] So irrelevant did market forces ultimately render AOL that in short order Time Warner removed AOL from its name altogether.

It's sad that what's so obvious must be stated, but if the Fed could actually prop up markets as the well-credentialed but thoughtless tell us, the U.S. equity market wouldn't be worth propping up. Repeat what's true again: markets are a look into the future. Implicit in the junior high notion that central banks rig equity markets is the belief that investors thrill at the idea of stasis, that they bid up what's already great. No. What's already great is already priced as already great. Investors are looking into the future for what will make yesterday look pretty average by comparison.

Which is why Chapter Eight's reference to 2000 is so useful in understanding what happened with markets in 2020. Looking back to the year 2000, GE, AOL, Enron, and others were the blue chips. Imagine where the economy would be to today if the Fed had had the capability to keep them at the top. Imagine the progress lost.

That's the case because in the year 2000, Apple was less than three years removed from near bankruptcy,[201] Amazon was unprofitably selling books, CDs, and DVDs, Google (Alphabet) was a largely unknown search company, Microsoft had just been pistol-whipped by the Department of Justice for the "crime" of being too successful, and Facebook didn't exist on account of Mark Zuckerberg still being in high school. In 2020, they were the five most valuable companies in the world. If the Fed had propped up the past, life still would be amazing, but it's what replaces the amazing that makes life truly grand. Crucial about this is that any Fed meddling in 2000 wasn't going to find the five companies mentioned. Again, Facebook didn't even exist, Apple was near bankrupt…

Going back to 2008, only Google and Microsoft were listed among the ten most valuable companies in the world. Number one in 2008 was ExxonMobil with a market capitalization of $492 billion. Number two was GE. Its valuation had fallen to $358 billion.[202] To believe the Fed narrative, central bankers not only rigged an artificial rally with their meddling, but they made sure to bid up the shares of Alphabet, Amazon, Apple, Facebook (oh wait, Facebook didn't float its shares until 2012!), and Microsoft, all the while putting out to pasture companies like GE and ExxonMobil in consideration of the stupendous decline in the valuation of GE and XOM to $183 billion and $58 billion respectively. No, such a view isn't serious.

If Fed officials could pick greatness, they wouldn't be at the Fed. There's too much money to be earned by investors capable of seeing what will thrive in the future and what won't.

Looking at all of this in terms of what caused the post-March 23 stock market rally, it was plainly *greatness*. The Fed had nothing to do with it. As of the end of April 2020, Alphabet, Amazon, Apple, Facebook, and Microsoft were up 10 percent for the year, while the other 495 S&P 500 companies were down 13 percent.[203] Remove them from the S&P, and there's not much of a rally to speak of. Considered a bit more broadly, through June of 2020 the fifty most expensive stocks in the S&P were up an average of 11.3 percent for the year, versus the fifty cheapest stocks that were down for the year an average of 16.8 percent.[204] By September of 2020, Apple's shares had soared 57 percent for the year and the company itself was worth more than all of the small companies in the Russell 2000 Index combined, or the FTSE index that measures the share prices of the London Stock Exchange's biggest companies. As for those five companies routinely mentioned, their valuation accounted for 23 percent of the S&P 500 index as of September of 2020.[205] If the market rally had been Fed-driven per Rattner, Thornton, and Dorn, it logically wouldn't have been so top heavy. Instead, there would have been uniformity to it to reflect the rally's artificial nature. Translated, corporate valuations of public companies would have risen in lockstep. And since central banks around the world were in QE mode, companies around the world would have been rising in lockstep with artificially valued American ones. Except that this wasn't the case. Throughout a top-heavy market rally, all-too-many companies in the U.S. and elsewhere flatlined, or declined, including former blue chips like GE and Exxon.

The notion that the Fed was behind the post-March 23 rally in U.S. equities never made sense, but commentators from all sides were generally too lazy to even lightly dig into the numbers, and more crucially into common sense, to figure this out. All stock-market rallies are generally a consequence of the vital few as the blue chips of today are replaced by the winners of tomorrow. Some stocks win seriously big in more than one bull market (see Microsoft), but it's generally the case that the future replaces the past. The Fed or any central bank couldn't have engineered any of this. The Fed is an arm of government.

Still, there's a remaining question of *why* this happened. The conventional answer to the post–March 23 rally was that investors sensed the big five previously mentioned (Alphabet, Apple, Amazon, Facebook, and Microsoft) revealed even greater market strength amid the lockdowns. Basically, investors fell in love even more. It seems like a reasonable explanation, but it's not as though investors forgot the genius of these businesses during the worst, most perilous days of the lockdowns.

The more compelling explanation is that, per Ken Fisher yet again, "stocks always look ahead, often fairly far." Bleak as the economic situation was in late March, there was light at the end of the tunnel. Specifically, it became more and more apparent about a virus that had all too many fearing for their lives quite simply wasn't very lethal. Just as the Chinese people weren't killed en masse by a virus that floated about seemingly undetected for quite a while, the same was found to be true elsewhere.

So while this book has promised to largely stay away from the medical aspects of the coronavirus, it's useful to point out from an economic/stock market angle that media of all stripes began to report a virus that, per former Stanford University Medical Center neuroradiology chief Scott Atlas, "99 percent of infected people have no significant illness from." Atlas added that half of those infected were "entirely asymptomatic," as in half of those infected with the virus exhibited no symptoms of it.[206] Some will respond that Atlas is associated with the conservative Hoover Institution, so let's consider a *New York Times* "Fact Check" of Donald Trump's assertion that "99 percent" of coronavirus infections were "totally harmless." Same result. As *Times* reporters Roni Caryn Rabin and Chris Cameron found after digging into Trump's assertion, the death rate was less than 1 percent; roughly 0.6 percent. Their source was Ashish K. Jha, faculty director of the Harvard Global Health Institute. Jha acknowledged that in terms of death rates "it's always tricky to do this in the midst of a pandemic." But he added, "Let's say you took 1,000 Americans at random who were all infected. Our best guess is that between six and 10 would likely die of the virus."[207]

As early as April 1, 2020, the *Wall Street Journal's* increasingly skeptical editorial page published an opinion piece by Stanford doctors Eran Bendavid and Jay Bhattacharya that asked, "Is Covid-19 as Deadly as They Say?" They indicated that "current estimates about the coronavirus fatality rate may be too high by orders of magnitude."[208] For those seeking seeming ideological balance, the *New York Times* published a piece by Dr. David L. Katz titled, "Is Our Fight Against Coronavirus Worse Than the Disease?" Katz looked at South Korea's numbers and indicated that "as much as 99 percent of active cases in the general population are 'mild' and do not require specific medical treatment."[209] Notable for understanding why sentiment among investors changed is that Katz's piece was published on *March 20, 2020*.

All of the above helps explain why stock markets were seemingly so "detached" from reality in the spring of 2020. Common sense, empirical realities, and the fact that the unequal always drive rallies easily discredit the Fed narrative that so typically reared its dopey head, after which it should be said yet again that equity markets never price in the present. While panicked politicians were needlessly and tragically suffocating U.S. and global economic growth, investors sensed a better tomorrow as reality intruded on the doings of nail-biting politicians. It seems markets were pricing in the highly unlikely odds of death related to the virus, which ensured an end at some point to the lockdowns. There's your stock market rally.

The tragedy is that there had to be a disconnect between markets and the economy to begin with. As Chapter One makes plain, there was already powerful economic evidence from China, the epicenter of the virus, that indicated it wasn't lethal. Had it been, U.S. shares once again would have corrected long before March 2020. China is where we'll head next.

Chapter Sixteen

CHINA

"[Napoleon] did not realize until it was too late that the only closed economy is the political economy in the world economy. Britain could not be starved into submission by blockade unless she were totally cut off from the world. As long as Britain could trade with any nation outside France, it was thus trading indirectly with France."

—Jude Wanniski, *The Way the World Works*

Kim Jong Il died on December 17, 2011. From 1994 until his death he was the supreme leader of North Korea.

Kim Jong Il was replaced as supreme leader by his son Kim Jong Un. And with good reason, if accounts from state media in the famously closed-off country are to be believed. In one biography of Kim titled, *The Childhood of Beloved and Respected Leader, Kim Jong Un*, it was reported that "he had perfect pitch, that he could ride the wildest horses at age six, and that, when he was just nine, he had twice beaten a visiting European powerboat-racing champion." It seems he'd driven at speeds of 125 miles per hour.[210] Oh, to have such talented leadership…

As most know, the realities of North Korea have long been much different. Overseen for decades by some pretty horrid people, life and living standards there have been awful. Such is life in parts of the world where government controls economic activity, all the while taking for itself the fruits of nearly all of it. Frequently such stringency leads to extreme poverty. Though the economy in North Korea is said to be growing by those who've long known the country, life has largely been tragic.

During the reign of Kim Jong Il, North Korea experienced some of its worst stretches of economic growth. Economic contraction of the *famine* kind. Despite this, it cannot be stressed enough that politicians always eat. And they eat well. Readers should never forget this. Politicians eat lavishly no matter the unemployment, desperation, and death they foist on their subjects. This was true during the coronavirus-related political crack-up (Fauci, Trump, Biden, Pelosi, McConnell, Newsom, and Cuomo never feared hunger or poverty), and it's always been true in North Korea.

Considering Kim Jong Un's father, he didn't just enjoy movies and women from around the world. According to *Washington Post* North Korea expert Anna Fifield, for two years amid what was a brutal famine suffered by North Koreans, Kim Jong Il "was the world's largest buyer of Hennessy Paradis cognac, importing almost a million dollars' worth of liquor a year."[211]

Funny about the imports is that Hennessy is a French product, yet France has a trading embargo on North Korea. What gives? Really nothing. When it comes to trade there's no accounting for the final destination of any good. What "France" won't sell to "North Korea" can be purchased by "North Korea" from those "France" *does* sell to.

It's a reminder of something ignored with not-so-surprising regularity by the small economic minds that the world of politics is so dense with. Embargoes are toothless. They achieve nothing.

Back in the real world, to produce is to express a desire to import. And when you import, the only limit to what you take in is how much you've produced, or exported first. With trade it's products for products. To import is to first produce something of exportable market value *so that* you can import roughly equal value.

Crucial yet again is that there's no accounting for the final destination of what you produce. While a Peoria, IL–based tractor manufacturer may theoretically only sell its products to other Illinois-based businesses, there's no controlling whom they sell to.

North Korea's supreme leaders vivify this truth well. Though the U.S. has maintained a trade embargo for ages with the Hermit Kingdom, Kim Jong Un grew up watching American movies, including *Ben Hur* and *Dracula*. He was known to pass the time listening to CDs by American songstress Whitney Houston too.[212] Part of his schooling in the 1990s took place in Switzerland, and a search on the internet will reveal a class picture that includes him in Nike gear.[213] Once Kim Jong Un ascended to supreme leader after his father's death, the jet that ferried him around (some apparently referred to it as Air Force Un) included a desk on which he typed out decrees on his Apple MacBook.[214]

Not terribly surprisingly, Iran is no different from North Korea. Even though the U.S. has a trade embargo placed on Iran, when Fifield's *Washington Post* colleague Jason Rezaian was on the verge of being arrested in Tehran in 2014 on false charges of espionage, his initial fear was the police discovering the hundreds of bottles of beer, wine, and liquor that he and his wife, Yeganeh, had stashed in their apartment's storage unit. Though liquor isn't for sale in Iran due to strict laws, it's surely for sale to Iranians outside of Iran… Though Apple can't sell to "Iran," Rezaian and others had iPhones.[215]

Stated simply, if you're producing something of value, you're selling to the world. Eventually everyone's trading with everyone. Embargoes are once again toothless.

Which brings us to an April 27, 2020, opinion piece written by Dr. Scott Gottlieb for the *Wall Street Journal*. At the time of the op-ed Gottlieb was a resident fellow at American Enterprise Institute, but he'd perhaps more notably been commissioner of the Food and Drug Administration under President Donald Trump from 2017 to 2019. Arguably even more notably, Gottlieb was a conservative in good standing, for what that's worth.

All of the above is mentioned mainly because Gottlieb's alarmism was very apparent. While former Stanford neuroradiology chief Scott Atlas was producing powerful data exposing fear of the new coronavirus as much ado about nothing, including an April 22 piece for *The Hill* in which he calculated the fatality rate among those infected as somewhere in the 0.1 or 0.2 percent range,[216] Gottlieb continued to write as though many millions of Americans alone were going to be directly brought to an early grave by a virus that had originated in Wuhan.

It didn't matter that there was no evidence of major death in China despite its population being hit by the virus wholly unaware, nor did stats produced at Stanford seem to compel him; Gottlieb continued to write as though the coronavirus was one of life's greatest foes. It was odd to say the least. After which it just became silly. Dr. Gottlieb started writing about economics.

In the aforementioned *Journal* piece, Gottlieb wrote that the "first nation to develop a vaccine for Covid-19 could have an economic advantage as well as a tremendous public-health achievement. Doses will be limited initially as suppliers ramp up, and a country will focus on inoculating most of its own population first." Don't worry, it got weirder. At op-ed's conclusion, Gottlieb wrote that "public health is part of national security." Eager for "America" to "win the vaccine race," Gottlieb argued that a "successful vaccine will allow Americans to reclaim the country's safety and sovereignty."[217] Books. Could. Be. Written. But this is just one book.

For one, explicit in Gottlieb's commentary was that government must centrally plan and help fund the creation of a coronavirus vaccine. Except that most anything of market value produced for us comes from private, profit-motivated individuals.

Really, if government could centrally plan a vaccine, logic dictates that the cure wouldn't be very difficult to achieve to begin with. What's transformative (think the iPhone, think Amazon, think Uber, think flight) usually doesn't come from government. It comes from live, profit-motivated minds outside of government. Even if you the reader believe that the federal government created the internet despite logic rejecting this most absurd of contentions, the reality is that the internet only evolved into something economically transformative thanks to genius individuals crafting market applications to it in the private sector.

So if a coronavirus vaccine represented "a tremendous public-health achievement" as Gottlieb ranted, then it wouldn't be planned by Gottlieb's cronies inside Washington. The very notion was absurd.

After which, it's a known quantity that every drug or vaccine has side effects. We know this from pharmaceutical ads. They always indicate potentially negative side effects that come with drugs that are said to protect us from something else.

Assuming a coronavirus vaccine, would "most" of a country's population vaccinate themselves against a virus that at least half don't know they have, that 99 percent experience no significant illness from, and that kills those infected at a rate somewhere between 0.1 and 0.2 percent? One guesses that "most" wouldn't bother, particularly if said vaccine brought with it side effects. To be clear, the latter is not an anti-vaccination statement. Thumbs-up to vaccines. But really, how many would broadly risk their health to protect themselves from a virus that was at least statistically so innocuous?

Gottlieb presumed some kind of "economic advantage" for the "nation" that developed a vaccine first, but why? Again, where's the advantage gained from vaccinating against that which isn't very lethal? And if there were an economic advantage, governments that create the greatest economic advantage for their country do so by virtue of getting out of the way, as opposed to planning outcomes.

The previous point was particularly important in consideration of Gottlieb's expressed fear that "China" was "making rapid progress, with three vaccines entering advanced development." For one, China's modern advance as an increasingly prosperous nation was plainly and logically a consequence of government more and more removing itself from commerce. That the latter needs to be said at all is a sad commentary on how little politicians and think tankers like Gottlieb understand about economics, but this is the world we live in.

To read Gottlieb et al., one who is ignorant to the twentieth century might believe China is still a "communist" country since the Chinese Communist Party still runs the country. No, China *was* a communist country in a collectivist, government-planning-economic-outcomes sense from the late 1940s to realistically the 1980s. That's why John Lennon could credibly write, "They're starving back in China so finish what you got" in 1980. At the time, China was a desperately poor country after communism had so thoroughly wrecked its economy up until then.

China has since freed its people to produce in profit-motivated fashion, and the result has been staggering economic growth. No doubt government inserts itself in economic activity in China, but so does that sadly happen in the U.S. China would be much stronger economically if government intervened less, "invested" less, and broadly made it its mission to leave people to produce as freely as possible. All the intervention, subsidies, and protection *weaken* China's economy, and the same *weakens* the U.S. economy. Imagine how much stronger both countries could be.

This requires mention in consideration of Gottlieb's 2020 nail bit-ing about "China" reaching a virus vaccine first. If it were government as Gottlieb presumed, then so what? If bureaucrats could quarterback a cure, then the cure wasn't a very distant object to begin with. If private, profit-motivated individuals could triumph, then so what once again. Really, why would any profit-motivated corporation produce something of value without a plan to sell into the richest market in the world? The question answers itself, at which point if a private company in China or Europe produces a vaccine, all the better. Any truly ambitious country always has a U.S. plan for obvious reasons.

Gottlieb's opinion piece contended that it "could be years before a vaccine is produced on a scale sufficient to help the entire world," but really, so what? If 99 percent of those infected never experience a serious illness from the virus, would it really matter if a vaccine were slow from a mass production standpoint?

In Gottlieb's case he alluded to a "national security" angle to that which had a death rate of 0.1 or 0.2 percent for those infected, and implicit there was that "China" would keep any presumed vaccine from "America," but that, too, would be of no consequence. Indeed, short of the Chinese crafting a coronavirus vaccine only to warehouse the doses, there would be no way for "China" to keep the vaccine from reaching "America."

Assuming high demand stateside for a "Chinese" vaccine, let's not forget that the Chinese are still quite a bit poorer than Americans are on average. This is important because assuming yet again high demand for a vaccine against a virus that doesn't cause serious illness in 99 percent of those infected, well-to-do Americans would vacuum up what's produced in China. There's quite simply no accounting for the final destination of any good, yet conservatives like Gottlieb who should have known better promoted what was preposterous.

Even more preposterous was talk of how "the Chinese" created the virus to weaken us economically. Yes, one might suppose some Chinese leaders don't think as Chinese entrepreneurs do, and that they're as brain-dead as certain American leaders and pundits are whereby they believe trade is war and that prosperity in other countries harms their country. OK, but such a belief would counter the view held by some on the right (probably the same people) that the Chinese have long been "cheating" us by "manipulating" trade agreements in order to inundate us with exports. OK, so which is it? The two absurd lines of thinking were, and are, rather contradictory. If the Chinese have all along been trying to hurt us by giving us daily raises through their export of increasingly cheap goods, why would they try to export a virus that, if actually lethal, would collapse an economy on which conservatives have long told us the Chinese are reliant for exports? Furthermore, if the goal were annihilation of the American people, why export a virus that thankfully killed so few and that also thankfully debilitated so few?

After that, why would the Chinese bother to try to weaken the U.S.? By the spring of 2020, hadn't American politicians done the latter on their own pretty effectively? What could the Chinese have done in addition? After the humiliation that American politicians foisted on themselves and their people, how could the Chinese political class have made things worse?

Yet silliest of all was the Gottlieb-driven assumption that was the theme of this chapter—that there was an economic and national security imperative to "America's" creation of a vaccine. Please. Such a view wasn't, nor is it, serious.

Thinking about this through an American prism, Los Angeles–based billionaire Patrick Soon-Shiong's source of immense wealth is among other things rooted in his development of the drug Abraxane. While it hasn't solved the killer that is pancreatic cancer, it's seemingly given those afflicted more of a fighting chance.[218]

And since pancreatic cancer knows no country borders, can anyone imagine people around the world refusing that which might save them solely because it was developed in the U.S.? Would people from China refuse the drug?

Interesting is that Soon-Shiong was born in China. That he was should have readers questioning some of the mindless rhetoric from before, during, and after spring of 2020 from Americans eager to shut down exchange between the U.S. and China, along with supply lines that make all manner of brilliant plenty possible. The only closed economy is the world economy as Robert Mundell long ago observed, and talented people whose genius will lift all of us come from everywhere. Abraxane is an "American" innovation insofar as Soon-Shiong created it in the United States, but then Americans aren't a race; rather, they're an ideal—a free ideal that includes openness to genius regardless of its origins. Assuming Soon-Shiong had stayed in China all of his business existence, would Americans facing a death sentence refuse what would instead be a "Chinese" innovation? The question is rhetorical.

Without China, the U.S. would be a much poorer country. And when there's less wealth, there are fewer resources to be directed toward the experimentation that turns today's viruses, disease, and killers into tomorrow's afterthoughts. Americans who should have known better wanted to somehow blame China for a virus that thankfully spared over 99 percent of those infected, but the better approach was to imagine how much poorer we would have been and how much less advanced we would have been on all manner of economic and health fronts sans the Chinese.

Still, China in 2020 was a political prop, particularly when it came to national politics, which is where we will briefly go next: Trump vs. Biden. Plus was there a constitutional aspect to the lockdowns? No constitutional scholar here, but it should at least be said that questions need to be asked.

Chapter Seventeen

IS THERE A CONSTITUTIONAL RIGHT TO WORK?

"The Founders didn't throw off a king only to enable a majority to do what no king would ever dare. No, they instituted a plan whereby in 'wide areas,' individuals would be entitled to be free simply because they were born so entitled—while in 'some' areas, majorities would be entitled to rule not because they were inherently so entitled, but because they were constitutionally authorized to rule. That gets the order right: individual liberty first; and self-government second, as a means toward securing that liberty."

—Roger Pilon, "Reclaiming the Constitution," *National Review*, 2002[219]

I n the movie and television industry, the ticket to work for aspiring actors is a

SAG card. SAG stands for Screen Actors Guild. It's a union. Some have negative views of unions; some view them positively. The view here is that if individuals operating without the force of government want to band together in order to attain wage floors and other work standards, then have at it.

At the same time, it should be said that actors unionize to limit the supply of actors and actresses who would otherwise work for nothing or who would quite literally pay famous directors like Steven Spielberg in order to act in one of his films. So much of life is getting one's foot in the door; an acting turn in a Spielberg film is the very definition of doing just that, so it's not unreasonable to suggest that without SAG cards that put floors on how little actors and actresses can be paid for speaking parts, that numerous ambitious actors and actresses would be working for less than nothing as the pathway to better things.

Major League Baseball, the National Football League, and the National Basketball Association similarly have players' unions. Those unions negotiate working conditions with the three leagues, along with minimum pay. Arguably the same applies here. Absent the minimums, more than a few players would offer up their services for next to nothing or less than nothing (pay teams for a spot on them) in order to get their feet in the proverbial door.

Away from acting, sports, and other forms of entertainment, it's not unreasonable to imagine more than a few enterprising individuals aggressively offering their toil to Jeff Bezos, Elon Musk, or Mark Zuckerberg for "negative" compensation. Why not? Think of what could be learned from all three, think of the future earnings that could be had from *paying* each to work for them in the early days.

So while it's a safe bet that Bezos, Musk, and Zuckerberg wouldn't take payment from ambitious young people eager to learn at their feet, all of what's been written is a long or short way of saying that in a perfect world, the minimum wage would be less than zero. As individuals, we should be free to offer up our services for as little or as much as we want.

Which brings us to May 2, 1895. On that day the state legislature in New York enacted a law that read as follows: "No employee shall be required or permitted to work in a biscuit, bread or cake bakery or confectionary establishment more than 60 hours in any one week, or more than 10 hours in any one day." As George Will described the legislation in his 2019 book, *The Conservative Sensibility,* "New York's legislature [ostensibly] limited the permissible work hours of bakery employees in order to protect the workers' health and safety."[220] Except that there was quite a bit more to the story than New York legislators taking up the cause of allegedly exploited workers, as Will made plain.

In truth, the law was meant to protect large, unionized bakeries against competition from what Will described as "small, family-owned, non-unionized competitors that depended on flexible work schedules."[221] If competitors not constrained by union-negotiated wage and working condition rules were free to compete, they just might topple those so constrained. New York's legislators wrote rules to protect them from competition. New York's state government was limiting the individual's right to work.

Specifically, Joseph Lochner's right to contract was limited. Lochner was an immigrant from Bavaria who owned a bakery in Utica, NY. He was fined fifty dollars "for violating the limits [the New York state law] it placed on the employees of his Utica bakery." As Will put it, Lochner argued "that he and his employees had a right, absent a compelling government interest, to voluntarily contract for longer working days and weeks." Translated, if Lochner freely entered into an agreement with similarly free employees to work more than sixty hours per week and more than ten hours per day, then employer and employee were acting on rights "natural and unalienable." Live and let live. *Always.*

Except that New York's legislators plainly disagreed. Lochner was as previously mentioned fined. Furthermore, wasn't there a "states' rights" angle at work here? About these questions, it's worth pausing to stress that your author is decidedly not a constitutional scholar. Not in the least. If there's an experimental chapter in this book, this is it. The chapter is written more as a way of hopefully unearthing questions from readers about what happened in the spring of 2020 when the right to work and the right to operate one's business were severely limited.

Back to states' rights, the Constitution's Tenth Amendment stated that "the powers not delegated to the United States by the Constitution, nor prohibited by it to the States, are reserved to the States respectively, or to the people." About the Tenth Amendment, it doesn't take a constitutional scholar to deduce from the amendment that it was meant to ensure that the vast majority of taxing, spending, and legislating would take place in states. The federal government would have very narrow, very defined, very *enumerated* powers, while the power of states would be more expansive. People could essentially choose the size and scope of government they wanted, or would tolerate, by their choice of state.

So why then did Lochner's case make it all the way to the Supreme Court? Weren't New York's legislators making laws locally, as was their prerogative? To read the quote that begins this chapter from the Cato Institute's Roger Pilon, the answer was, and is, no. As he explained it about states' rights, there are limits. "The Founders didn't throw off a king only to enable a majority to do what no king would ever dare. No, they instituted a plan whereby in 'wide areas,' individuals would be entitled to be free simply because they were born so entitled." Yes it's true that states trump the federal government the majority of the time, but with certain things "individuals would be entitled to be free simply because they were born so entitled."

Your author won't presume to speak for the brilliant Pilon, but the Supreme Court seemed to agree with him over one hundred years ago in *Lochner v. New York*. As Will explained it, the New York state law limiting work hours and the length of a work day in bakeries amounted to "an unconstitutional 'interference' with the liberty of contract."[222] So when states trample on the doings of free people, it's arguably the job of the federal government or the Supreme Court to step in and be activist in protecting the rights of people to live and do as they want so long as what they do doesn't hurt others.

Looked at through the prism of 2020, someone working or a business operating logically wouldn't hurt others. Really, if an individual feared individuals out and about working and potentially contracting the coronavirus, the response was simple: they could stay at home. Just as government shouldn't be able to force people to not work, to not operate their business, and to not live as they want, so should government not be able to force individuals fearful of those living as they wish to be out and about around them. Yet again, live and let live.

With *Lochner*, employer and employees were *voluntarily* entering into a work arrangement. Constitutionally empowered states couldn't interfere with this right to contract. The Supreme Court confirmed this truth with its ruling. Limits on freely arrived at work hours and conditions amounted to an "'interference' with the liberty of contract." From a modern angle, *Lochner v. New York* reads as an indication that employers and employees alike should be free to contract with each other as they wish and without governmental interference on any level.

In 2020 politicians had arrogated to themselves the right to "allow" some businesses to remain open, some partially open, yet some deemed "non-essential" or unsafe were forced to shut down altogether. The simple act of sitting down to eat in a restaurant was no longer allowed. The very humans who drive all progress and whose historical innovations had pushed all manner of life-ending maladies into the proverbial dustbin of history were now seen as a lethal menace to one another. To walk by someone on the street amid the coronavirus meltdown was to witness people rushing from the sidewalk onto busy streets in order to maintain "social distancing." Yes, it was the Twilight Zone. It was a nut show. Those who lived it knew, and will forever know, the behavioral oddities that massive human delusions unearth in people.

For the purposes of this chapter, local and state decrees had shuttered all manner of businesses on the way to rampant bankruptcy and unemployment—unemployment of the tens of millions kind. As this was happening, many understandably reacted very negatively. The richest country in the world was being forced into economic contraction by witless politicians. More than a few asked if President Trump could do something about it.

Could a locked-down nation be unlocked? More specifically, could Trump have ordered the U.S. back to work? Walter Olson, constitutional expert and a senior fellow at the libertarian Cato Institute, said no. In a March 30, 2020, opinion piece for the *Wall Street Journal*, Olson firmly stated that the president "can't legally order the nation back to work. The lockdown and closure orders were issued by state governments, and the president doesn't have the power to order them to reverse their policies."

Olson went on to write that "in America's constitutional design, while federal law is supreme, the national government is confined to enumerated powers. It has no general authority to dictate to state governments. Many of the powers government holds, in particular the 'police power' invoked to counter epidemics, are exercised by state governments and the cities to which states delegate power."[223]

To be clear, Olson is a substantial constitutional scholar. And while it's not the place of your author to question what he deems constitutional truth, an argument will be made here that it was never about Trump ordering "the nation back to work" even if Trump felt he had such powers. It wasn't because no reasonable person would dispute Olson's constitutional point that the power resides in states. Thank goodness for that. States should be policy laboratories, as opposed to one-size-fits-all enforcers of federal decrees.

As opposed to Trump or any president having the capacity to demand Americans get back to work, the bigger question is one of whether Americans had the right to work; as in were they per Pilon "entitled to be free simply because they were born so entitled"? And per *Lochner v. New York*, were they free to work simply because states lacked the constitutional power to interfere with "the liberty of contract"? Translated, if business owners and employees agreed to continue operating, how was it the state's prerogative to interfere?

Pilon himself weighed in on the discussion in an April 3, 2020, piece for *RealClearMarkets*. Full disclosure: your author edits *RealClearMarkets*, and Pilon's opinion piece was contracted by me in response to one written by me in which I questioned whether there might be some sunlight on the issue of federal power over state lockdowns between Cato colleagues Pilon and Olson. In his response, Pilon sided with Olson:

> The Constitution makes federal law supreme in its domain, to be sure, but it divides powers between the federal and state governments, leaving most powers with the states or, as the Tenth Amendment says, with the states or the people. Federal powers are thus limited.... Everything else belongs to the states, including, especially here, the general "police power," which governors wield to protect the rights, health, and safety of their citizens. That's why most criminal law, for example, is enacted and enforced by the states and state executive agencies. Again, in principle, the federal government, including the president, has limited authority over such matters because there is no general federal police power—Wally's main point.

At the same time, Pilon seemed to indicate that there was room for courts to strike down state limits on workers going to work. In his words, "Even if the courts were to strike down a state statute, as in *Lochner*, or a governor's order, as here, that would not empower the *president* to act." Yes, many times over. Again, this was never a question about Trump's being able to order a nation or individual back to work as much as it was about whether or not federal power that's both limited and supreme might be able to free individuals and businesses that were suddenly limited in their ability to respectively work and operate.

So while Pilon seemingly left open the possibility that the federal government could intervene in defense of individual liberty and property rights, this was ultimately "an area where, quintessentially, state police power to regulate the health and safety of citizens comes to the fore. And it's an area where reasonable people can have reasonable differences."[224] *Precisely.* Or maybe?

"Reasonable people" can certainly have "reasonable differences" about politicians decreeing businesses nonessential or even unlawful. Which spoke to an opportunity at the time for President Trump *not* to order the nation back to work, but instead for the president to empower his Department of Justice, solicitor general, and seemingly everyone else with legal power inside his administration to file lawsuits in defense of property and individual liberty anywhere in the U.S. where they were being violated.

Unknown to this day is why Trump didn't do just that. Why didn't he make it apparent from day one of this lapse of reason that his administration would not let hysteria about a virus get in the way of the very freedom and economic progress that has so successfully felled killers of the past?

Some may respond that Trump couldn't act rationally amid all the irrationality in consideration of how the media and his political opponents would have treated him, but such a response is much less than compelling. It is simply because the media were going to vilify Trump no matter what, as were his political opponents. Each did, even though Trump tragically joined them in panicking.

It was a monumental political blunder, but for Trump it was a much bigger economic error. For Trump, an economic error amounted to a major unforced *political* error when it's remembered how very much Trump aimed to define his presidency in terms of the economy.

Some may respond yet again that Trump lacked the power to order a locked-down nation back to work, but the argument misses the point.

It does because, per Pilon, reasonable people disagreed about the constitutionality of the lockdowns.

Some, including former New Jersey Superior Court Judge Andrew Napolitano, felt that the city and state lockdowns amid the coronavirus meltdown were blatantly unconstitutional. Napolitano lamented that in closing "most businesses, public venues and houses of worship, prohibited public assembly and restricted travel—all of which they have unilaterally decreed to be nonessential," the "governors of all 50 states and the mayors of many large cities have assumed unto themselves the powers to restrict private personal choices and lawful public behavior in an effort to curb the spread of COVID-19."[225]

Pilon at least saw reasonable constitutional objections to the lockdowns; Napolitano saw those same lockdowns as rather blatant in their violations of rights, but then law professor Kimberly Wehle (author of *How to Read the Constitution—And Why*) argued in *Politico* on May 15, 2020, that federal power is absolute, that "during the next pandemic—which is all but inevitable—Washington can and should impose an immediate, nationwide program of contact tracing and mandatory quarantine for infected people."[226] Though Wehle's view of federal power reads as terrifying, "reasonable minds" can once again disagree.

Which is the point. Had Trump not panicked, his administration could have at least put up a fight across the country for the workers and business owners who saw their livelihoods and life's work being cruelly taken from them. In filing lawsuits around the country, the Trump administration could have at least bought time for workers and business owners, plus its efforts would have given skeptical-about-lockdown governors and mayors national cover of sorts. Alas, that didn't happen.

Rather than being himself, and violating historical presidential norms by not "doing something," Trump acted like modern presidents always do. His administration would support the lockdowns, and worse, Trump made constitutionally illiterate comments about his power over governors that included, "The president of the United States calls the shots.

They [governors] can't do anything without the approval of the president of the United States." When "somebody's the president of the United States, the authority is total."[227] Again, a huge economic opportunity missed, which meant a huge political opportunity missed for Trump.

Rather than pushing back against the authoritarian ways of mayors and governors, the at times tone-deaf Trump used the imposition of economy-wrecking state force to try to one-up the wreckers when it came to who had the most power. And then a week later, when Georgia Governor Brian Kemp showed Trump where the power in fact resides by virtue of reopening the Peach State, Trump stepped on yet another opportunity to appear reasonable amid a near total loss of reason by telling the media that "I disagree with him on what he is doing."[228]

In Trump's defense, his opponent for the White House in 2020 was no better. Joe Biden acted as though presidential power was absolute, too, in childishly criticizing Trump for having done "next to nothing" in response to the virus.[229] If only! *New York Times* columnist Michelle Goldberg, who wrote weekly about Trump's failings, claimed that the forty-fifth president's "incompetence" in response to the virus "has wrecked us." She called for him to resign.[230] She was not alone. For the supercilious members of the left, the man who had built a global brand, executive-produced a top TV show, and got himself elected president was somehow flamboyantly stupid. On its own the argument was ludicrous, only for it to become more ridiculous amid the coronavirus meltdown.

Indeed, while Trump revealed his own ignorance about the Constitution in laughably contending that his power was "absolute," his opponents unwittingly revealed ignorance that exceeded Trump's with their illiterate assertion that the president had absolute power such that "America's" alleged failures in fighting that which had a death rate of somewhere between 0.1 and 0.2 percent were somehow indicative of Trump's weaknesses as president. As mentioned before, there was stupidity all around in the spring of 2020. Any worthwhile discussion of the presidency would conclude that virus fighting doesn't list as one of the president's responsibilities. Really, what halfway sentient human would expect the politically skillful to have virus savvy? This isn't a political statement. Consider what Ron Klain, Biden's chief of staff during Obama's presidency, said about the Obama administration's handling of the H1N1 virus: "We did every possible thing wrong. Sixty million Americans got H1N1 in that period of time, and it is just purely a fortuity that this isn't one of the great mass-casualty events in American history. [It] had nothing to do with us doing anything right; just had to do with luck."[231] Political operatives say the darndest things!

That they do is a reminder that any reasonable discussion of presidential performance would be in terms of how much the White House occupant protected broad freedoms so that cities and states could be laboratories in the fight against or the dismissal of the virus. Nothing more. Nothing less. But again, the conversation was remarkably obtuse back in 2020.

Worse was that there were very real victims of the stupidity. Naturally they weren't the well-to-do for whom politics is sport. In truth, it was those who, at least by U.S. standards, were not well-to-do. In flyover country, but also on the coasts...the mouth breathers for whom work was—gasp—a destination would suffer the idiocy of a pompous political class. Which is where this book will head next.

Chapter Eighteen

#RICHMANSCORONAVIRUS

*"You have to disobey. You have to do what's best
for your business. You have to do what's best for
your employees and your customers. You have to do
what's best for your livelihood, for your families."*

—Wayne Hoffman, president of the Idaho
Freedom Foundation[232]

"That's what I got busted for. I was ordering away." Those were the words of U.S. Senator Joe Manchin, a West Virginia Democrat. Manchin was describing an April 2020 conference call he was on with his Democratic colleagues, one that he participated in while ordering lunch at an Arby's drive-through in his home state of West Virginia.

"Silly" Manchin. He didn't realize that he wasn't on mute while ordering a King's Hawaiian Fish Deluxe sandwich. The senator joked that the sandwich was "a big piece of fish and it has a big slice of cheese. They were just jealous they weren't getting the good sandwich."[233]

In so many ways the lockdowns were all a big laugh for the well-to-do.

Along these lines, there's a story, perhaps apocryphal, about Jock Whitney. The well-born Whitney was among other things the original private equity investor, and the story goes that he was speaking at the graduation of a top Ivy League school. As he spoke, Whitney referenced the "Grand Tours" the grads were soon to take before getting on with real life. Apparently there was a bit of chuckling in the audience. Even in the rarefied Ivy League, the idea of a months-long and rather fancy tour of the world's great capitals was beyond the imagination or finances of most. Whitney seemingly imagined *everyone* was like him.

This came to mind during the lockdowns. What could those who imposed them have been thinking? It seemed the elite just assumed everyone locked down was just like them, that shelter-in-place rules would amount to a minor imposition. *They can just work from home, can't they?*

In Manchin's case, he could do his job from *anywhere*. He could even do it while in the drive-through of an Arby's. For the well-positioned economically, work for the most part continued during the lockdowns. Most often from home. And while waiting in line at fast food locations. Or from a second, third, or fourth home.

Rich parts of Manhattan somewhat emptied out during the lockdowns. People couldn't expect the NYC borough's captain-of-the-universe-style residents to shelter in place around big crowds, could they? So 10021 and other prominent zip codes went quiet.

One account of Manhattan amid the lockdowns went like this: "A late morning drive down Fifth Avenue, starting at the Metropolitan Museum of Art, where the lanes are normally choked with inching traffic, now passes by almost impossibly quickly."[234] With the city empty, small businesses throughout the city died. According to Yelp, 2,800 New York City businesses closed between March 1, 2020, and August 1, 2020.[235]

A *New York Times* headline said it all: "Even Art Is Leaving for the Hamptons." As *Times* reporter Ted Loos explained it, "With vacation homes becoming full-time residences during the pandemic, galleries are adding outposts to be near top buyers."[236] The art migrated to the buyers, and the buyers had left Manhattan. Well, *of course* they had! Their jobs were portable like Manchin's. *Wasn't everyone's job like that?*

Actually no. While technological advances had made it possible for 37 percent of U.S. jobs to be done at home (more on this in a bit), the rest could not be.[237] Jobs were a *place*.

This isn't to say or to presume that the hysterical reaction to the coronavirus by the political class didn't bring stress to the well-to-do, and this is certainly not meant to be construed as a call to arms against the rich. The rich get that way by improving the living standards of everyone else. It's not their fault that their achievements made it possible for witless politicians to force needless economic damage on tens of millions (more on this in a bit too). At the same time, it should be said that what was difficult for the prosperous was something quite worse for the common man. Stated simply, COVID-19 was in so many way's a rich man's virus and a rich man's hysteria that would be suffered by those with the least.

Up front about this chapter, there's a personal quality to it. All books are personal simply because they're "as things happened" through the eyes of the person explaining what happened. In this case, occasional personal recollections will be woven into observations of what happened that are always implicitly personal, if not explicitly.

At lunch at the great McLean Family Restaurant during the early days of the lockdowns, an old friend, who is the former head of a major Washington, DC, think tank, talked of how his daughter had been working as a hostess at one of the most famous restaurants in a southern city known for its famous restaurants. She'd just been laid off, as had millions of other Americans as a consequence of "non-essential" businesses being forced into shutdown, or forced into limited operational capacity.

Notable is that this daughter of a pretty major Washington personage didn't hole up in her apartment out of fear of contracting the virus, nor did she come home to wait out the health scare with her parents. She was with her boyfriend at the family's vacation house in Florida. Her restaurant job wasn't a career as much as it was work for extra pocket money ahead of finding a "real job" that correlated with her college-educated status. Though the layoff hurt (really, they all sting), bills would be paid. Meals would be eaten. Once again, she would wait out at least the early days of virus hysteria with her boyfriend in the sun.

In Washington, DC, in many ways the epicenter of the political freak-out over the coronavirus, it was fascinating to watch well-heeled shoppers at the city's grocery stores. Even though the shelves were largely well-stocked, with the exception of paper products, the well-to-do were buying indiscriminately, loading their carts up with hundreds of dollars' worth of grocery items. It should be stressed that they were doing this even though store aisles didn't look all that different on March 23 compared to February 23.

Those two anecdotes rate mention for what they perhaps said about the economic state of a country that was in the midst of a panic over a virus. In a very real sense, there was a part of the U.S. that was so comfortable that the whole "shutdown thing" was a bit of a vacation—a time to decompress, catch up on books, binge-watch shows, and get to know neighbors during daily long walks through the neighborhood.

For the American professional class, they would buy enormous amounts of food that would to varying degrees perish; that, or they would buy nonessentials to cook simply because they would finally have time to do so. As a stocker at Safeway indicated to me amid the virus's apex, cake, cookie, and muffin mixes were flying off the shelves. For the affluent patrons of all too many grocery stores in Washington, DC, they would buy food they didn't necessarily need while buying other mixes and ingredients with an eye on fulfilling their inner baker as they comfortably waited this one out. Sadly, it was those affluent types who in a broad sense were making brutal economic decisions for those not so flush.

Parents would get to spend more time with kids than ever before because suddenly they were no longer expected at the office. Have Wi-Fi and work from anywhere. The lockouts were again more of a hindrance than a job-destroying disaster for the well-to-do.

The thing is that the poor didn't realistically have backstops like abundant savings, second houses well away from the crowded cities, or parents' savings and lodgings to rely on. Their jobs were, and are, their safety nets, but thanks to an economic shutdown overseen by an out-of-touch and affluent political class, the poor increasingly didn't have jobs. That was especially the case because their jobs were service jobs, often the kind that involved interaction between the server and the serviced. This was a major challenge in consideration of how intent politicians (who never feared the loss of a paycheck) were on keeping cities and states shut down. If a business is closed, then it's closed. Millions of the lower-middle and poor had been working for businesses that met the consumptive needs of individuals. Many were deemed "non-essential" as evidenced by the tens of millions suddenly out of work. Their jobs were—gasp—a *destination*.

No, they couldn't do their work remotely from a vacation house, or while in the drive-through at Arby's, or even necessarily from their homes. Maintaining payments on those homes was suddenly a challenge (assuming they owned) as evidenced by banks tightening credit (see Chapter Fifteen). As for renters, *Forbes* estimated in October 2020 that 1.3 million devastated households would owe $7.2 billion in unpaid rent by year end.[238] And while some readers will point to safety nets in the form of unemployment insurance, PPP, and Main Street Lending, it's a safe bet that many of the suddenly jobless were "illegal" workers who couldn't access what wouldn't have been necessary if the shutdowns hadn't happened as is.

The empirical data supported the observational or personal. One Federal Reserve study that detailed March 2020 layoffs revealed that "almost 40% of households earning less than $40,000 a year experienced at least one job loss in March, versus 19% of households earning between $40,000 and $100,000, and 13% of those earning more than $100,000."[239] In Kentucky, the *Wall Street Journal* reported, nearly a third of its labor force had "filed for unemployment insurance, the largest share of any U.S. state."[240] Eternally beaten down Michigan wasn't much better off. Amid a jobless surge that could be measured in the million-plus range, nearly one-quarter of the state's labor force was rendered jobless in sickeningly rapid fashion.[241]

A *Wall Street Journal* headline from June 2020 noted, "Coronavirus Obliterates Best Black Job Market on Record." *Journal* reporters Eric Morath and Amara Omeokwe wrote, "Near the end of decade-long economic expansion, African-Americans were finally finding some financial stability. Unemployment had reached record lows, and their wages had begun rising modestly."[242] The crazed reaction to the coronavirus wiped away a lot of that progress.

Considering the hotel industry, suddenly travel of any kind was viewed as one asking for a death sentence. Those with the least were hit hard again as hotel companies like Marriott furloughed or laid off thousands.[243] While they accounted for 17.6 percent of the total U.S. workforce, Hispanics were roughly *half* of all maids and housekeeping cleaners.[244] They bore a disproportionate brunt of the forced contraction, and their struggles bled into other countries as a future chapter will reveal.

Restaurants were hit hard, but imagine the caterers providing food and drink at anniversary parties, graduation parties, charity dinners, weddings… Remember, politicians decided that human beings were essentially walking, talking carriers of death such that they needed to be separated, quarantined, you name it. Which meant bartenders, waiters, and others who picked up cash in the $60 billion (annual revenues) catering economy were viciously idled.[245]

In Blacksburg, Virginia, Virginia Tech comprises over half of the town's economy. But with the school shut down by the virus, so went an economy. What was vibrant was suddenly vacant. Businesses near wholly reliant on tens of thousands of students well-to-do enough to attend college were suddenly empty. As a *Wall Street Journal* front-page story described it, "What is happening in Blacksburg is playing out in cities from Ithaca, NY, to Pullman, Wash., where the pandemic hasn't only shut down businesses but also emptied out college campuses."[246]

Where it gets really sad is that small college towns were only beginning to feel the hit to their economies. Indeed, politicians had at least in the early days promised that the lockdowns would be short, given their decadent pursuit of a flattened COVID-infection curve. Translated, the economic hit to businesses and workers for whom work was a destination would reach its endpoint quickly. That all changed.

Somewhere along the way politicians forgot something that was all too obvious to the great Holman Jenkins of the *Wall Street Journal*. Though shelter-in-place and other lockdown rules might delay the spread of the virus, that was it. Jenkins reminded readers that blocking out reality wouldn't alter reality. Assuming quarantining worked in delaying infection, eventually things were going to have to get back to normal, and in getting back to normal, people were going to be infected with the virus. Some responded happily to the latter given the historical truth about "herd immunity," but that was really not the point. The point was that eventually everyone was going to be exposed to the virus. Thank goodness it was much less than 1 percent lethal and that somewhere around half were asymptomatic.

The shame was that politicians forgot all this. As lockdowns and other tyrannical takings of liberty ended, it was only natural that coronavirus cases would increase. Rather than celebrate this truth in the way that mothers would make sure that one sick brother or sister would infect the others, politicians locked down again. This matters simply because college football conferences like the Big Ten and Pac-12 began canceling

WHEN POLITICIANS PANICKED

nonconference games ahead of the 2020 season, and then whole seasons, thus laying an even bigger wet blanket on college town economies reliant on the arrival of prosperous alums from around the country.

It wasn't just small towns and small businesses that suffered there. Small football schools did too. You see, smaller college football teams (think Bowling Green, Kent State, Eastern Washington—schools like that) pay the bills each season by traveling to the big schools (think Alabama, Texas, Ohio State) for games that are seen as easy wins by the big schools. But with the cancellation of nonconference games, small schools faced big financial hits that imperiled their very survival.[247]

To be clear, those with the least endured this lapse of reason most cruelly. Government spending on its own is economically damaging as past chapters have made apparent, not to mention how *psychologically damaging* it no doubt was for millions to essentially be forced onto the dole. Really, what could individuals and businesses do? The economic collapse was so quick as to not leave time for any response other than just taking what little was being thrown their way. This tragedy will on its own be discussed in greater detail in future chapters.

Still, in closing this chapter it's important to contemplate what's already been discussed: lockdowns that were supposed to end quickly, quite simply did not. For those for whom the lockdowns were a minor hindrance, all too many wanted them extended without endpoint. Or at least until a vaccine could be found. Why not? The lockdowns didn't hurt the well-to-do in the way they harmed those not as financially set. Once again, *can't everyone work from home?* These people brought new meaning to #richmanscoronavirus.

Which is why it's worth closing with more thoughts on the lock-down-at-all-costs crowd. They rate some questions and comments in retrospect. In particular, for those who were "sheltering in place for humanity" and who thought skepticism about quarantines and lock-downs was the stuff of anti-science mouth breathers, they might stop and think about their 2020 stridency. What would all those self-proclaimed humanitarians have done if the new coronavirus had reared its head in 2000 instead of 2020? Assuming anyone would have noticed, how evident would their reverence for science and the "experts" have been then?

Those are questions worth asking simply because "sheltering in place" in 2000 would have been an entirely different concept. Some would argue that it would have been an impossibility.

For one, it was more than a challenge back then for the virtuous in our midst to signal just that. How could they?

Looking back once again to Chapters Eight and Fifteen, Mark Zuckerberg was still in high school in 2000. Facebook didn't open its proverbial doors until 2004, and even then it was still only envisioned as a social network for college kids. Basically those so eager amid the frenzy of the pandemic to demand that we *all* stay home and be *safe*, all the while endlessly advertising to all of us how much they *felt* as they stayed at home wouldn't have had a megaphone in 2000 to project just how deep their feelings were. Really, where's the fun in being more virtuous than all of us if no one knows about it?

What about all those amazing meals the deep believers in experts and medical science were making from home with the freshest, most organic of organic ingredients? Ever mindful of the importance of "flattening the curve," they made sure to order the "dolphin-free" version of everything they purchased *online*. Pretty amazing stuff, but perhaps those who never left their residences for groceries amid the coronavirus meltdown were unaware of how the biggest of the early online grocery businesses, Webvan, went bankrupt in rather splashy fashion back in 2001, well before its services reached even a small fraction of the U.S. Translated, grocery shopping back in 2000 was largely *in person*—out of necessity.

Of course, there were times during those oh-so-humane lockdowns during which the endlessly militant grew tired of cooking and doing dishes (going back and forth about whether washing by hand or dishwasher was best for the environment), so they ordered something healthy on their smartphones from Uber Eats, Postmates, Grubhub, or some other delivery service. No doubt it was a potential death sentence for *the believers in science* to be out breathing the air that others breathed and touching all manner of common hands or gloves as they purchased hot meals, but it was surely OK for the subhumans who probably didn't much care about science as is to risk *their lives* so that the "humanitarians" sheltering in place could take a night off from the rigors of cooking. Just as long as those "delivery people" didn't enter any houses or apartments. Thank goodness that online ordering provided ways for online buyers to send notes to the "drivers" with commands such as "leave the food on the doorstep!!!"

Technological advances also enabled great binge-watching amid all the healthy eating. Back in 2000, movie-and-TV fanatics still for the most part drove to a physical location to pick up VHS tapes and DVDs. In 2000, there was no *Tiger King* because it didn't exist but also because internet service was too slow back then for streaming. "Blockbuster Nights" were the primary non-cable option in May of 2000, and there was driving involved...

But wait, the haughty might say, the lockdowns weren't all about eating and television. All this was combined with exercise. Except that going outside was so risky back in 2020! So many science deniers running and breathing without masks! Capitalists to the rescue again. They combined exercise bikes with high-speed internet access on the way to businesses like Peloton that enabled virtual exercise classes all the time at all hours. In 2000, Peloton and its workouts from *anywhere* at *any time* were an impossibility thanks to slow internet speeds, among other things.

Work from anywhere at any time would similarly have been a challenge. Not only was internet service much slower twenty years ago, not only was so much dial-up, most if not all online connections involved a cord. No moving around the apartment or house to work from anywhere. Assuming the corona-adamant had home internet, it was going to be utilized from a specific location and at speeds that no internet user would come close to tolerating in 2020. Zoom? Sorry, it was a long way off. No work meetings from home, no gatherings of old friends during which rather gauche notions of curve flattening were discussed over craft beers and other creations of the profit-motivated.

Most of all, not much of Amazon either. Though the Seattle-based retail giant thrived amid the lockdowns, back in 2000 Amazon met very narrow consumer needs very unprofitably. Absent patient investors who grew very rich for being patient, the Amazon of 2020, whereby its sale of seemingly everything made quarantining a snap, likely doesn't exist.

So yes, the poor suffered the most amid a tragic economic crack-up authored first and foremost by elite politicians who, arguably influenced by how their own work could be shut down or done remotely without loss of job, decreed that the work of others could be similarly discontinued or done remotely for stretches. Politicians weathered this lapse of reason with ease, as did the well-to-do who saw their work transformed by billionaires whom many of the merely well-to-do oddly despise. The poor: they got the *fist*. And really they got worse than the fist as the next chapter will make plain. Work is more than a paycheck, or a check, despite what politicians think.

Chapter Nineteen

WRAP YOUR GENIUS IN PLASTIC

"As I look back over a misspent life, I find myself more and more convinced that I had more fun doing news reporting than in any other enterprise. It is really the life of kings."

—H. L. Mencken[248]

"I can't *not* act. It's what I was made to do."[249] Those are the words of Jennifer Lawrence, one of the highest paid actresses in the world. They're from a *Vanity Fair* interview conducted in 2014.

Lawrence is lucky enough to live in a time and place where what she was made to do also affords her a living. Since she "can't *not* act," it's not unreasonable to speculate that Lawrence puts herculean effort into her craft. Loving what animates her, work is an expression of her unique genius. Indeed, as she acknowledged in the aforementioned interview, acting is the "only thing I'm good at."

To be clear, Lawrence is an outlier. That's well understood. At the same time, Lawrence's passion is a reminder that arguably the greatest gift of economic growth is the growing ability of people to showcase their individual skills and unique *intelligence* while on the job.

This wasn't always the case. Before automation, and yes, global trade, the vast majority of human exertion was directed toward the creation of food. Work was life, albeit not in a happy way. People worked dawn to dusk six days per week in order to survive. Most worked until they died.

Thanks to automation and trade, it's more and more the case that people can "outsource" to others their need for food, shelter, clothing, transportation, and the like. Think about what that means. If it's hard to contemplate, stop for a minute and imagine what your hair would look like if you had to cut it or what your clothes would look like if you had to make them.

That we can buy from others doing what they do best means we have much greater odds of specializing in the work that we "can't *not* do." This is the stuff of economic growth. Specialized workers are productive workers.

Importantly, there's a human side to all this. More and more of us will work until our last days not because we have to, but because we *want to*.

And because work for all too many is more and more about doing what we *want to*, it should be stressed that work is increasingly the stuff of *happiness*. Work reinforces what we're good at, which means it's hard for a growing number of us to not be working.

This wildly uplifting truth about work is something else tone-deaf politicians plainly missed in their hysterical responses to the new coronavirus. Having panicked over a virus that thankfully sickened very few, and that very thankfully killed even fewer, politicians expressed their alarm through frenzied limits placed on work. Unnerved by something they didn't understand, they substituted their extraordinarily limited knowledge for that of the marketplace on the way to putting tens of millions out of work in the U.S. alone.

Tragic about all this is that politicians aren't just alarmist. They're also self-unaware. Having engineered an economic contraction that wiped out the livelihoods of tens of millions, those same politicians then doubled down amid their stupor as they extracted trillions of dollars from the private economy in a panicked effort to throw money indiscriminately at a problem of their own making. Yet in attempting to buy calm after their act of economic terrorism, they just added to their insult of the workers they devastated. Think about it.

It's not just for money that we work. That's why when politicians suffocate economic growth under the pretense of protecting us from our allegedly stupid selves or stupid others, we lose much more than income. So many of us lose what causes us to excitedly get out of bed each morning.

Work is once again happiness. Figure that Warren Buffett could, if he wanted to, retire thousands and thousands of people to lives of monetary splendor. But he couldn't give them happiness. Happiness comes from work done well.

Politicians shut down "non-essential" businesses and then paid those whose jobs vanished a pittance to soften the blow of their unemployment. But these endlessly oblivious legislators missed that jobs are so much more than money. Work is where people get to be stars and superstars.

Writing about the men and women crafting amazing dishes in his super-high-end kitchens in *32 Yolks*, legendary chef Eric Ripert described their "dangerous, rock star charisma that comes from those who are truly good at what they do."[250] Ripert's book should be required reading for every politician.

Though most would likely gloss over the essential truths about passionate work, a light bulb might come on in the heads of some. They might see that work is so much more than a way to pay the bills. Thanks to economic growth that has nothing to do with politicians and everything to do with entrepreneurs outrunning their outstretched hands, more and more of us get to be truly good at what we do.

Not after March 2020. Politicians implicitly said workers couldn't be trusted and that businesses couldn't be trusted to remain open amid what they proclaimed a pandemic. Their message was we'll "shut you down for your own good, but pay you while you're idled."

How they missed the point. Precisely because so many modern workers love getting to do what "they're truly good at," they would have made all manner of changes to their daily routines just so that they could continue to work. Just as athletes play while hurt all the time simply because they can't *not* play, free workers would have made all manner of adjustments to how they worked amid a spreading virus just so that they could do what made them stars.

The problem yet again was that politicians on all levels panicked, and having panicked, they foisted cruel, one-size-fits-all solutions on their constituents that resulted in sick-inducing job loss and bankruptcy. In the process they robbed millions of what gave them daily *meaning* and happiness, and others of the chance to eventually find work that uniquely suits them, but that is invariably a consequence of the economic growth that politicians so obnoxiously snuffed out. What of Ripert's charismatic chefs? They were insultingly told to wrap their genius in plastic.

Chapter Twenty

PERISHING AMID OVERPOWERING, ODIFEROUS SLUDGE

*"I can't stop. If I don't sell, I don't
eat. It's as simple as that."*

—Leonardo Meneses Prado,
as he desperately tended his hamburger
cart in a locked-down Mexico City[251]

"After hearing of the deaths in the gutters, I think about what will happen to my family if I die." Those are the words of Jamshed Eric, as expressed to *New York Times* reporters Zia ur-Rehman and Maria Abi-Habib. Eric is a Pakistani Christian, and his religion requires mention since Christians are so low in the Pakistani social order that they're routinely slotted to work in the *gutters*.

Yes, you read that right. Pakistan still maintains an implicit caste system. Manual "sewer cleaners" are those in the lowest of Pakistani castes, as in "the most untouchable of the untouchable Hindu castes." Christians once again work the gutters. It's a generational thing.

So what are these gutters Eric talks about? Readers can perhaps guess. Pakistan suffers levels of poverty that would stagger the poorest of poor Americans, and its primitive sewer system is reflective of the country's desperate economic condition. Eric works daily to keep Karachi's sewer system flowing, using his hands to "unclog crumbling drainpipes of feces, plastic bags and hazardous hospital refuse."

Remarkable in consideration of how Americans and others lucky enough to live in the developed world were wearing masks out of fear that other humans in public places were a mortal threat to them, ur-Rehman and Abi-Habib reported that Eric wore "no mask or gloves to protect him from the stinking sludge and toxic plumes of gas that lurk underground." Worse is what happens at night. Eric told the *Times*, "When I raise my hand to my mouth to eat, it smells of sewage."[252]

Notable is that Eric in a sense feels lucky to be living with the constant sewage stench. It means he's *living*. The death rate of sewer cleaners had picked up around the time he was interviewed.

Reading about Eric, it was hard not to wonder how Americans would react to the kind of work that pays him the equivalent of six dollars a day. In college football parlance, fans talk about where they wouldn't be "caught dead." University of Washington fans won't be caught dead at Autzen (where the Oregon Ducks play), and for the longest time Alabama fans wouldn't be "caught dead" at Jordan-Hare (Auburn's stadium). First world problems, or grievances. Something like that.

Back to the realities of other parts of the world, how many Americans can imagine clearing out sewers full of the waste of others, let alone be caught dead in one? Thankfully Americans don't have to contemplate such horrendous working conditions in return for a wage.

The reason they don't is thanks to economic growth. Economic growth is a consequence of economic freedom. When people are broadly free to produce sans overbearing barriers of the tax, regulation, trade, and floating money variety, they prosper. In all-too-many instances they get to do work that would have caused members of past generations to ask something along the lines of "they pay you to do that?"

Crucial about this growth as the previous chapter argued is that the nature of work is constantly changing where economies are growing. Translated, jobs are being destroyed all the time, only to be replaced by new, better forms of work. All of this must be considered with Eric in mind. He's "now been forced into the same work his Hindu ancestors had tried to avoid through religious conversion."[253]

Pakistan's still encouraged caste system is on its own a tragedy, but much worse is the static nature of work whereby generation after generation does the same thing. There's a myth that poverty correlates with unemployment. No, "unemployment" is a rich country concept. In poor countries everyone is working, all the time. Worse is that the work is passed down through generations.

That would be impossible in the U.S. simply because what's work now most likely won't be ten, twenty, and thirty years from now. And what's work now in so many instances wasn't ten, twenty, and thirty years ago. Thanks to abundant economic growth, backbreaking work of the past like farming and coal mining is largely in the past. And while some still farm and mine in the U.S., *they don't have to.* Since they're part of the greatest zone of prosperity the world has ever known, and since they can migrate freely within this fifty-state zone, Americans can essentially *choose* the kind of work they'll do. In other words, if they're farming or working in a mine, they're doing so by choice.

Alexis de Tocqueville observed about Americans in the nineteenth century that they're "restless amid abundance."[254] By the latter, the French chronicler didn't mean that Americans were bouncing from sewer job to sewer job. Where there's freedom, there's also economic progress. And where there's economic progress, the range of ways in which individuals can offer up their skills expands in happy fashion.

Thinking about all this in terms of the hideous lockdowns, it's not just that they indiscriminately destroyed tens of millions of jobs and millions of businesses. That was the damage they did in the present. That the imposition of command-and-control needlessly destroyed jobs and businesses was a given. Slow to shrinking economic growth is awful in so many ways right as it happens, but it's arguably most awful for it shrinking and slowing our ability to showcase our unique skills and *intelligence* in jobs that continue to evolve for the better. Growth often erases the work of the past, only to free us to do new work in the future unimagined in the past.

The coronavirus story is still being written as this book is, and it will continue to be written decades into the future, but the undeniable truth in the spring and summer of 2020 was that economic growth in the developed world would be restrained. The only disagreement was about how much. Not discussed much was the argument being made here: slower growth slows the happy process whereby the work of the past is replaced by the much better work of the future.

Of course, an extraordinarily bad economic day in the United States represents smile-inducing boom times most anywhere else in the world. America's poor would be middle class most anywhere else. America's poor have cars, air conditioners, mobile phones, and all sorts of luxuries that were largely nonexistent for the richest of the rich one hundred years ago.

Figure that the first window unit air conditioners didn't go on the market in the U.S. until 1932. The problem was that almost no one could afford them. They retailed anywhere from $10,000 to $50,000.[255] Thank goodness that rich, "venture buyers" established the value of what was out of reach for 99.999 percent of Americans. The desirability of air conditioners to the superrich existed as a market signal for entrepreneurs who began producing them in more affordable fashion. Fast-forward to the present, and the window units that formerly signaled unimaginable wealth are most often seen in the poorest of U.S. neighborhoods. Such is the genius of economic growth. Looking back to Chapter One, luxury is "historical." Where there's freedom, growth is the logical result. From that emerges plenty of what used to be scarce. That air conditioners are the norm in free societies is a reminder of how very compassionate are freedom and growth.

This serves as a good jumping-off point as we consider the panic about the coronavirus in a global context. It was disastrous.

Precisely because Americans consume so much of the world's plenty, when growth slows stateside it's felt around the world. Americans are huge consumers of much that is produced around the world, often in poorer places. Wildly productive American "hands" working feverishly also enable much greater productivity by non-American "hands." But there's more to it. Americans, along with citizens in other developed countries, are *producers* for the rest of the world too. That they are has loomed large in the happy reduction of poverty around the world in modern times.

In a 2015 piece for *Investor's Business Daily*, Cato Institute senior fellow Marian Tupy noted that, according to World Bank estimates, 50 percent of the world's population lived in absolute poverty as recently as 1980. By 2015 that number had plummeted to 10 percent, and it was falling.[256]

Which speaks loudly to the tragedy of the coronavirus panic in 2020. What happened in the United States had a global impact, one that was explanatory about so much, including monetary policy. To understand this, it's first useful to travel to El Salvador.

Amid the economy-sapping U.S. lockdowns in the spring and summer of 2020, a lack of production in the U.S. was felt rather acutely down in Central America. As the *Wall Street Journal's* Santiago Perez explained it in a June 2020 report, the "slum in El Salvador where Maria

Graciela Barrera lives is dotted with white flags, outside homes, serving as distress signals that people inside don't have enough food."

In Barrera's case, she was "no longer getting the $50 a month that two of her grandchildren send from Los Angeles." Barrera told Perez that "since they lost their construction jobs because of the coronavirus, we are adrift." More broadly, Perez reported that as "the jobless rate among Hispanics in the U.S. surged to close to 20% in April, remittances to El Salvador plunged 40% from the same month last year."[257] As this book has stressed throughout, all demand is a consequence of production first. *Of supply.* Demand for food in El Salvador didn't just happen; rather, it was to a high degree a consequence of production that took place elsewhere—much of it in the United States.

U.S. production has long informed Salvadoran demand, which is just a reminder of how worthless are numbers like GDP that excite economists so much. GDP is consumption-focused, which means it's largely a consequence of production. Applied to El Salvador, a not-insubstantial portion of its GDP doesn't even take place there. This truth requires a brief digression into monetary policy. Rest assured, it's brief. But important. And also useful. It's a reminder that money creation doesn't stimulate economic growth as much as it's a consequence. Money *finds* the fruits of production, as opposed to money stimulating it.

Think back to Chapter Sixteen. In that chapter we went over how U.S. products can be found in countries like North Korea and Iran even though the U.S. maintains a trade embargo against both. There's no accounting for the final destination of any good, which means American products find their way to "enemy" countries. So do American dollars.

Money is an agreement about value that enables exchange or trade. With trade it was historically products for products. Translated, trade was barter. The problem was one of wants that weren't always coincident. The bread maker didn't necessarily want the vintner's wine, thus making trade among producers more of a challenge. Money erased this problem. Though trade is *still* about products for products, the existence of an agreement about value (money) means that the bread maker can still trade with the vintner even if he solely desires the butcher's meat. Movements of money reflect the movements of real goods and services; money once again simplifying things for it enables producers to trade with anyone, and without regard to the actual wants of those transacting.

The U.S. dollar can be found all over North Korea precisely because the dollar is trusted around the world.[258] Unsheathe it anywhere, and producers will exchange real goods, services, and labor for it. That's why the dollar factors into nearly all global trade. Since trade is once again products for products, the handing over of products for dollars is a trustworthy deal for the person handing over real goods for the paper (the dollar). It can summon resources anywhere. North Koreans use it over the local currency (the won) as a result.

The digression into money was necessary simply because some monetary theorists (they call themselves "market monetarists") believe they can plan country GDP growth through control of so-called "money supply." Basically they aim to plan a backwards-looking statistical aggregate that is the consequence of actual growth via the planning of money in an economy. The joke's on them.

Indeed, while El Salvador's country currency (the colón) was replaced by the dollar in an official sense in 2001, simple logic tells us that the dollar was the official currency of Salvadoran exchange long before 2001. Logic reigns here because trade is once again about products for products. Money just facilitates the exchange so long as it's credible. The dollar long ago replaced the colón owing to the basic truth that the dollar readily commands goods and services wherever it's offered. In short, El Salvador's switch to the dollar back in 2001 was an acknowledgment of a long-standing reality.

It's a reminder that even if the colón were still the country's official currency, dollars would still liquefy trade in the country. The dollar is not just an accepted medium of exchange among Salvadorans, it's also the currency that is regularly remitted to the Salvadoran people by their more economically productive relatives up in the United States. Translated, the so-called "money supply" that lifts Salvadoran GDP isn't a consequence of the Fed or "market monetarists" advising the Fed on how many dollars to "supply" through "open market" operations with Salvadoran banks; rather, it's an effect of U.S.-based production that is rewarded with dollar compensation that ultimately flows to El Salvador.

Money and so-called "money supply" is production determined. Without production, money logically would have no use. Money flows once again signal the flow of real goods, services, and labor. Where there's none of the three, there is no money. In their focus on numbers like GDP that are an upshot of growth and various forms of monetary sorcery, economists put the proverbial cart before the horse. *Production first, then money.* Without production stateside, there were logically fewer dollars in El Salvador. Very sadly, it wasn't just El Salvadorans who suffered the U.S.'s economic contraction.

Simply stated, U.S. production has long been the driver of "demand" and GDP in other parts of the world too. So has production in other, more developed parts of the world been the source of "demand" in less developed locales. But in the spring and summer of 2020, developed countries the world over shut down economic activity to varying degrees. Politicians panicked globally.

Whereas in 2019 tens of millions of "Indians, Filipinos, Mexicans and others from developing countries working overseas sent a record $554 billion back to their home countries," the lockdowns put tens of millions out of work around the world. The result was greatly reduced remittances. Basically, the white flags seen outside of houses in El Salvador could be seen around the world in a figurative sense. A *Wall Street Journal* headline chronicling this global disaster got right to the point: "Countries Lose Billions Sent from Workers Abroad."[259]

It cannot be stressed enough that GDP is the consumptive result of production, and with so much global consumption a consequence of production in the developed world, GDP was plummeting in poor countries solely as a reflection of reduced production in the economically advanced ones. To give readers an idea of just how much the poorer parts of the world are reliant on the developed world, the $554 billion in 2019 remittances was greater "than all foreign direct investment in low—and middle—income countries and more than three times the development aid from foreign governments." [260]

So while global liberalization had surely brought on plummeting global poverty since 1980, arguably the bigger factor had been stupendous growth in the developed parts of the world—growth that increasingly lined the empty pockets of the world's poorest. Decadent lockdowns in the rich world that drove unemployment surges in them were going to hurt the world's poorest the most. Let this tragic development in 2020 exist as a reminder of a certain truth that the left would rather not acknowledge: wealth creation is the greatest enemy of poverty, *by far*. Wealth isn't a fixed pie that is taken; rather, wealth is created. And when it's created, the whole world benefits.

A World Bank projection as global panic in response to a virus raged was that global remittances would decline by 20 percent in 2020.[261] With fewer dollars, euros, pounds, and yen being earned in the developed world, there would be reduced "supply" of those currencies in the poorer parts; the supply not a consequence of central banks, but plainly a result of former production that led to a shift of those funds to the needy. Sad examples abounded.

Bangladesh is increasingly the "sewing machine" for the developed world, but lockdowns led to an 85 percent decline of clothing exports in April 2020 alone. In concert with the aforementioned drop, remittances into the country declined 24 percent.

In total dollars, India takes in the biggest number annually. In 2019, $83 billion was remitted. The expectation for 2020 was that the number would decline by 23 percent.[262] This money wasn't remitted to pay for trips to amusement parks and movies. It's no reach to say the money was sent to help some very desperate people desperate to feed themselves.

Considering the Philippines, 10 percent of Filipinos live outside the country, or lived. Thanks to slowing global growth, the projected remittance decline from overseas Filipinos was 20 percent. Combining anecdotal with the statistical, the *Wall Street Journal's* Jon Emont interviewed Mitzie Espiritu, a thirty-four-year-old Filipino who had moved to Dubai where she worked as a fitness center employee. Her earnings supported a niece and nephew back in the Philippines until her job was terminated. With no work options in Dubai as the economy contracted, she returned home to the Philippines. It's sad to contemplate her work options there since her home country itself had such stringent lockdowns.

The tragedy was that the political panic wasn't limited to the rich countries. "No one dies from a fever" became a popular saying in the same Philippines that Espiritu returned to. The saying caught on simply because a country as poor as it plainly lacked the means to do something so decadent as to lock down its citizens in the face of a virus. Really, what could President Rodrigo Duterte have been thinking? As a *New York Times* report from mid-April 2020 pointed out, presumably with a hint of sarcasm, "Fever, body aches and coughs were commonplace long before the virus came."[263] Poverty hurts; it's dirty, it's crowded, which means it's *already* the stuff of spreading viruses.

The Philippines situation spoke loudly to the shocking lapse of reason that defined the times. As the previous paragraph makes plain, the country's impoverished masses suffered fever, body aches, and coughs in general, so the country's politicians were going to force them to stay locked down in closed quarters to somehow avoid the symptoms of COVID-19? Sorry, but the Filipinos couldn't afford to shelter in place or any other gauche activity dreamt up by alarmists in country and around the world who never had to fear a loss of paycheck or a missed meal. They needed to work in order to survive. As Analyn Mikunog, a mother of four, bleakly put it to *New York Times* reporter Jason Gutierrez, "Sometimes we talk, and wonder how long this lockdown will last. Will we die hungry?"[264] Exactly.

So much effort was spent on modeling projected deaths from the virus or actual deaths. Did they ever stop to model the many multiples that die every year from poverty?

Venezuela was instructive in this regard. Already in desperate shape due to socialist policies that prevailed long before lockdowns, Venezuela's collectivism had long been repelling its best and brightest people. Nelson Torrelles was one of those who had left; in his case for Colombia. Except that he was forced to leave his adopted country as the lockdowns spread globally, and in ways exponentially more crushing of spirit and life than the virus ever could.

"I wanted to stay put in Colombia to build a better future for my daughter, but we have to go back." So said Torrelles to *Wall Street Journal* reporter John Otis. As Otis reported in the August 31, 2020, edition of the *Journal*, the "haggard and hungry" Torrelles, along with his wife and five-year-old daughter, was walking back to Venezuela on a Colombian highway.[265]

They'd initially moved to Colombia to escape Venezuela's socialist hellhole, only for Torrelles to get a job as a waiter at a barbecue restaurant in Bogotá. But when Colombia joined much of the rest of the locked-down world, Torrelles lost his job and soon enough the family apartment that he couldn't make rent on. Hard as it may be to imagine for those of us lucky enough to live in the developed world, the hungry Torrelles and his family were moving *back* to Venezuela.

Please stop and think about this for a minute. Please stop and imagine the pain Torrelles was in. It surely extended well beyond hunger. Imagine not being able to adequately provide for your family, including a daughter too young to understand that your failures are largely beyond your control. Words don't begin to describe what Torrelles must have been going through, nor can someone lucky enough to live in the United States or some other prosperous part of the world understand just how awful things must have been for Torrelles and his family. The lockdowns were sickeningly inhumane to those with the least.

Politicians in the U.S. and around the world kept congratulating themselves on the hard work they were doing to "flatten" the infection curve, and in pretending they were helping, they only succeeded insofar as they revealed just how staggeringly unaware they were of what was actually happening. Anthony Fauci told the *New York Times* that the new coronavirus had "in a period of four months…devastated the whole world."[266] Was he serious?

While acknowledging up front that all lives matter, as of mid-July the number of COVID-related deaths *worldwide* was roughly 593,000. About the previous number, it's worth reiterating yet again that a numbers contest is a loser's game. This is a book about the tragedy of the lockdowns, and it can't be said enough that the lockdowns still wouldn't have made sense even if global deaths had been *5.9 million* versus 593,000. The bigger the threat, the less the need for force.

Still, what could Fauci have been thinking? The new coronavirus had "devastated the world"? What could he possibly have meant? Could he really have been so ignorant to the basic truth that poverty's body count over the millennia rendered suffering from the new coronavirus the proverbial ant on the elephant's gargantuan bottom? You quite simply cannot compare the devastation brought on the world by the coronavirus to the historical, murderous cruelty that has always been poverty.

If anyone doubts the above truth, they need only contemplate the global reaction if as opposed to the virus spreading in 2020, or 2000, what if it had reared its head in 1920 with the same death rate that was somewhere between 0.1 and 0.2 percent? The answer about the 1920 reaction is that there wouldn't have been one. Life would have gone on. Period.

Fauci bit his nails about the world being "devastated" by the virus, and in doing so he glossed over the tragic truth that *135 million human beings* faced starvation as a result of a global economy that was being destroyed to fight that which as of mid-July 2020 was associated with 593,000 deaths. Is 135 million deaths not enough for you? Are you still "standing with Fauci" regardless? OK, what about a doubling of the number? Arif Husain, chief economist of the United Nations' World Food Programme, projected in April 2020 that *285 million people* could be pushed to the brink of starvation by the end of 2020.[267] About Husain's projections, economists are most notorious for being wrong about nearly everything. At the same time, one had to wonder. Even if Husain had been extraordinarily wrong, deaths from starvation brought on by global economic contraction were still going to make corona deaths microscopic by comparison. Yet Fauci kept talking about black vs. white death rate comparisons and the need for a vaccine for a virus that thankfully wasn't terribly lethal. Why? As of now we still don't know.

What we do know is that in response to a new virus that largely visited death on very few very old people with preexisting conditions, politicians and experts the world over foisted brutal economic contraction on the world. And as is always the case, those with the least were hit from all sides.

The slower global growth that was a certain and logical consequence of global lockdowns was going to slow the economic evolution that would free the children of Jamshed Eric from the disgusting, inhumane, and life-threatening work done by generations of the Eric family. Eric *père* worked the gutters each day, but he was striving mightily to get his kids educated so that they wouldn't have to do the work that he was doing. Eric was trying to break the cycle of poverty that is defined by hideous work being passed down through the generations. Tragically, the lockdowns would make an escape from Dad's work by the Eric kids less likely. For one, their continued education was surely rendered less likely thanks to a global contraction authored by elite hysteria. As the *New York Times* reported in late September 2020, school closures and the need for money meant that "at least 24 million children will drop out [of school] and that millions could be sucked into work."[268] Work stasis would be the cruel long-term "reward" for the world's poorest thanks to rich, witless politicians panicking in response to a virus. Readers can only hope the Eric kids weren't among those knocked off the course out of poverty set for them by their loving, gutter-working father.

In a broad sense, hundreds of millions of the world's poorest faced a return to the poverty and starvation that they'd been rapidly escaping. Tens of millions would have probably preferred quick death over the horrid fate they faced.

Why again did this happen? All these allegedly compassionate politicians, all these experts working together to fight a virus? Why did their efforts result in a poverty and starvation inducing global crisis? The previous question will be addressed in the next chapter.

Chapter Twenty-One

EXPERTS AREN'T THE ANSWER TO CRISIS, THEY *ARE* THE CRISIS

"There are more people killed by good doctors than by good generals."

—Bartlett

I n 1949, Antonio Egas Moniz, a Portuguese neurologist, won the Nobel Prize in Medicine. Why was this highly regarded doctor honored in such a grand way? In Moniz's case, the Nobel's jury members were very taken by his development of the lobotomy.[269]

The present rarely predicts the future. This is true in sports, entertainment, commerce, and really all walks of life. Brokerage employees are required to tell clients that past performance should not be construed as indicative of future performance.

Knowledge is similarly not always forward looking. New information reveals itself on the way to changing how we see things and understand them.

Disease is instructive in this regard. Let's think about AIDS. In thinking about it, let's consider Anne Glenconner. She was the eldest child of the 5th Earl of Leicester. Anne (her maiden name was Coke) grew up at Holkham Hall, which was ten miles from Sandringham, the king and queen of England's estate. Her family was so aristocratic that when Queen Mary contacted her great-grandmother about visiting Holkham with the king of England, her great grandfather could be heard complaining, "Come over? Good God, no! We don't want to encourage them!"[270]

Anne Coke wound up marrying Colin Tennant, the 3rd Baron Glenconner, and who was best known later in life as the man who built the Caribbean island Mustique. Before marriage, Coke was maid of honor at Queen Elizabeth II's coronation, plus she served Princess Margaret as her lady-in-waiting until the princess's death in 2002.

Some readers may find the royals fascinating, others might find the very idea of prestige by birth offensive, and others are perhaps indifferent. But that's not the point, really. The reason Glenconner's remarkably aristocratic and royal background is referenced has to do with when her son, Henry, contracted AIDS in 1986.

One might assume based on who Henry Tennant was, along with who his mother was, that they would have had access to those who had sophisticated knowledge of a disease that originated in the Democratic Republic of Congo sometime in the 1970s. Except that they didn't. As Anne Glenconner explained it in her 2020 autobiography, *Lady in Waiting*, "no one knew how it was caught" when Henry made his announcement.[271] Though it was heavily linked to gay men, the lack of a cure had people very scared. And with hysteria at a high in the mid-1980s, lots of incorrect assumptions were made.

In Michael Fumento's 1990 book, *The Myth of Heterosexual AIDS*, the epidemic expert referenced one Dr. Robert Redfield on no less than twenty-four pages. Redfield, among other things, declared the chance of "male-to-female vaginal HIV to be 50 percent per contact." Except that Fumento cited widely available data at the time that rejected the eventual CDC director's alarmism. The data showed that "if neither partner had genital sores or other openings, odds approached zero."[272]

The thing is, *no one knew*. It didn't matter if you were rich or poor, gay or straight, there quite simply wasn't enough knowledge yet. Look back to Chapter Ten and the mention of Anthony Fauci's assertion about AIDS in a 1983 paper that he authored on his own, that AIDS might be passed around by the infected through "routine close contact, as within a family household." Those were the assumptions back then, inside and outside science.

Doctors and experts didn't know, yet despite not knowing, this didn't stop them from speculating. And in speculating, they created unnecessary hysteria.

In 1985, a sickly looking Rock Hudson kissed Linda Evans's character Krystle Carrington on the smash ABC hit show *Dynasty*. He did so despite knowing he had AIDS. In an autobiography he coauthored with journalist Sara Davidson, Hudson acknowledged that the day of the kiss "was one of the worst days in his life," that he used "every gargle, mouthwash and spray he could get his hands on" ahead of the kiss, and he took all the aforementioned precautions because he worried he would pass the disease onto Evans.[273] Information was limited when Hudson caught the disease that eventually killed him. He sadly died worried he'd infected his friend in Evans. Again, people didn't know.

In 1986, the year that Henry Tennant contracted AIDS, the British government started a major ad campaign with the warning that "one in five people would contract HIV."[274] The ad's tagline was "Don't die of ignorance," but as we know in retrospect, it was the medical experts in England, the U.S., and everywhere else who were ignorant. Goodness, by the early 1990s Redfield was still so terrified by AIDS that he backed federal legislation that, according to Fumento, "would have subjected people with HIV to forced testing and the loss of their professional licenses and would have effectively quarantined them—for a disease essentially transmitted by anal sex and transfer of blood and blood products."[275]

To be clear, this isn't to say that Great Britain's National Health Service experts were all idiots, that Fauci is a dolt, and that Redfield is an authoritarian dolt. One senses they're all very smart. But as the introductory chapter contended, "In relying on experts to understand the present, we're expecting them to digest voluminous information produced around the world on the way to coming to some kind of knowledgeable conclusion. We ask too much of experts."

In relying on experts, it cannot be stressed enough that we plant the seeds for crisis. That we do is a statement of the obvious.

To see why, let's assume that the hysteria about the coronavirus dies down enough that we can eventually get back to normal. Normal would include capacity crowds at stadiums. Assuming there's a normal 2021 professional baseball season and noted Washington Nationals fan Fauci attends a game at Nationals Park, it's not unreasonable to suggest that he will be the smartest individual in the stadium. Some say his intelligence is formidable.

At the same time, Fauci's mental capacity will be very small relative to the combined intelligence of every fan cheering at Nationals Park. Whether eighteen thousand are in attendance, or there's a full-house of 41,313 (maybe the Yankees are in town for an inter-League matchup), one remarkable mind is no match for the collective wisdom of the masses. Their combined knowledge puts them at a major advantage against one or, for that matter, *many*.

All of the above very neatly explains why free, unfettered markets correlate so well with positive economic outcomes. Market signals are arrived at through the combined knowledge, wants, and skills of tens of thousands, millions, and *billions* of human beings.

At the same time, it hopefully also explains why central planning always fails in miserable fashion. It's not that there weren't intelligent people running some of the Iron Curtain countries of the late twentieth century, and it's not that those in power didn't avail themselves of expert opinion at times. The problem then was that individual genius, no matter how substantial, couldn't come close to measuring up to the combined knowledge of the masses of people who make up what we call a market.

This rates prominent mention in consideration of how much members of the political class were relying on experts in pursuit of an effective response to the new coronavirus. In empowering individual genius, it's logical to assert that politicians created a crisis where there otherwise wouldn't have been one.

Consider Fauci yet again. In a press conference toward the end of April in 2020, he said it would be necessary for coronavirus testing to double so that the lockdowns' asphyxiating economic activity could be lifted. Was Fauci correct? It's fairly easy to say he wasn't, and not just because he supported the lockdowns.

It's likely Fauci was incorrect simply because the information he had at his disposal was so limited. That he was so wrong about AIDS in the 1980s is instructive. It's just so difficult to know.

Furthermore, just as central planners routinely failed when it came to planning economic outcomes in the twentieth century, so did that same central planning fail in 2020. Fauci may have been brilliant, but he was no match for the collective wisdom of hundreds of millions of Americans making infinite decisions born of what they knew, every second of every day.

What applied to Fauci similarly applied to another known genius in Bill Gates. Some believed in 2020 that his undeniable brilliance as a businessman positioned him to knowledgeably opine on how the U.S. and the rest of the world could come back from the virus. Gates argued that it was "important to realize" that the economic contraction wasn't just the result of "government policies restricting activities," that when "people hear that an infectious disease is spreading widely, they change their behavior."[276] OK, but going back to Chapter Ten, if behavior changes in response to an infectious disease, as in if people with even a small clue decide to be careful in response to something spreading as is, why the need for lockdowns? Gates, like Badger and Parlapiano in Chapter Ten, never bothered to answer the obvious contradiction to his thesis, one that exposed rather quickly the truth: one-size-fits-all policies from government *did* kill tens of millions of jobs and millions of businesses.

Absent force, individuals and businesses would have had a fighting chance to innovate around the limits imposed by the virus. We knew then, and know now, that this is true in consideration of how grocery store chains like Safeway and Whole Foods thrived during the political crack-up despite moderating customer flow, as did fast-food chains like McDonald's, big retailers like Walmart, online retailers like Amazon, and others. In August 2020, retailer Target reported "the strongest quarterly growth in its history," while "chains like Kohl's Corp. and T.J. Maxx that had to temporarily shut their doors posted sharp sales declines."[277] In 2020 politicians were to some degree dictating who could, and couldn't, meet the needs of customers. Earnings reflected this sad truth. So no, Gates was flat-out wrong that the existence of the virus itself was going to crash the economy such that "there was never a choice to have the strong economy of 2019 in 2020." Parts of the economy were wrecked in 2020 precisely because parts of the economy never had the chance to work around the virus. Experts and politicians picked winners, as is their wont.

It's also worth pointing out a blinding known, that Gates is, and was, one of the world's richest men. This requires mention when it's remembered that the expert in Gates felt the lockdowns should continue on indefinitely until such a time that the U.S. and the world were better situated in terms of a vaccine. Yes, lockdowns wouldn't shrink his material comforts in any major way.

Still, was Gates right? It's once again difficult to know in total. For one, his analysis ignored the "unseen"—as in what would individuals and businesses have done had the response of politicians to the virus been something like, "You're all adults. Be careful."

If so, as in if Americans hadn't been so lucky as to have surely "amazing" political figures like Nancy Pelosi, Mitch McConnell, Donald Trump, Chuck Schumer, Jay Pritzker, Ron DeSantis, Gavin Newsom, and Andrew Cuomo holding their hands, it's not unreasonable to suggest that Fauci, Gates, and other intelligent individuals would have strongly called for Americans to shelter in place, and tens of millions would have done just that. At the same time, Elon Musk and investors like Michael Burry might have responded in more intrepid fashion, calling for individuals and businesses to work around a virus of unknown lethality.

And with the truth about the virus surely vague, some businesses would have shut down in total, wholly fearful of brand risk related to "hot zones" emerging on their property. Others, perhaps staring bankruptcy in the face, would have risked the reputational pitfalls related to the new virus spreading on their property. Other businesses might have tried something in between. The main thing is that the varied responses, which could only have emerged from a less muscular response from experts and politicians, would have produced essential information about what the best economic solution(s) to the virus might be.

It should be added that "venture buyers" would have helped guide the decisions of businesses. We all know some individuals who, upon being made aware of the virus, bought weeks' worth of groceries, hand sanitizers, books, and hand soap with an eye on quarantining for weeks. At the same time, others continued to live as they did before, patronizing any business, park, public or private place that would have them. Crucial about the actions of free people is that their surely varied reactions in response to "You're all adults" would have amounted to highly valuable market intelligence for businesses.

Which was the problem with expert-driven government solutions no matter how locally they were made. What's one-size-fits all amounts to politicians and those close to politicians substituting their highly limited knowledge for that of a marketplace that incorporates the knowledge of *everybody*. In other words, reliance on experts for decisions about how we should live and protect our health in an all-new era leads to a blurry picture. Very blurry.

Just as centralized decision-making by the very few led to immense desperation during the twentieth century, so logically did it lead to sub-optimal outcomes in the twenty-first. For the lockdown skeptics in the spring and summer of 2020, more than a few pointed out that the response to the new coronavirus or the attempted political cure for the virus was worse than the disease, which was really a blinding glimpse of the obvious. Anytime the possible brilliance of the few is substituted for the decentralized knowledge of the marketplace, odds are high that something resembling "crisis" will reveal itself. Experts are routinely called on as the answer to "crises" when it's more realistic to assert that the experts *are* the crisis.

So were Fauci and Gates wrong, or were Musk and Burry incorrect? Should local, state, and national politicians have quickly called for economic reopening, or was this virus so lethal that the lockdowns should have continued per Gates until a vaccine was produced? The simple truth is that no one knew. And since no one knew, it was much better for governments and experts to do nothing so that well-informed markets could have brought clarity to that which was opaque.

All this also speaks to a problem already alluded to, which was the power of people like Fauci and Redfield amid the crisis. It's not just that their expert opinion held so much sway such that their narrow views were substituted for the combined wisdom of every American.

It's also worth stressing yet again that as federal employees, they didn't feel the stifling heat of the marketplace itself. When they were wildly wrong in the past about AIDS, it's not as though they lost their jobs. In Fauci's case, Donald Trump was the sixth president he served. Assuming they were wrong about the coronavirus, it's not as though they were going to be out on the street, jobless.

This is important mainly because imagine if Fauci worked for Walmart, Target, Amazon, or McDonald's as one of those company's top infectious disease experts. If so, the room for error, including the room to call for stifling lockdowns regardless of their economy-crippling impact, would have been quite a bit narrower. If Fauci had been wrong while in the employ of a major company, the company's shares would have plummeted, and yes, Fauci would have been rapidly unemployed. This is a *feature* of the marketplace, not a bug. The marketplace elevates those who are right and shines a harsh, unflattering light on those who are wrong.

Markets also force us to moderate our behavior, and yes, our rhetoric. Some might respond that Fauci would have been less trustworthy while in the employ of say, Disney, simply because he would have been shilling for a corporation reliant on abundant crowds for a substantial portion of its earnings. Such a view is brain-dead. It implies that Disney is so short-sighted in its pursuit of profits that it would risk killing its customers just to get them into its parks and into movie theaters. Or at the very least that Disney would risk making its customers sick in order to maintain ticket sales. This kind of thinking isn't fit for serious discussion. Readers know why.

Think back to Chapters Two and Three. Ideally they made a pretty strong case that stock markets are *forward looking*. Translated, they never price in the present. Applied to Disney, and if Fauci were in its employ, the doctor would have to be *extra* careful. He would simply because an errant read while working for Disney could be a brand killer. Indeed, imagine the headlines if, thanks to Disney being solely focused on the here and now, hundreds or thousands of visitors to Disney World got sick or died from a virus contracted while at Disney World.

So no, it's much less than serious for some to incoherently presume that the nonmarket aspect of government work renders the experts in its employ more credible in the face of the spreading of a virus. Quite the opposite. Precisely because government workers don't suffer falling share prices and unemployment if they over- and underreact, their projections about anything serious aren't as meaningful.

As for businesses in the proverbial arena, it's very costly for them to be wrong. Which is why they're so much more reliable. When they're wrong, they must fix their mistakes quickly or else risk obsolescence. This is true regardless of size.

To offer up a much smaller anecdotal example that shows how some business owners think, consider Atlanta's Plaza Theatre. Georgia was one of the first U.S. states to "open up" after the lockdowns. Yet not every Georgia business reopened despite it suddenly being "legal" for Georgia businesses to operate again. The Plaza Theatre was one that stayed closed.

As owner Chris Escobar explained it to Brooks Barnes and Nicole Sperling of the *New York Times*, "I want to be back in business right this second. But we've got to be smart about it. What happens if we open too soon and contribute to an outbreak? Traced to the Plaza Theater! You know what that would do to my business? I wouldn't have one."[278]

In staying closed, Escobar made an economic decision. Much as he wanted profits, he deduced that ticket sales in April 2020 would potentially come at the expense of greatly reduced sales down the line. So he delayed reopening.

In Escobar's case he was being careful with one movie theatre in Atlanta, Georgia. This is worth considering with Disney and other companies top of mind. If the Plaza Theatre is wrong, maybe ten or twenty people suffer job loss, plus a business perhaps closes. With Disney, being wrong means that massive business lines employing hundreds of thousands around the world will suffer, which is why an incautious Fauci at Disney seeking to inform worried or oblivious customers would be rendered rapidly unemployed if he got a virus wrong.

Which is again the point. The economy didn't just suffer expert opinion in contractionary fashion in 2020. Much worse was that it suffered expert opinion that was in no way governed by the markets in 2020.

Looking back to Disney specifically in 2020, it almost certainly would have closed its U.S. parks in the spring of 2020, at least for a time. It would have because the brand risk of Disneyland becoming a hot zone would have been too great. As is, Disneyland Tokyo announced its March 2020 closure in late February, meaning it did before politicians panicked in the U.S. Disney had a brand to protect. At the same time it's entirely possible that Disney reopens its parks much sooner while moderating crowds in much the same way as, or perhaps differently from, the businesses that were actually allowed to remain in operation. Or maybe Disney doesn't open at all, having concluded that the brand risk related to any kind of virus spread on one of its properties is too great. If so, fine. An economic decision would have been made that produced abundant information.

No one expects brand protection from those in government. Its reputation with the people is bad, and it is regardless of ideology. When cash for operations and payroll are a given no matter performance, urgency to perform is logically reduced. Yet it was people working in government like Fauci and Redfield who had enormous sway over politicians with the power to render cities and states lightly comatose. A dangerous combination. There's so much they don't know, and worse, there's so much they don't need to know since a failure to be right in government doesn't lead to a crashing share price and job loss.

To which some readers might reasonably ask me about the experts *I've* cited. Great question. Though this book promised to for the most part avoid endless commentary on the infection and death rates related to the coronavirus, it has for instance quoted doctors like Scott Atlas, David Katz, and Ashish K. Jha in Chapter Fifteen to make a point that on the left and right, in the *New York Times* and the *Wall Street Journal*, there was a consensus early on and throughout spring and summer of 2020 that the coronavirus wasn't terribly lethal. So what if they were wrong?

Again, a great question, albeit one that supports my argument about expert opinion. Experts are working with highly limited information, and they're in the business of making predictions or assertions with that limited information. These predictions and assertions often don't age well. See once again what was assumed about AIDS in the 1980s. See 2020, as the view about the efficacy of masks seemingly changed by the day. In a March 30 news conference, Dr. Michael Ryan of the World Health Organization said, "We don't generally recommend the wearing of masks in public by otherwise well individuals because it has not been up to now associated with any particular benefit."[279] Yet in later months, experts claimed masks were essential to restrain the virus's spread. The experts knew so little in the '80s, and they knew so little nearly forty years later.

Fast-forward to the spring and summer of 2020, experts were yet again weighing in on a virus; the difference in 2020 versus the 1980s was that politicians were literally shutting down economic activity based on potentially limited knowledge about the virus. The results were, as previously mentioned, predictable. Experts *are* the crisis precisely because they're no match for the information producer that is the market itself.

This isn't to say we should ignore those with substantial knowledge of any issue at hand. At the same time, *it is* to say that crisis will often be the result if the genius or expert standard is substituted for freedom. Freedom works. Always, always, always. The greater the presumed risk, particularly if the risk is seen as lethal, the more important that freedom is.

Just when we needed to maximize freedom, politicians ineptly shrank it—which is why the next chapter will return to a discussion begun in Chapter Eleven about political inaction as a virtue. Once again, the correct response in 2020 would have been if politicians had done nothing in response to the virus.

Chapter Twenty-Two

THEY DIDN'T NEED A LAW

*"I'm telling you that the cure is the disease. The main
source of illness in this world is the doctor's own illness;
his compulsion to try to cure and his fraudulent
belief that he can. It ain't easy to do nothing."*

—The Fat Man, *The House of God* [280]

In 1968, there was a rather substantive pandemic in the United States. According to Jeffrey Tucker, the great economics writer who was instrumental in the spring and summer of 2020 when it came to exposing the political crack-up over the coronavirus, the "flu spread from Hong Kong to the United States, arriving December 1968 and peaking a year later."

Tucker noted that the flu "ultimately killed 100,000 people in the U.S., mostly over the age of 65, and one million worldwide." Since the U.S. population at the time was around 200 million, Tucker extrapolated the 1968 death toll to the equivalent of 250,000 in 2020. "So in terms of lethality, it was as deadly and scary as COVID-19 if not more so."[281]

Yet very little was done as the flu spread. Life went on.

Tucker wrote that "nothing was closed by force. Schools mostly stayed open. Businesses did too. You could go to the movies. You could go to bars and restaurants." Some schools closed based on absenteeism, but that just supports the point that people got it then just as they got it in 2020. They took precautions on their own.

When you think about it, what choice did politicians have but to do nothing? Though the U.S. was the richest country in the world in 1968, life was relatively primitive. Schools stayed open alongside businesses in 1968 out of necessity. Leaving the liberty implications of all this aside for the moment, lockdowns quite simply were not an option in 1968. If you believe Chapter Eighteen, the lockdowns would have been extraordinarily difficult to impossible for impatient Americans as recently as the year 2000. 1968? Forget about it. Work was realistically a destination for everyone then. Many fewer could afford babysitters. More than most want to admit, school is daycare.

Stay-at-home orders would have rendered the vast majority of working Americans unemployed, which means they couldn't have happened. Only in an era of remarkable technological advance that enabled a growing elite to work from everywhere could lockdowns have happened. Americans needed to work in 2020, and so did they in 1968. The 14 percent unemployment rates that prevailed during the worst days of the 2020 lockdowns would have been exponentially higher in 1968 and quite a bit higher in 2000. Translated: no way.

It's also worth pointing out that viruses were viewed differently then. In families with two or more kids, it wasn't uncommon if one child picked up an illness for the parents to order the other kids to sleep next to the ill. Better to develop immunity sooner rather than later. Tucker described his own parents as having had what they deemed a "sophisticated" view of viruses: contraction among young people was a *good thing* for its signaling growing immunity.

Needless to say, a virus coursing through the U.S. that was more lethal at a time when medicine was much less sophisticated didn't result in mass shutdowns or stock market crashes or any kind of economic crisis. As Tucker's essay about 1968 noted, Woodstock happened in 1968. No "social distancing" there! As the previous chapter made plain, crises and crashes are the stuff of intervention by those with extraordinarily limited knowledge relative to the "masses."

So why the big difference between 1968 and 2020? Some will say it was media—that media caused an overreaction in 2020 that didn't happen in 1968. It's not unreasonable to speculate that some readers have been wondering all along why this book hasn't blamed the "liberal" or "mainstream" media for instigating a political crack-up. The answer is that the blame-the-media narrative isn't very compelling.

Going back to 1968, and realistically 2000, what was mainstream and media was quite a bit more powerful. In 1968 there were the three networks (ABC, NBC, and CBS); there was the *New York Times*, and there was PBS. Those mentioned largely drove the news cycle. There was no internet then or Fox News or talk radio. There was no Facebook or Twitter or YouTube whereby knowledgeable and dense people could beam their knowledge or lack thereof around the world in an instant. This matters simply because if we're honest, those who were skeptical about the lockdowns in 2020 had voluminous media at the ready to cite in support of their skepticism. Those who thought the lockdowns necessary still had the *Times* and other media sources that viewed the virus with alarm. It's all a long or short way of saying that "the media" was much more capable of causing a societal or political crack-up in 1968 than it was in 2020.

Which brings us back to the tragic lockdowns that unemployed and bankrupted so many Americans and that brought hundreds of millions around the world back to poverty. The view here is that they were a consequence of an upper middle class elite that was making decisions for everyone, and for whom the lockdowns were a mere inconvenience at worst and a vacation at best.

Much as technological and economic progress is beautiful, there's a trade-off to everything. The wondrous living standards brought to us by the centimillionaires and billionaires of Silicon Valley also made the hideous lockdowns possible. They made working from home, working out at home, eating at home, and being entertained at home a possibility. And for those unemployed Americans for whom work had once been a destination, Congress had access to markets willing to lend to the richest nation on earth so that some of the newly jobless could be bought off. In short, the lockdowns happened because they *could* happen.

For the longest time chin-scratching intellectuals have searched for signs of "decadence" in the United States. The view here is that the U.S. officially happened upon it in the spring of 2020 when, in response to a virus, well-to-do politicians with access to trillions decided to take a months-long vacation from reality. Imagine just shutting things down over a virus. Sicker than that, imagine blithely shutting things down on the way to pushing hundreds of millions around the world back into poverty. Let them eat cake?

Proper history will indicate that what took place in 2020 was a global debacle—a human rights tragedy of remarkable scale. *When politicians panicked*, those with the least suffered in unimaginable ways. Consider the unseen globally. What the U.S. does *matters*. The U.S. is the ultimate global influencer. What if the U.S. political class had broadly concluded that the most foolish way to fight a virus would be through economic contraction? The speculation from your author is that a brave face from the U.S. would have given politicians around the world the necessary cover to avoid economy-wrecking lockdowns. More locally, the speculation domestically is that if President Trump hadn't panicked, he could have given all manner of red (and blue) states cover to avoid that what was so economically crippling.

What makes it all so much worse is that the suffering was so unnecessary. If people had just been allowed to adapt, a global contraction could have been avoided. If anyone doubts this, they need only consider yet again the businesses and sectors that were "allowed" to remain open. They adjusted and did just fine. Never forget that businesses became going concerns not based on their ineptitude but because they figured out ways to meet the needs of their customers. The great ones also figured out ways to *lead* their customers in new directions. See Steve Jobs and the iPhone.

So a virus came along and people were scared. Here was the chance for businesses to try all manner of approaches to the virus, including shutting down altogether for some. But when the chance existed for them to respond to a customer base that was changing, and also lead that customer base to a new place based on a virus that was perhaps changing the world, the expert standard replaced the market standard. And so a crisis was born.

This was all unnecessary simply because businesses and business owners are expert at adapting, and even anticipating changes among customers. Take Danny Meyer as an example. Readers were first introduced to the creator of Shake Shack (and numerous high-end restaurants) in Chapter Twelve.

Meyer's first New York City restaurant was Union Square Cafe. Notable about what quickly became one of the city's top restaurants is that Meyer banned smoking in it. He did so for a variety of reasons, including that the drift of smoke proved a negative for some of his non-smoking patrons. Perhaps most interesting about Meyer's decision to ban smoking was that he did so in *1990*, twelve years ahead of New York City passing a law. As Meyer explained it in his 2006 biography, *Setting the Table*, "It's my opinion that you can do anything you want in your own place of business. I didn't need a law."[282] Amen!

Realistically, most don't need a law to do well by their customers or, in Meyer's case, to improve the environment for customers in ways they perhaps hadn't imagined he could. It used to be accepted that smoking happened inside restaurants and bars and even airplanes, but some were ahead of the law. That's how it should be. Let businesses be individual laboratories.

Some will—*gasp*—allow smoking. Some will allow pets, while others won't. Applied to the coronavirus, some would have limited crowds by decree, and some would have used surge pricing to moderate crowds. Sure enough, once "allowed" to reopen, One Manhattan Dental in New York City offered a $1,500 private appointment to patients eager "to be the only one in the office" versus $295 for a cleaning in an office populated by other patients.[283] Some businesses wouldn't have made any rules at all only for customers to set crowd size on their own (haven't we all walked into a restaurant only to walk out?), some would have served packed crowds, and some would have shut down altogether. You need all kinds in order to learn what customers want but also what works.

Cafe Milano, arguably the most celebrity-laden restaurant in Washington, DC, purchased a new technology that enabled customers to "virtually" open its menu on their own smartphones while at the table. Spoons, forks, and knives came in plastic. Overdoing it? Possibly. Or maybe not. And that's the point. The beauty of freedom is that people are free to innovate. Or think differently. The future is opaque. Lest readers forget, around the time of the iPhone's rollout RIM Blackberry CEO Jim Balsillie concluded that "The recent launch of Apple's iPhone does not pose a threat to Research In Motion Ltd.'s consumer-geared Blackberry Pearl and simply marks the entry of yet another competitor into the smartphone market."[284] Whoops!

TEAM Schostak Family Restaurants in Ypsilanti, MI, created a "hands-free door pull" at its Applebee's restaurants so that customers could enter with the "touch of an elbow or forearm to its extended, apple-shaped handle." Even though the at-the-time consensus was that the coronavirus didn't seem to trouble young people, high chairs were wrapped in plastic. The disinfecting of tables at the 170 TEAM

Schostak restaurants was a three-step process. Its executive chairman, Mark Schostak, told the *Wall Street Journal* that "we want to be the safest restaurant on the block."[285]

Gravity Fitness reopened in downtown Atlanta on May 11, 2020. Initially the fitness center followed rules set by the State of Georgia, including an employee taking everyone's temperature upon entering the gym. The problem was that the gym's members were unsatisfied. You see, the state's rules *weren't stringent enough* in consideration of the fact that a lot of Gravity members were fifty years old and older.

One thing that worried many of the older members was that Gravity employees were required to wear masks per state protocols, but patrons were not. Responding to customer need, the gym instituted a rule that from 8 a.m. to noon on weekdays, masks would be required for everyone.

Notable about Gravity Fitness was that it was a local business, as opposed to a national fitness company. This is worth mentioning because as of mid-May, some of the larger, more nationally known chains such as Equinox and SoulCycle had delayed reopening. They had done this even though it was legal for them in parts of the U.S. to reopen.[286] This was perhaps as it should have been. National companies with bigger brands to protect were, to varying degrees, going to allow smaller businesses to essentially conduct their market research and virus-spreading research for them. No doubt they would potentially lose market share in the near term, but they might gain over the long term by understanding better the risk involved in opening with a virus spreading.

At the Gaylord Texan resort in Grapevine, TX, members of the resort's housekeeping team wore gloves and masks, plus there were over two hundred signs posted around the property asking guests to remain six feet apart. In the resort's gym, every other treadmill was turned off "to support social distancing," plus the Gaylord's 1,815 rooms were readied for guests based on a twenty-eight-page booklet put together by Marriott International. U.S. hotels needed to adjust quickly based on the 25 percent occupancy rates that prevailed in April 2020; this despite the closure of over five thousand U.S. hotels in March and April. An overreaction? Some might say yes, but hotel companies weren't taking anything for granted with so many hotels closed, or running on fumes, not to mention the million-plus lodging employees that were still jobless.[287]

Notable about this is that Salesforce, a fifty-thousand-employee global software behemoth, required adjustments that make the previous ones mentioned seem positively anarchic by comparison. Salesforce employees would no longer be allowed to talk in the elevator, there wouldn't be hugging, and there wouldn't be "communal snack jars" full of treats like Gummy Bears.

While waiting for elevators, Salesforce employees were required to wait on "social-distancing floor markers," plus stand on other ones once inside. Of course, just getting to the point of being on the elevator was its own achievement. Before then, employees had to fill out online health surveys, they would have their temperatures taken, they'd have to provide a good reason for coming into the office, plus company management was scheduling office visits in shifts.[288]

On the other side of the world in Melbourne, Australia, the thirty-five-years-running Australian soap opera *Neighbours* resumed shooting in May 2020. Imagine that. Shooting a soap opera in the age of "social distancing." But as the *New York Times* reported, the producers adjusted. Cameras were "positioned to make the cast appear as if they were standing or sitting closer to one another," there were no extras, and while soaps are known for heavy embraces, there would be "no touching and no physical intimacy." Instead, the camera would "cut away in the cliff-hanging moment before a kiss or a punch."[289]

Really, if a soap opera could adapt to a post-COVID reality, couldn't any business? Tragically, this question was never answered. The lockdowns just happened. Politicians and experts operating with limited information simply decided what could operate and how, and what could not. So while some businesses "legal" to operate ultimately innovated, even then they did so with guidelines from the state.

Unknown was why. As Salesforce's stringent requirements revealed, businesses didn't need a law. Their customers and their employees were too important to them. Regardless of one's views of the virus, businesses were going to respond in ways well beyond what politicians required just because that's what they do. Better yet, they were going to respond in ways that politicians could never *imagine* requiring them to respond. And that's the point. A crucial one. Government is lousy at running businesses as anyone who's spent time in the post office, DMV, or passport office knows well, but suddenly government was empowered to shut down or keep open businesses and sectors, and also tell them how they could operate once open? Again, the months surrounding the coronavirus hysteria were defined by a lapse of reason that they'll marvel at in the future.

Strange was that even the *Wall Street Journal's* excellent editorial page, despite being openly hostile to the lockdowns by April, still found itself stuck in the government-knows-best mindset as late as April 15, 2020. In the closing sentence of an editorial that revealed growing skepticism on the part of the editorial page, it was written that "politicians and public health officials need a plan to reopen the economy."[290] No! The world's most important editorial page missed the point.

To see why, let's for fun travel back in time to April 2020 and imagine a sudden declaration of freedom from coronavirus decrees on local, state, and national levels. If so, how many readers would have in *April 2020* immediately reverted to the "old way" of doing things, including close-talking, packed bars, sold-out movie theaters, infrequent hand-washing, and biggest gasp of all, *shaking hands*?

Just the same, how many businesses wouldn't have evolved once free to operate again? The ability to adapt to change is such a known driver of long-term commercial success *in good times* that it's almost a cliché. Figure that the good businesses nowadays disrupt *themselves* (think Netflix taking out Blockbuster DVDs by mail, only for Netflix to erase its own DVD-by-mail model with streaming) with survival in mind, so is it unreasonable to suggest that, if free to operate once again, businesses wouldn't have overseen all manner of changes meant to please *and lead* consumers who had also changed?

In the same week as the aforementioned editorial, *Journal* editorial columnist Holman Jenkins referred either sarcastically or critically to the "mythical 'do nothing' strategy" in response to the coronavirus, but your author chose to believe he was being sarcastic given the impossibility of "do nothing."[291] There is no "do nothing" simply because humans have evolved as a species presumably because it's in their DNA to do that which elongates their existence. And as evidenced by the copious savings that individuals and businesses are able to draw on in order to innovate, we humans are careful people. To varying degrees we save for the possibility of a "rainy day" without coercion, which is just more evidence that in a broad sense we the people get it. We don't need a law to do what's in our interest.

To which some will key on the "in a broad sense" line to point out that not everyone is as wise as the COVID-obsessed in 2020 were, which means everyone had to endure draconian, economy- and freedom-crushing rules so that the few who needed hand-holding could get it. "We're all in this together," or something like that. Such a view wasn't serious. As is, all too many of us had long been unwilling to limit ourselves to the mood-altering substances that politicians "allowed" us to consume, some of us are only interested in surfing and skiing when conditions are most life-threatening, and some of us can't stand the thought of not hugging, shaking hands, or missing the excitement of a loud—and very packed—party, bar, stadium, or arena.

Just the same, some businesses won't change either. Frustrating as they are, some will never rid bathrooms of the hand dryers that are said to spread germs, some will never demand that their customers maintain distance from other customers or demand that they wait outside altogether, and some will refuse to refuse customers even if it means people aren't SIX FEET APART.

What cannot be stressed enough is that if the goal is figuring out the best way to combat a virus with no known cure, those who don't follow norms are as crucial producers of information that will enable victory as those who do. Precisely because they don't follow the unwritten societal rules, their contracting of the virus (or not), their sickness (or not) from ignoring broad convention, and their death rates relative to the COVID-obsessed would hopefully give those searching for solutions exponentially more to work with.

What applied to individual decisions freely made also applied to businesses. As this book has continually stressed, no one knew. It was all somewhat of a speculation amid the virus's spread. As evidenced by how many businesses went above and beyond government requirements, few knew what customers wanted and would want in the future. Yes! Trite as it sounds, and is, it's not unreasonable to suggest in 2020 and beyond that we will forever hear about how "COVID-19 changed everything." Absolutely. And because it perhaps changed everything, it was essential that there be a "do nothing" approach from politicians given the certainty that free businesses would try all manner of things in order to win back customers either shell-shocked a little, a lot, or not at all by the past. As previously mentioned, some would perhaps even give the finger to illiterate rules against "price gouging" such that they would institute surge-pricing at their businesses as a way of controlling crowds via *market signals*.

Stating what should be obvious, the one-size-fits-all lockdowns imposed on Americans by politicians were *blinding* those same Americans to the information necessary to successfully beat an unknown. Freedom isn't some feel-good, amorphous chant. It's in fact pro-life and pro-growth simply because free people acting without forced limits show us through their successes and failures how to get by, and thrive, in life. Conversely, government plans just produce darkness. In 2020 the U.S. and the world needed "do nothing" so that people could *see*.

It cannot be stressed enough that the unknowns and misunderstand-ings about the coronavirus *in 2020* were likely vast. Just as AIDS was wildly misunderstood in the 1980s relative to the present, it's not unrea-sonable to suggest as the previous chapter did that some of the most confident comments about the coronavirus will not age well. What will age well is freedom. Free people doing as they want create clarity. Bank on it that this book's main thesis will stand the test of time.

About this hopefully muscular call for freedom, some readers will point out that as the lockdowns began to be relaxed by the summer of 2020, COVID cases spiked to record levels; their view being that more freedom correlated with more infections. Such a stance misses the point. For one, no one ever said that the virus was just going to just magically go away. Goodness, the Hong Kong flu is still with us decades later. A vaccine was never developed.[292] One guesses a lot of Americans were infected with that, which killed over one hundred thousand in the late 1960s.

In short, the expectation was always that COVID cases would rise simply because if it's assumed stay-at-home orders even worked, we weren't going to be able to stay at home forever. Eventually the decadent lockdowns were going to have to end out of economic necessity. No nation could consume its way to prosperity from home! See Chapter Ten again if you've forgotten that consumption is a consequence of economic growth, not a driver.

Luckily, returning to reality wouldn't be terribly painful mainly because the lethality of the virus hadn't changed. By late July the research continued to show that five to ten died for every one thousand infect-ed.[293] But again, a numbers argument is a loser's argument. Assuming the virus had been killing people of all ages indiscriminately, any lockdowns would have been wholly superfluous. Most of us generally don't go out of our way to die. The stay-at-home orders became less necessary the more lethal the virus was.

Yet this one wasn't lethal, and we once again knew this truth back in January. We did because if it had been, there's no way China, South Korea, and other countries early to the virus could have kept this truth quiet. Yet politicians still panicked. Oh wow, to be alive hundreds of years from now to read historians writing with awe that politicians could be so ridiculous.

In the next chapter some of that ridiculousness will be discussed. Indeed, it wasn't just politicians who lost their minds in the spring and summer of 2020.

Chapter Twenty-Three

FROM RIDICULOUS TO SAD TO RECOVERY

"Each of us had been misunderstood, misjudged, dismissed.
Shunned by bosses, spurned by luck, rejected by society,
shortchanged by fate when looks and other natural graces
were handed out. We'd each been forged by early failure."

—Phil Knight, about the early days of Nike [294]

After shutting down spring training and postponing the season's start in March 2020, Major League Baseball finally got the regular season started on July 23, 2020. Except that fans weren't allowed into the stadiums. Yes, you read that right.

The hysteria that began in March 2020 still reigned in July. A few media members would be allowed into stadiums so that the games could be televised and written about, obviously umpires had to be—*gasp*—near the players, but people were still a lethal menace to one another. Falling death rates and the stubborn reality that those dying from or with the virus tended to live in nursing homes,[295] over 40 percent according to the *New York Times*,[296] didn't deter the alarmists. The very *New York Times* that reported death rates from virus infection well south of 1 percent ran a front page story on baseball's opening day with a "Surge Pushes U.S. Hospitals Close to Brink" title.

Just once it would have been great if the *Times* had added to its alarmist front page headlines something like the word "Expected" next to "Surge" as a way of properly informing readers. Indeed, it had long been made clear on the CDC's website that a surge would occur. *That was the point.* Holman Jenkins reminded readers that for months the CDC's website very clearly explained that "in the coming months, most of the U.S. population will be exposed to the virus." You can't block out reality. It's going to happen. Jenkins added for readers that it wasn't just the 1968 Hong Kong flu that a vaccine was never created for. The 1918 and 1957 viruses were similarly never "cured." As the *Wall Street Journal* columnist put it, "They ended when people decided to accept and adapt to the virus's existence."[297] Assuming they thought about them at all: see the previous chapter, Jeffrey Tucker, and Woodstock.

The strange thing was that the lack of crowds in stadiums was perhaps the most normal thing about Major League Baseball at the time. The coronavirus meant all-new rules for players if they actually wanted to get on the field. Players hoping to play would be required to begin their mornings with two tests of their temperature in rapid succession. They would do so with "contactless" thermometers issued by the MLB, after which they would be allowed to commute to the stadium if their temperature was below one hundred degrees. Transportation by taxi, Uber, and public transport was not allowed. They could only commute to work in their own cars (no word on whether the players' cars would be "contact traced") or on the team bus.

Once at the stadium they would be tested twice more for fever in case they contracted one sometime after the morning, and if they passed again, they would be allowed into "Restricted Areas." You know, the clubhouse, fitness room, dugout...places like that. Fear not, it gets even weirder.

As the *Wall Street Journal's* Jared Diamond reported about the league's guidelines (scary is that Diamond seemed to write his report with a straight face), once the playing actually began, "Any baseball put in play and touched by multiple defenders" would be "removed and exchanged for a new one." It's hard to type this without laughing, or crying, but the guidelines also "strongly discouraged" infielders "from throwing around the horn after an out." Don't worry, players were expected to wash and disinfect their hands every half inning.[298]

In Canada, the federal government there ruled that the Toronto Blue Jays wouldn't be allowed to play home games at all. How could they? The rule on players arriving from out of town was that they would have to self-isolate for two weeks. Writing about it for the *National Post,* columnist Lorne Gunter mused that "if ball players flew into Toronto, the pilots and flight attendants who brought them wouldn't have to self-isolate. The players would."[299]

Some will latch on to all this as a way of pointing out that it wasn't just the government—that private businesses were on their own exercising extraordinary caution that will surely entertain future generations needing a laugh or two, and that pushed businesses into comatose states. It's a fair point, but one that probably best underscores how terrified businesses were of government in 2020. Their capacity for damage was limitless when it's remembered that they can, among other things, jail the noncompliant or take from them or limit their ability to operate at all. Have readers forgotten Chapter Four and how for instance Los Angeles Mayor Eric Garcetti threatened to shut off electricity to businesses that continued to operate without his permission? So while it's not unreasonable to speculate that some of the MLB owners bought into the corona delusion, their willingness to be ridiculous was about protecting their billion-dollar-plus properties. Get on the wrong side of political power, and those in government might shut you down altogether. So the MLB abided the lapse of reason within the political class.

The NBA brought playoff teams to a "bubble" of sorts in Orlando. The players would similarly be tested with great regularity, they would eat in a league-sanctioned restaurant, and their access to the outside would be strictly limited. About the latter, ESPN's Stephen A. Smith had a good laugh about the comical notion that players used to having a girlfriend, or two or three, in every city were suddenly going to shelter in place.[300]

At the same time, readers can rest assured that politicians continued to not disappoint. On July 23, 2020, Washington, DC, Mayor Muriel Bowser instituted a "universal masking order" that mandated "the wearing of masks in all indoor and outdoor settings." Failure to abide the rule came with fines up to $1,000. But before readers become too enraged by Bowser's decree, they can perhaps rest a little bit easier that she oh-so-surprisingly exempted lawmakers, judges, and federal employees from the rule.[301]

In Michigan, Governor Gretchen Whitmer decreed that it was OK for citizens to launch a rowboat, but not a motorboat. Gradually she caught up to the shocking stupidity of such a rule. On the New Jersey Shore, the *New York Times* reported that "ocean rescues" by the Avalon Beach Patrol were "contactless," lifeguards were required to "shower and sanitize equipment afterward," and most mindless of all, "mouth-to-mouth resuscitation" was "now done with a face mask equipped with a manual pump."[302] Yes, you read that right. To allegedly protect swimmers from a virus that half of those infected didn't even know they had, New Jersey would place limits on those trying to save swimmers from drowning. It's just speculation, but does anyone want to bet that most swimmers in Avalon weren't day-trippers from nursing homes?

In Colorado a father was arrested "for not social distancing while playing with his wife and child while at the park."[303] In Malibu, CA, a paddle boater was arrested for having the temerity to exercise amid a stay-at-home decree in the Golden State. One supposes the message was "We're protecting your health by not allowing you to do what's good for your health." South of Malibu in San Clemente, officials there, presumably fearful that skateboarders would have too much fun on the way to ignoring "social distancing," proceeded to idle a local skatepark by filling it with thirty-seven tons of sand.[304] On October 3, 2020, California governor Gavin Newsom's office sent out a tweet telling Golden Staters, "Don't forget to keep your mask on in between bites."[305]

In Chapter One, Imperial College epidemiologist Neil Ferguson's famous projection of 2.2 million U.S. deaths directly from the coronavirus was mentioned given how quickly his ultimately walked back projections inspired lockdowns around the world. The problem was that he couldn't abide what his hysteria had helped bring about. It seems desire got the best of the expert. He was discovered to be having an affair with a married woman who broke stay-at-home orders in England in order to be with him. To be fair to Ferguson, his behavior wasn't unique for its being hypocritical.

When 250 individuals traveled to Michigan's state capital in order to protest lockdowns that had caused 25 percent unemployment in the state, those maskless individuals were vilified in the media as the "abhorrent" source of virus spread. But as the great *Wall Street Journal* columnist Andy Kessler pointed out, much bigger protests not long after in pursuit of social justice "were given a hall pass."[306] One supposes "it depended on your definition of 'hypocritical.'"

Not enough for you? Let's consider college campuses. In July 2020 Harvard University announced that it would open up its campus for incoming freshman, but according to *Harvard Crimson* reporters Juliet Isselbacher and Amanda Su, sophomores, juniors, and seniors would be required to "seek approval to return." With its remaining spots, Harvard would allow those lacking a "sufficiently updated computer, fast internet, a quiet place to work," and whose situation was otherwise compromised away from campus back onto campus. Seniors would also get to "petition" for the right to attend Harvard at Harvard but with no assurances. Notable about Harvard is that the school announced it wouldn't change tuition despite the new rules.[307]

To be clear about the lost class time, there will be no tears shed here for the learning that Harvard and other college students would forego given the lapse of reason on campus. And the previous statement is not about ideology. Right and left have long overstated the value of what's learned in college, and they've long been positively delusional in their assertion that campus learning has had something to do with future life and work achievements. College in particular is a signaling device. Merely "getting in" to Harvard says a great deal about you. In short, the tears shed here have to do with how mass hysteria was going to deprive so many of what has historically been an amazing experience.

Add to the amazing experience the tears shed by parents as they drop their loved ones off at school. First world, very American problems for sure, but the drop-off has long been a big deal to parents. In 2020 that was all due to change. As one parent joked to the *Wall Street Journal's* Nancy Keates about bringing her son to Amherst College, "We'll slow the car down as we go by so he can jump out the back."

Keates went on to write that "what had morphed into an all-day occasion in recent times, with family picnics, informational sessions for parents and matriculation ceremonies, will be a mostly students-only, efficiency-oriented process this year." The latter would reveal itself through many colleges "not allowing parents in the dorms, or, in some cases, even on campus."[308]

Which brings us to alarmed citizens. "Community surveillance" really picked up during the corona meltdown. The *Wall Street Journal's* Yoree Koh wrote of concerned citizens reporting "offenses" like teenagers having the temerity to high-five on a basketball court, others playing soccer at a public park of sorts, and then a surely evil mother entering a closed park with her sons. Koh noted that some of those triggered even "called the police" for offenses like the ones listed.

Koh wrote of a Stephen Lukasewycz, a forty-three-year-old doctor in Edina, MN, who threatened to call the police when roughly six teenage boys rode past him on bikes and skateboards despite them not being socially distanced enough in the eyes of the doctor. The surely traumatized Lukasewycz ultimately chose not to call the police, but "concerned citizen" that he was, he made sure to report the incident on Nextdoor given his hope that "any adult in the community would be present and willing enough to speak up for the community."

In Toronto, one Caroline Kaiser shamed one Maria Shkolnik on Nextdoor for taking her two- and four-year-old boys to a park that was closed for renovations. Kaiser didn't do so because the threesome might disturb the renovations, but told Koh she did so given nerves related to her immune system.[309] It apparently never occurred to these neighborhood activists that rather than tattle on or lecture others, they could simply stay inside.

In Bethesda, MD, it was announced by midsummer that public schools would instruct online in the fall of 2020. One mother of a high school senior commented in heartbreaking fashion that her child had just started to fit in at school given the teen's participation in the high school's marching band. Tough on the student one supposes. Don't get in the way of the compassionate when they're trying to "save" you.

In New York, by July 2020 Governor Andrew Cuomo had seemingly moved on from the humility of March that caused him to admit that he didn't "even know that it was the best public health policy" to "quarantine everyone" and "close everything down."[310] The previous admission was Cuomo's way of perhaps obliquely acknowledging that locking everyone down while destroying businesses and jobs, or slowly destroying businesses by forcing them on the dole, was perhaps not the best strategy.

By July Cuomo was full authoritarian again. Luckily by July the *Wall Street Journal's* editorial page was fully against the disastrous lockdowns and other attempts at control by government. Writing about Cuomo, the editors observed that "nothing's harder to sate than a taste for power." In Cuomo's case he decreed no indoor dining in New York City, plus he declared that alcoholic drinks couldn't just be served to patrons.[311] Some kind of meal or snack had to come with it.

Cuomo's reasoning about drinks being served with what he classified a meal or snack was that his rules would keep New Yorkers from getting too close to each other such that they would spread the virus. You see, without politicians leading them around, New Yorkers would just go crazy in order to contract something that politicians said was disastrous to contract? Does the shocking stupidity of all this not cause mouths to open at least somewhat in surprise? Again, if the virus were truly deadly, or even if it caused major illness, what was the point of the rules? Even getting sick is very inconvenient. Who would need force to avoid such an outcome or death? But if contraction of it was going to be meaningless for half of those infected, why *wouldn't* people congregate? Or at least be allowed to. Furthermore, what difference would it make in terms of virus spread; you know, the masks, hand sanitizer, six feet apart, and all the other stuff people were told to do if those at a bar just had a Miller Lite versus a Miller Lite with a cheeseburger and French fries? Rest assured these simple questions were never answered. Power has an effect on people. Among other things, it can cause them to separate themselves from most forms of reason. And it wasn't just Cuomo.

While Cuomo was declaring chips or peanuts with an alcoholic drink noncompliant, San Diego County ruled that all restaurants had to be closed by 10 p.m. even though late-night diners had been a good source of income for them before the lapse of reason. No evidence that late eating spread the virus. In Chicago, restaurants were "allowed" table umbrellas but not tents meant to protect customers from the elements. In Oregon, pool tables were disallowed, but juke boxes and coin-operated arcade games were allowed. Lottery kiosks were naturally allowed.[312] Politicians weren't going to let a virus shut off all of *their* sources of income. Lost revenue is what *businesses* were supposed to endure. Don't you get it: governments have a lot of jobs to maintain and mouths to feed! And that was really the point.

As politicians foisted more and more limits on suffocated businesses, the news got worse and worse. Tragic really. The Independent Restaurant Coalition, an entity that represented five hundred thousand small businesses, released a projection in the summer of 2020 that up to 85 percent of independent restaurants faced the possibility of closure by year's end.[313]

Pleasurable as reading can be, including newspaper reading, it became a daily source of sadness in the spring and summer of 2020. The stories of businesses shuttered were endless. "Our whole lives went into this." So said Jodi Fyfe, co-owner of Chicago-based restaurant, Eden. It closed in July 2020. Fyfe and her husband did everything they could to keep the restaurant afloat, including not taking paychecks from March through mid-July. But with Chicago having disallowed indoor service, there wasn't much they could do.[314]

Out in Northern California, Chris Mittelstaedt witnessed sales plummet at The FruitGuys, the business he'd been building for over twenty years. He had expected sales to be over $40 million in 2020 only for hysteria about the virus leading to the closure of offices and schools. Talking about it with the *Wall Street Journal*, Mittelstaedt admitted that he "was in tears…. I spent every day for 22 years of my professional life building a family business with people I love." But in order to keep the business above water, he was forced to lay off almost half of his 163 person team.[315]

Tragically, tears were being shed all over the United States. Oxford Information Technology, a research outfit that follows over thirty-two million businesses of varying sizes, estimated as of late July 2020 that 1.85 million U.S. businesses had suspended operations or shut down altogether. The forecast from Oxford's president was that 2020 would eclipse the 2008 contraction, when 4.5 million businesses vanished.[316] As always, one of the most certain signs of economic decline is when the businesses in operation are the same for decades. In a dynamic economy, it's the prosperous norm for the present to routinely be replaced by the future in terms of businesses and commerce. The tragedy in this case is that dynamism wasn't at work. Politicians panicked, only to pick winners and losers in a stupor that was impressive even for them.

About some of the businesses mentioned, it's perhaps easy to most tug on heartstrings with stories of small businesses going under. At the same time, it's important to remind readers of what was discussed in greater detail in Chapter Twelve, that small businesses are frequently a consequence of big businesses. They tend to cluster around them. In that case, the bigger 2020 tragedy was the big businesses weakened and bankrupted by a tragic lapse of reason on the part of politicians.

As was stressed in Chapter Twelve and the chapters about the PPP and Main Street programs, some of the companies that filed for bankruptcy perhaps would have anyway. Again, this is the norm in a progressing economy. At the same time, we can't know which ones failed on their own and which were brought to an early death by the matchless stupidity of politicians who decided to fight a virus with economic desperation.

Needless to say, Kroger, Chuck E. Cheese, Sur La Table, and Brooks Brothers joined previously mentioned retailers like J.Crew and Neiman Marcus in bankruptcy.[317] Multibillion market cap home "sharing" company Airbnb announced on May 5, 2020, that it would lay off 1,900 employees, one-quarter of its workforce.[318] The following day Disney reported a quarterly profit decline of 90 percent given the closure of theme parks and movie theaters. One hundred thousand workers were furloughed, and company executives suffered steep pay cuts.[319]

It's the sad norm for politicians to presume that a "big business" can handle huge body blows by virtue of its being big, but consider the meaning of such childish thinking in a city like Orlando, Florida. How many businesses of all sizes chose Orlando and its surrounding areas precisely because of Disney's massive presence there? It cannot be stressed enough that what harms the large is felt most acutely by the small given the basic truth that small businesses are so often given life by the big.

At the same time, there was a dopey pretense about the programs that rendered the already senseless even more so. Specifically, they were geared to make sure the biggest and best would get little to nothing so that the small could get the most. PPP was "designed" to feed companies with five hundred or fewer employees, and then Main Street was for companies with up to fifteen thousand employees or $5 billion in revenues. Publicly traded companies were mostly pushed aside in terms of funding—probably to their betterment or, more realistically, *certainly* to their benefit. Still, the presumption that Congress, the Treasury, or the Fed should be playing investor at all was much, much too much. Those trying to lend the money of others were in a sense studious about feeding the mediocre that were a consequence of the big. Companies with high debt levels were similarly excluded, but some frequently have lots of debt precisely because markets trust their long-term plans.[320] Debt can often be a very positive sign, but it can also be negative. Markets figure this stuff out. Government bureaucrats can't.

Worse was that amid all this tragedy and carnage, Congress was debating extracting another $3 trillion from the U.S. economy on top of the previous $3 trillion. Worse than worse was that the Republicans went along with the Democrats in pursuit of trillions of wealth always and everywhere produced in the private sector. As the *Wall Street Journal's* Kimberley Strassel lamented about a prostrate, allegedly limited government Republican Party, "Who needs Nancy Pelosi demanding more spending, more unemployment benefits and more union payoffs when Steven Mnuchin and Mitch McConnell will do it for them?"[321] In 2020, both sides operated under the delusion that government spending and waste would boost the economy. They got it backwards. Government spending logically can't stimulate growth; it's only a somnolent, but most important of all, the spending is always a consequence of *growth that already happened.* Congress was spending the wealth consequence of growth, thus shrinking the amount of precious investment capital available to businesses and entrepreneurs pursuing growth *that hadn't yet happened.*

So while things looked bleak and felt bleak in the spring and summer of 2020, it cannot be forgotten that forward-looking markets were optimistic. They were because shocked as investors were by the ability of politicians to truly outdo themselves with inept lockdowns, those would eventually have to end for countless reasons, the most obvious one being that consumption driven by stay-at-home rules amounted to a cessation of economic growth as Americans consumed the fruits of past efforts. Translated, there's no such thing as consuming oneself to prosperity, despite what economists and politicians naively believe. There was also the happy truth that tragic as the political panic was for so many Americans on so many levels, this crack-up didn't result in war that would cut short way too many young, eventually productive American lives. After that, it's not unreasonable to remember that misguided as the political hysteria was, American entrepreneurs stare death in the face every day even in the good times. They would not be suffocated by politicians. No chance.

For some colorful background, Ron Farmer will first be mentioned. This is one of those "cutaways" where yours truly points to a personal anecdote. In this case, Farmer is a Houston-based serial entrepreneur of remarkable energy. Back in 2009, and when the U.S. economy was gasping for air after a 2008 political crack-up that subsequently led to financial and economic terror, I asked Farmer how he felt given the economy's disastrous shape. Could we recover? His response was uplifting.

Paraphrasing Farmer only slightly, he quickly replied, "Are you kidding me? I'm way too smart for Obama, and I was way too smart for Bush." Farmer didn't have time to be pessimistic. His belief in his ability to meet the needs of customers was powerful. Farmer was certain he would be able to work around existing and future governmental incompetence.

Ken Fisher has long said the same, albeit in a different way. Though a billionaire several times over today, Fisher hasn't forgotten when his eponymous firm had but $250 in capital. Yes, that's *250 dollars*.

Fisher's lived through uncertainty about the viability of his creation; he knows from the early days what it's like to stare potential failure in the face, and this may explain what he's long said about government: capitalists always outrun politicians. Entrepreneurs routinely overcome enormous obstacles to achievement including, but not limited to, near universal skepticism about what they're trying to do. More important, they spend many nights worrying the next day will be the last for their business. All of this is very crucial in consideration of the outlook in the spring and summer of 2020. Awful as times were, America's entrepreneurial class had been through worse by virtue of being entrepreneurs.

For one, capitalists routinely overcome obstacles erected by others along with ones of their own making. While errors in government are generally never fixed as a consequence of government enjoying privileged access to the production of others, in the profit-motivated world entrepreneurs must realize their mistakes and correct them quickly. Unlike government, entrepreneurs can only innovate as long as they have investors willing to let them. This relentless pressure forces constant improvement.

For two, entrepreneurs are battle-hardened. Most successful entrepreneurs can remember many days, years, and even *decades* of wondering whether their creation would last. Awful, incompetent, and inexcusable as the actions of politicians were, they weren't going to break the spirit of individuals for whom looming failure was the constant rule to the success exception. Consider Blackstone cofounder Stephen Schwarzman. In the early days of what is now a global financial behemoth, Schwarzman was turned down *seventeen* times for every yes he received when the former M&A investment banker had the nerve to try and raise a billion dollar private equity fund, despite no background in private equity.[322] In his spectacular memoir, Schwarzman recalls how he "began to feel dizzy" one night as he sat alone with his thoughts, worried that he was "failing on every count."[323]

In his similarly spectacular memoir, Creative Artists Agency cofounder Michael Ovitz recalls the "folding chairs and card tables for desks" that were the nascent talent agency's office furniture when CAA opened its doors in 1975 in a "bargain bin" building on "the very edge of Beverly Hills."[324] And even when it became more apparent that CAA might survive the relentless attempts by global agency William Morris to vanquish the agenting upstart, the brilliant Ovitz writes that "there wasn't a day when I didn't walk in the door and get hit by a rush of anxiety. What idea can I come up with today to pay the overhead?"[325]

Nike cofounder Phil Knight spent many, many years up late at night, wondering if the next day would be Nike's last. He didn't even pay himself a salary until Nike's eighth year,[326] but long after that he recalls reassuring his wife, Penny, nearly every night about Nike's ongoing viability "with optimistic words that I didn't wholly believe."

Fast-forward to May 2020, and Tesla founder Elon Musk thumbed his nose at corona-fearful local authorities when they told him he couldn't reopen Tesla's Fremont, CA, manufacturing plant. The pugnacious entrepreneur did anyway, telling authorities that "if anyone is arrested, I ask that it only be me."[327] Even Musk's longtime critic in Holman Jenkins was thrilled. He commented that Musk was perhaps the only operator of a public company "who has decided to risk his livelihood being destroyed by infringements on the most basic rights of U.S. citizens; to leave their homes, to engage in trade, to work and receive pay."[328]

These stories are a reminder that whatever needless barriers politicians can—and will—throw in the way of America's entrepreneurs, they've seen and overcome much worse. Unspeakable and as unnecessary as the 2020 political crack-up was, it was just another barrier to overcome for the frequently rejected, the mocked, for those "forged by failure." They always do overcome, and when they do, the world's most dynamic economy would attain levels of progress that would make the past look primitive by comparison.

In short, panicky politicians with endless "plans" were no match for the actual creators of economic growth. They were going to bail out the political class again.

Chapter Twenty-Four

IF LOCKDOWN CRITICS MAKE THIS A NUMBERS DEBATE, THEY ENSURE FUTURE LOCKDOWNS

"What America is about is a nation that will protect our rights to life, liberty and the pursuit of happiness. I would much rather have somebody who is just a utilitarian, who just thinks live and let live, hasn't thought about the philosophy, just believes freedom works."

—Ed Crane, cofounder of the Cato Institute

In May 2020 the *Wall Street Journal* reported that French doctors had "discovered a case of the new coronavirus dating from late December in a man who was hospitalized near Paris, the earliest publicly identified COVID-19 infection outside China."[329] Two months later *Wall Street Journal* editorial page writer Allysia Finley wrote that scientists had found "traces of the virus in wastewater samples collected in Italy as early as mid-December and in Brazil beginning in late November."

Finley wasn't surprised when it's remembered that Chinese doctors identified the first coronavirus case in November 2020, only for the country to not lock down the presumed epicenter of the virus until January 23. About this, Finley wrote that "for two months direct flights ran from Wuhan to 30 cities outside China, including London, New York, Paris, Rome and San Francisco."[330] Finley's conclusion from all this was that "tests may significantly underestimate the number of people who have already been infected with Covid-19, especially if they had a milder strain." From there she concluded that "herd immunity" in July 2020 may have been closer than presumed.

Readers can rest assured that while this chapter will make no such conclusion, that it should not in any way be construed as a critique of Finley's speculation. Maybe she was right. Certainly doctors and scientists were certain themselves of a fast-spreading virus, so if it began to spread in November or sooner, it's not unrealistic to guess that it had made its way around the world long before it was a news item. There's no pretense of scientific or medical knowledge in this chapter and hopefully none in this book. When it comes to the virus, the book aims to report on what was being reported or editorialized.

Still, judging by the frantic responses of doctors, scientists, and politicians to the coronavirus in March 2020, what Finley described should cause anyone, regardless of background, to ask questions. The virus had all along been said to be a fast-spreading one, which was one of the justifications used for the lockdowns in March 2020. If readers forget, the argument was that so quickly did the virus spread and cause so much sickness, that we needed stay-at-home orders to slow the flow of infected people into hospitals.

OK, but using the alarmism expressed stateside in concert with what we know—that the virus was spreading from a city with global ties for months unchecked—can't we at least wonder? This isn't a medical or scientific presumption. Once again, if doctors in China first began identifying coronavirus cases in November, and if the U.S. didn't lock down en masse until mid-March, wouldn't the virus have already spread pretty substantially in a country with so many flights to and from China? Had the virus been lethal, wouldn't global deaths from some kind of unknown have surged?

It's worth wondering about because the global economy was crushed to limit the spread of something that seemingly had already begun spreading. Why? And if the answer is that experts were caught unawares only to catch up, such a response is insufficient. Do we require force to avoid sickness or death? The question answers itself.

So while this chapter will once again not get into health or disease from a medical point of view, it will point out discoveries that reporters made in pursuing this story. It will make a case that so much is unknown; the only known being that the virus isn't terribly lethal. We know that from China. As Chapter One argues, and has been argued at times throughout, even if China's reported death statistics were total fabrications, market signals along with the rapid-fire spread of information care of smartphones would have exposed much that Beijing allegedly wanted to hide—if there had been something to hide. It should be added that despite the rehashing of statistics unearthed from around the world, this chapter will conclude with an argument that numerical battles are a waste of time. About what's ahead, in most instances date of statistic and publication in which the statistic was found will be mentioned. This is purposeful. It gives readers a chance to decide for themselves the validity of the information reported.

On July 22, 2020, *New York Times* reporter J. David Goodman published a report about neighboring Houston, Texas–area communities, Gulfton and Bellaire. As Goodman described it, in Gulfton "more than 45,000 restaurant workers and housekeepers, immigrants and refugees live close together, mostly in shadeless two-story apartment blocks. At least 965 people have been infected by the virus in the ZIP code that covers the area, far more per capita than the city as a whole; 12 people have died."

Yet in neighboring, well-to-do Bellaire, a locale that "feels suburban and is home to mostly white and Asian professionals," there had been as of late July 2020 about "67 cases, about a third of the per capita rate for Houston."[331] The knee-jerk response to this disparity from readers might be, "Duh, Gulfton is more crowded. People living close together spread the virus much more easily and lethally."

It's not an unreasonable response given some of the assumptions about how the coronavirus spread. Certainly experts feared quick infection among the citizenry in New York City because of subways and population density, but then what would explain Thailand? Geographically it was much closer to the virus's epicenter, and per Hannah Beech at the *New York Times*, it confirmed "the world's first case of the coronavirus outside of China," which isn't surprising since Thailand experienced "an influx of foreign visitors early in the year from countries badly hit by the coronavirus." It should also be added that Bangkok, Thailand's capital city, is intensely crowded. All those months of visitors from the country where the virus took flight, yet as of July 17, 2020, Thailand, according to Beech, had "recorded fewer than 3,240 cases and 58 deaths."

Myanmar, Cambodia, and Laos border Thailand, but as of July 17, 2020, confirmed cases of the virus in those countries were respectively 336, 166, and 19. Vietnam? It's less than one hundred miles from Thailand, yet as of July 17, 2020, the country had "not recorded a single [coronavirus] death and had "logged about three months without a case of community transmission."[332]

The above examples at least call into question the notion that crowded cities are the source of spreading or that poverty is the root cause of spread (see Myanmar most notably) or that lockdowns prevent spread. With these countries we're talking about ones that experienced "an influx of foreign visitors early in the year from countries badly hit by the coronavirus" when no one knew a virus was in our midst.

Apoorva Mandavilli of the *New York Times* described India, which is poor and crowded, on October 1, 2020, as "a hospitable environment for infectious diseases of every kind" with "1.3 billion people jostling for space." But the "per capita number of cases reported daily" in the still very poor country were "lower than in Spain, France, or even the United States." Better yet for a country full of crowded, desperately poor cities, its deaths as of October of less than 100,000 had "surprised some scientists" since, per University of South Carolina infectious disease specialist Dr. Krutika Kuppalli, India "is a place where you would expect a disease like this to roar through."[333] Except that it hadn't.

China calls into question the city density argument. In late April of 2020 Holman Jenkins of the *Wall Street Journal* reported that China could claim *eight cities* larger than New York City. Jenkins added that China was able to restart its economy without a major testing regime. This is presumably the norm for poorer countries than the U.S. The cost alone of testing a big portion of the population would have been daunting.

It raises a question about the U.S. The *Wall Street Journal's* Allison Prang and Jennifer Calfas reported on July 28, 2020, that "the U.S. accounts for about a quarter of the more than 16.2 million [coronavirus] cases worldwide."[334] OK, but isn't such a sentence a bit misleading? Implicit in it was that there was a defect in the U.S. such that the virus spread with abandon. Isn't it more realistic to say that the U.S. is the richest country in the world, so naturally there are much greater means for more people to be tested? Indonesia helps answer the previous question. An October 9, 2020, report by the *Wall Street Journal's* Jon Emont indicated that the country, a nation of 270 million people, had "tested a smaller share of its population than every other major economy." Indonesia had tested 8 citizens for every thousand, compared to 34 per thousand in Philippines, 13 per thousand in Mexico, and 60 per thousand in India. Though Indonesia estimated 11,000 deaths related to the virus, who really knew since so few had been tested?[335] It's no reach to say the more you test, the more cases you're going to find. By October the U.S. could claim 7.5 million infected with the virus. Did this signal coronavirus failure stateside, or was the richest country in the world the location of most testing? As the indispensable Jenkins put it in an October 9, 2020, column for the *Wall Street Journal*, "We know the real number is probably ten times higher" than 7.5 million.[336] The big country that tests the most will have the most cases. The U.S.'s prosperity and its ability to mobilize quick testing were being used against it by the alarmists. On October 30, 2020, Jenkins reported that there had been over 150 million coronavirus tests conducted in the United States; something on the order of nearly one test for every two U.S. residents.[337] Do readers perhaps see now why the U.S. had so many cases, and so many reported deaths when other countries didn't?

Indeed, what if the virus had reached the U.S. in 1968 or 1918? Assuming any kind of response, it can at least be pretty confidently stated that there would have been exponentially fewer tests, and by extension many fewer cases for cost of testing alone. Maybe this explains Myanmar and Cambodia, and perhaps Thailand? Of course, if true, perhaps this speaks to a virus that is even less lethal and less likely to spark illness than thought? Indeed, on July 22, 2020, Mandavilli of the *New York Times* quoted CDC researcher Dr. Fiona Havers as saying what Jenkins had said in so many words, that "the number of people who have been infected with the virus that causes Covid-19 far exceeds the number of reported cases," and that "many of these people likely had no symptoms or mild illness and may have had no idea that they were infected."[338] Try to consider this in terms of the two to three months when the U.S., a country routinely visited en masse by the world's citizenry, was the recipient of arrivals from around the world. Yet there were no major spikes in illness or death during this time despite no virus-related precautions and certainly no lockdowns to fight the spread of something that was largely unknown.

Speaking of lockdowns again, *New York Times* reporters Norimitsu Onishi and Constant Méheut relayed to their readers on May 28, 2020, that France had endured "one of the world's strictest lockdowns, two months during which people had to fill out paperwork just to step out of their homes."[339] Conversely, *New York Times* Tokyo reporter Motoko Rich relayed to readers on April 20, 2020, that Japan's coronavirus "state of emergency" was comparatively light, that it only empowered governors to *"request* [my emphasis] that people stay at home and businesses close," and that Tokyo's governor had "asked people to refrain from going out at night."[340] Despite this lighter touch, the *Wall Street Journal's* Alastair Gale reported that as of May 22, 2020, Japan could claim a relatively meager "777 deaths attributed to Covid-19."[341]

Looked at just in the U.S., New York famously locked down while Florida was one of the last states to do so and one of the first to reopen. And while the media's role in the coronavirus lapse of reason is yet again overstated, it's useful to point out that when coronavirus cases and deaths ticked up in July 2020, the media reporting gave off the impression of the Sunshine State's being paralyzed by relentless death, bodies in the streets, packed hospitals turning away patients... Headlines and analyses included "Florida Sets Yet Another Coronavirus Record: 173 Deaths in a Day," and "A record 173 Floridians died from the virus Thursday, an average of more than one every eight minutes."

But as *Issues & Insights*, a website founded by former *Investor's Business Daily* editorial board members pointed out, the "record" number of deaths did not take place in a twenty-four-hour period. On the "record day" nineteen Floridians actually died. The "record" of those dying with the virus in Florida remained July 16, when 114 were known to have died.

None of this is meant to minimize the deaths, but it is meant to at least provide context. While largely unlocked, Florida's worst death day was 116, and while 45 percent of Florida's coronavirus-related deaths "involved residents and staff at long-term care facilities," heavily locked down New York could claim multiple one-thousand-death days in April alone despite a population that was 9 percent smaller than Florida's. Heavily locked down New Jersey had 59 percent fewer residents than Florida, but its peak day was 523 deaths on April 20. The editors at *Issues & Insights* noted that Florida-based deaths per million amid the "surge" were 273. The previous number was used to damn Florida, while elevating New York—except that deaths per million in New York were 1,680. In New Jersey the number of deaths per million came in at 1,785.[342]

And then there's old people. Deaths from the virus kept pointing back to the seriously old. That they did placed the state of Florida as an obvious locale for relentless dying. Particularly since the state was once again so slow to lock down and so quick to reopen. As *Wall Street Journal* reporters Arian Campo-Flores and Alex Leary pointed out on May 4, 2020, "People aged 65 and over make up 20.5% of Florida's population, the second highest proportion of any state in the U.S., after Maine."[343] Keep in mind that Florida sits only behind California and Texas in terms of population. Yet according to Statista, the online stat service used by the *Wall Street Journal's* editorial board, deaths per one hundred thousand amid "record" virus cases in late July 2020 was 27. New York's was once again 161. Maine's was 9. Deaths per one hundred thousand in Texas, a state full of "science deniers" and a state that never took well to lockdowns or masks, was 18.

To which some will reply that Texas is spread out. Yes it is, but Thailand isn't. Neither is Vietnam. Neither is Tokyo. Neither are China's cities.

And even still, unknown even now is how many people who died *with* the coronavirus as opposed to *because* of it were counted as coronavirus deaths? Jenkins pointed out in a September 9, 2020, column in the *Wall Street Journal* that "some people who died of gunshot wounds, drug overdoses and motorcycle accidents have been categorized as Covid victims in the U.S.," given the broader tendency of Covid-related deaths to have fallen on those with "multiple serious health conditions."[344] Along those lines, on May 18, 2020, Rick Rojas and Melina Delkic of the *New York Times* reported a complaint lodged by Colorado's Democratic Governor Jared Polis about the CDC's death statistics; the "criteria include anybody who died with Covid-19. What the people of Colorado want to know is how many people died *of* Covid-19." A worthy question indeed considering how deaths were so highly concentrated among the seriously old who already had preexisting conditions.

Sweden is perhaps a useful example when it comes to preexisting conditions along with dying with the virus as opposed to dying as a direct consequence of it. Readers may remember from Chapter Ten the discussion of Sweden and its decision to largely avoid lockdowns. It was as though proponents of the latter were praying for disaster there for the country's politicians having the temerity to trust the people. And when deaths in Sweden picked up, the digs at Sweden's decision increased. OK, but as a *Wall Street Journal* editorial from July 29, 2020, noted, deaths per one hundred thousand in Sweden were 56,[345] versus 44 in heavily locked down France. It's maybe compelling at first to some, but as the same editorial went on to point out, two-thirds of the deaths in Sweden were "among those over age 80." Here it's useful to look back to Chapter Eleven's discussion of Sweden, and the *New York Times* stat about over 40 percent of COVID-related deaths having occurred in nursing homes. The *Times* reported much the same about COVID-related deaths in the U.S. Paraphrasing Polis, did they die with COVID-19, or because of it? Most famously, the CDC reported in late August 2020 that 94 percent of Americans who had died with the coronavirus had at least one other substantial preexisting condition. At the very least, the previous revelation underscored how unreliable the coronavirus death count in the U.S. was. More than most want to admit, it was seemingly old people dying with the virus. This isn't to minimize the death of the elderly, but it is to say that when those in nursing homes pass it's sad, but rarely—if ever—a tragedy.

On July 28, 2020, *New York Times* reporter Julie Bosman began a story about the spread of the coronavirus in Illinois that was unsettling. In her words, "The latest count of new coronavirus cases was jarring: Some 1,500 virus cases were identified three consecutive days last week in Illinois, and fears of a resurgence in the state even led the mayor of Chicago to shut down bars all over town on Friday." Scary stuff, right?

But with the *New York Times* and the coronavirus, scary headlines and worrisome story introductions frequently obscured happier truths within. As Bosman went on to write, "Deaths from the virus statewide are one-tenth what they were at their peak in May." Michael Fumento predicted as much in April 1, 2020, piece for *RealClearMarkets* in which he wrote that "diseases nab the 'low-hanging fruit' first (in this case the elderly with co-morbid conditions), but then find subsequent fruit harder and harder to reach."[346]

On July 29, 2020, *New York Times* reporter Edgar Sandoval published a piece with the title, "Overwhelmed Funeral Homes in South Texas Struggle to Keep Up." In the article, Sandoval wrote about how the coronavirus was "tearing through" the Rio Grande Valley in Texas and that "a surge of virus cases" had "set off a flood of deaths." But then if the reader continued reading, rather than perhaps put down an article that was sad, the reader would have found out that despite Hidalgo County in South Texas having "one of the highest per capita death rates in the state," it worked out to "one of every 2,000 people" dying from or with the virus.[347] As always, none of this is meant to minimize death, but "one of every 2,000 people" hardly correlates with a "surge" or a "flood of deaths," and it probably doesn't associate with "highest" anything. On August 7, 2020, a front page *New York Times* story by David Leonhardt led with the headline, "U.S. Is Alone Among Peers in Failing to Curb Virus." It all sounded so disastrous, but buried deep in Leonhardt's attempt to indict the U.S. was an acknowledgment that the virus "kills only a small percentage of people who get it."[348] Actually, much smaller than small. Thankfully the coronavirus was much less than lethal. That journalists felt the need to create their own narrative of bodies in the street remains disturbing, particularly in consideration of what the lockdowns meant for the most vulnerable around the world.

All that's been mentioned in this chapter so far brings us to a May 21, 2020, front page *New York Times* story by James Glanz and Campbell Robertson. They cited Columbia University disease modelers who, in the telling of the reporters, asserted that "if the United States had begun imposing social distancing measures one week earlier than it did in March, about 36,000 fewer people would have died in the coronavirus outbreak."[349] Except that there's no reasonable way to make such an assertion.

Implicit in it was that the coronavirus had just begun to spread in March in one of the world's most open countries to people from foreign countries. So one week was the difference for 36,000 people living or dying even though global rates of infection and death are all over the map? Thinking about the Columbia study in terms of Florida, 20 percent of its population is sixty-five and above, and Florida didn't lock down until April 3. What explains death rates there that were so much lower than states like New York that locked down mid-March?

Furthermore, the study's conclusions ignored how the virus spread throughout parts of Asia that didn't lock down at first because they didn't know of the virus's existence right away (Thailand, Cambodia, Myanmar, and the like); that, or they knew about it but largely left it up to their people to be careful (Japan). Such a view also ignores how exponentially more people died in locked-down New York versus much more open Texas. It leaves out how the virus hit heavily locked down France much harder than it did an open U.S. state like Florida that was dense with old people.

In short, for every alleged "certainty" about the coronavirus, there's a "Yes, but." Which is why the speculation here remains that so many assumptions about the coronavirus will not age well.

That there's arguably so much we don't know speaks yet again to the importance of freedom, of live and let live. Free people experimenting in 330 million different ways in the U.S. and billions of different ways globally are the producers of information necessary to bring clarity. Some would lock down and never see the outside for months, some would go in between, and some would throw caution to the wind. *Precisely.* Find out from people living as they want to what tends to attract the virus and what doesn't. This way the skeptics can live as they want, but so can the alarmists. If they're worried, they needn't leave home. Most don't want to get sick or die, which probably means all 330 million would take at least some precautions. And if not, good. You can't force people to protect themselves. For those who choose to ignore spreading viruses altogether, how foolish to muzzle this approach. Better to learn from it.

And then there's the unseen to learn from. Applied to the panicked response to the coronavirus, it's not unreasonable to speculate that it was tragic.

The risk now is "an epidemic in a few months' time that will kill more children than Covid." So said Chibuzo Okonta, president of Doctors Without Borders in West Africa and Central Africa, to *New York Times* reporters Jan Hoffman and Ruth Maclean. Okonta was referring to the spread of preventable illnesses like polio and measles in her June 15, 2020, interview.

You see, the World Health Organization had warned in the spring that the coronavirus pandemic "could spread swiftly when children gathered for shots," which meant that many countries subsequently suspended their inoculation programs. And then even in countries that tried to keep the inoculation programs going, "cargo flights with vaccine supplies were halted by the pandemic and health workers diverted to fight it."

Hoffman and Maclean found that diphtheria (remember from Chapter Two, "the winter-time murderer of children") was returning to Pakistan, Bangladesh, and Nepal; cholera in South Sudan, Cameroon,

Mozambique, Yemen, and Bangladesh; polio in more than thirty countries; plus measles was found to be "flaring around the globe." They cited a projection from the Measles and Rubella Initiative that 178 million people were "at risk of missing measles shots in 2020." Please keep in mind that the suspended efforts, or those suspended by diversion, were credited with preventing "35 million deaths in 98 countries from vaccine-preventable diseases."[350] And while tuberculosis is thankfully no longer the biggest U.S. killer, it remains the world's biggest (1.5 million deaths per year) thanks to a failure in the poorest parts of the world to tame it. Still, as an August 3, 2020, *New York Times* report from Apoorva Mandavilli explained, the infectious disease had been "on the run," having reached a nadir in 2018. And then COVID-19 happened. With it "consuming global health resources," tuberculosis was making a comeback along with AIDS and malaria.[351] Call it the tragic law of unintended consequences.

Oh well, the experts are experts. The view in 2020 was that skepticism about their alarmism reduced one to anti-science crankery. Even though the coronavirus had spread for months in China without killing too many people, the experts at WHO decided to protect the young around the world from crowded places where vaccines could be administered…

Back in the U.S. people were said to be safer at home for being away from potential virus spreaders, but according to Maria Cramer of the *New York Times* on May 27, 2020, sales of beer, wine, and liquor were "much higher" than the previous year. So much of life is trade-offs. Stay-at-home orders theoretically protected people from the virus (though not apparently in New York where, as of May 6, 2020, two-thirds of COVID patients had been sheltering in place beforehand), but the loneliness of being at home or boredom or depression seemed to facilitate other self-destructive behaviors.[352] Those behaviors included opioid abuse. According to a September 29, 2020, report by Hilary Swift and Abby Goodnough in the *New York Times*, "In the six months since

Covid-19 brought the nation to a standstill, the opioid epidemic has taken a sharp turn for the worse. More than 40 states have recorded increases in opioid-related deaths since the pandemic began, according to the American Medical Association."[353] Apparently suicides spiked too. Dr. Michael deBoisblanc of the John Muir Medical Center in Walnut Creek, CA, told reporters that he'd seen a "year's worth of suicides" in a four-week stretch from April to May.[354] Similarly in Tennessee, suicides outpaced coronavirus deaths.[355] Coincidental? Who knows?

Traveling back to the previous chapter, Holman Jenkins once again alerted readers to the CDC's assertion that "in the coming months, most of the U.S. population will be exposed to the virus." This rates repeat mainly because the lame justification for unjustifiable lockdowns was that they would slow the spreading of the virus, and as a consequence "ease the burden" on hospitals. But as an April 19, 2020, editorial from the *Wall Street Journal* noted, "Thousands of hospital beds are empty in places with few Covid-19 patients." The editorial cited an Oxford Economics forecast that "1.5 million 'non-essential' health-care workers" would lose their jobs in April 2020 alone. Government services are routinely awful and then thoroughly ghastly when there's a surge in usage, yet it was government telling hospitals how to handle what the experts predicted would be a big surge in hospital use. More realistically, empty beds quickly became the norm alongside hospitals around the U.S. being pushed into bankruptcy. According to a May 16, 2020, account in the *New York Times*, empty and/or underutilized hospitals were "losing an estimated $50 billion a month." In Minnesota, the prestigious Mayo Clinic had "postponed lucrative surgeries to make way for coronavirus victims" that never materialized. The Mayo Clinic stood to lose $900 million in 2020 after producing $1 billion in net operating revenue the year before.[356] The *New York Times* kept running alarmist headlines about virus surges and hospitals allegedly strained by them, but the actual hospitalization rate from the virus according to the CDC was 0.1 percent.[357] Tragically, it didn't stop there.

According to Yves Duroseau, chairman of emergency medicine at Lenox Hill Hospital on New York's Upper East Side, this purging of emergency rooms was resulting in "excess deaths." Duroseau described the latter in a May 20, 2020, opinion piece for the *Wall Street Journal* as "deaths beyond what would normally be expected" for a specific period. Between March 11 and May 2 there were 5,293 "excess deaths" in New York City that didn't "necessarily have much to do with the virus." Duroseau chalked the latter up to would-be patients who chose "to stay out of emergency rooms" out of fear that time in them would "put them at a greater risk of contracting the coronavirus."[358]

A month earlier, former U.S. Senator Bob Kerrey (D-NE) wrote in a April 21, 2020, *Wall Street Journal* opinion piece that government officials, including Surgeon General Jerome Adams, "urged a halt" to "elective surgery in U.S. hospitals and ambulatory clinics" out of "concern they'd spread the coronavirus and strain hospital capacity." According to Kerrey, thirty states followed the directives from health experts on the federal level. Kerrey's piece made plain that these bans meant to somehow "protect" hospitals from more business actually forced on them "a contraction of $45 billion a month." Worse, they were foregoing procedures meant to treat the biggest annual killers in the U.S. like cancer and heart disease.[359]

On May 7, 2020, the *Wall Street Journal's* Sharon Terlep reported on how CVS executives had warned of an "impending surge in medical problems unrelated to the coronavirus." As an owner of health insurance provider Aetna, CVS was privy to the buying habits of those it insured. In the words of Terlep, it detected in April 2020 "fewer new prescriptions, as many have started fewer new treatments and seen doctors less frequently—a concern especially for patients who have chronic conditions such as diabetes and heart disease."[360] Looking into the future, how many killer diseases went undiagnosed as resources were directed toward the coronavirus, only to be discovered too late? Indeed, as the tragic finances of hospitals during the corona hysteria loudly indicated, health care spending by Americans during the pandemic plummeted.[361]

The great George Gilder asked the simple question that Governor Polis in Colorado broached: were people dying *of* the coronavirus or *with* it? In an April 25, 2020, piece for *RealClearMarkets*, Gilder pointed to CDC data indicating that "overall death rates from all causes show no increase at all. Deaths [in 2020] are lower than in 2019, 2018, 2017 and 2015, slightly higher than in 2016. Any upward bias is imparted by population growth." In short, deaths recorded as caused by coronavirus meant that fewer people were dying of other maladies, meaning Polis was on to something.[362] So seemingly was Gilder. The death rates attributable to the virus were lower than even the lowest estimates.

Trade-offs. Big-time trade-offs. To protect against a virus that hadn't revealed much in terms of lethality way back in January, experts imperiled the financial health of hospitals, scared and sometimes mandated the unhealthy away from surgeries, emergency room visits, and drug treatments, plus globally they sidetracked a vaccination program credited with having previously prevented thirty-five million deaths. What to say about this? Will the experts who did so much damage ever be called on to explain themselves? Will they suffer even a fraction of all the agony their alarmism brought to the rest of the world? The "seen," or the consequences of their actions, is already tragic, but what of the "unseen"?

What would businesses and people have done, and how would they have innovated if they'd been left alone to work and live around the virus? Or would they have innovated at all? Maybe experts toiling under the hot and bright lights of markets would have called for a great deal more calm such that the new coronavirus largely passed without incident. It's surely possible, but we'll never know. And what about the economic growth lost and the businesses suffocated—businesses that might have minted a future multibillionaire or two such that hundreds of millions of more investment in health care advances might have been funded. The latter is a speculation based on how the superrich have historically invested in and given a lot to medical concepts meant to advance the science.

The problem was that in 2020, the solution from panicked politicians was to wreck the global economy, induce potential starvation for hundreds of millions, and create mass desperation in order to fight a virus. The words are hard to type, so shockingly obtuse was the political response.

All of which speaks to why, compelling or unpersuasive as the previous numbers in this chapter might be, a numbers argument is no way to win an argument like this one. In the future, we must lead with freedom first.

To see why, it's important to close with commentary about a piece written by economic commentator Richard Rahn in the May 25, 2020, edition of the *Washington Times*. He asserted that "if you are under 65, in reasonably good health and do not have a Vitamin D deficiency, you only have a tiny chance of dying from COVID-19. And if you are younger than 34, your chances of dying from the virus are so small as to almost be statistically undetectable."

Some might say the statistician in Rahn very skillfully exploded the alarmism that has surrounded the spread of the new coronavirus. As he calmly put it, it's quite simply not much of a threat unless you're eighty-five or older, live "in a nursing home, [and] have serious health problems including a Vitamin D deficiency." Rahn thankfully noted that only "a tiny portion of the population" was "in such a condition."[363]

So while Rahn's statistical breakdown of C-19 read as comforting news, and a validation of the point that this book makes in Chapter One that the virus was never a major killer, the view here remains that there are dangers that come with turning debates about freedom into statistical battles.

Indeed, Rahn was plainly of the view that the lockdowns cruelly foisted on the electorate by local, state, and national politicians brought incalculable damage to the U.S. economy. No argument there. The lockdowns were, and are, a tragedy.

That they were so disastrous speaks—at least partially—to why it was so dangerous to make the COVID argument or realistically any argument that involves freedom into a statistical one. To see why, consider what many well-meaning people no doubt did with Rahn's piece that yet again exposed the virus's microscopic lethality: they passed it around as an argument for ending the lockdowns. It all makes sense at first glance. But only at first glance. Think about it.

On second glance, it's easy to see just how dangerous such an approach is. That's the case simply because COVID-19 won't be the last virus to work its way around the world. Rest assured that when the next one rears its ugly or largely benign head, alarmist scientists, doctors, and self-styled experts will quickly have scared-of-their-own-shadow politicians lusting to "do something" to protect us from illness and perhaps death.

Which is why those properly horrified by the lockdowns of 2020 should refocus the argument on freedom. And they should do so quickly.

If not about freedom, what happens if the expert conclusion about a future virus is that it's most lethal for those under thirty-four? Implicit in all the statistical back-and-forth is that lockdowns might be justified then. Right? Young people are America's and the world's future and all that. Right? We need to lock down to protect the future! Wrong. Governments have no right to take away our freedoms. Period. That the takings blind us just adds insult to injury.

Looking back to 1793, that year Philadelphia endured a yellow fever pandemic. Writing about it on June 8, 2020, in the *Wall Street Journal*, Michael J. Lewis indicated that "desperate citizens fumigated their rooms, tied bags of camphor around their necks, and soaked handkerchiefs in vinegar—the face masks of the day. None of this did the slightest bit of good, for the disease was transmitted by mosquitoes, something that was not *discovered for a century*."[364] The emphasis at quote's end is mine. The speculation here once again is that so much that was assumed about the coronavirus and how to prevent infection in 2020 won't age well. Which is why freedom is the first, second, and last answer to what is said to imperil us. Freedom isn't just correct. It cannot be stressed enough that it also produces clarity.

Assuming what seems likely, that a future virus materializes, imagine once again if experts tell us "this time is different"—that the virus will hit thirty-four and under the hardest. If so, freedom will be the answer precisely because some youthful types will dismiss the alarmism. These "venture livers" will be knowledge givers. Without their defiance, we can't really know the truth about why the virus spreads and who is most endangered by it. Say it over and over again: free people produce information.

It's all a reminder that lockdowns aren't just inexcusable because they destroy jobs, businesses, and the human spirit. What takes away freedom is also anti-life. Lockdowns blind us as to what is best for us and what will keep us safest when our health is most imperiled.

In short, if we make the C-19 argument solely about numbers, we hand the very politicians who created so much personal and economic misery the power to do so again. Let's not do that. But let's most crucially not allow lockdowns again because what crushes freedom also crushes the knowledge necessary to elongate life.

CONCLUSION

"When history passes its final verdict on John D. Rockefeller, it may well be that his endowment of research will be recognized as a milestone in the progress of the race. For the first time, science was given its head; longer term experiment on a large scale has been made practicable, and those who undertake it are freed from the shadow of financial disaster. Science today owes as much to the rich men of generosity and discernment as the art of the Renaissance owes to the patronage of Popes and Princes. Of these rich men, John D. Rockefeller is the supreme type."[365]

—Winston Churchill

On the evening of July 4, 2020, fireworks lit up the sky of Southern California. Throughout Los Angeles, for miles and miles, fireworks could be seen.

These weren't the usual Independence Day shows that Californians were used to. They had been canceled, including the Rose Bowl's annual fireworks extravaganza in Pasadena, CA. The shows were shut down because people were yet again a presumed menace to one another. The view was that humans connecting with other humans would lead to mass illness and perhaps death. And since humans apparently couldn't decide for themselves whether to risk contracting what most didn't know they had, politicians felt it was their duty to protect Californians from themselves.

In response, Californians decided to stage their own fireworks shows. Videos that went viral on social media revealed Southern California skies lit up.

Except that we're getting ahead of ourselves in a sense.

On November 29, 2017, Farhad Manjoo published a column in the *New York Times* lamenting the internet's eventual disappearance. The cause? Manjoo felt that allowing the very owners of the proverbial internet "pipe" into the home to charge different users different rates for usage, including higher rates for better access, would cause the internet to disappear. The hyper-emotional columnist titled his rant, "Without Net Neutrality, Say So Long to the Internet."[366]

Manjoo's name perhaps rings a bell for readers. He was first discussed in Chapter Four. The often wrong but rarely in doubt columnist was actually correct about the coronavirus at first by virtue of him calling for calm. To refresh the memories of readers, in January 2020 he warned against "unnecessarily severe limits on movement and on civil liberties" and that politicians might "begin pushing for travel bans, overbroad quarantines, or other measures that might not be supported by the science." Manjoo was so right at the time, which explains why he soon enough backtracked. He's uncomfortable being correct or insightful about things.

Needless to say, Manjoo's alarmism about the internet was as dopey as his eventual alarmism about the coronavirus. In his defense, this book speculates (see, for instance, the previous chapter) that most assertions about the coronavirus won't age well. As for the internet, Manjoo's speculations aged very poorly.

As Chapter Fifteen recounted in some detail, internet stocks like Facebook, Amazon, and Google had actually performed quite well amid the lockdowns. With personal interactions limited, along with retail access very limited, the businesses that could bring life's comforts to the home did well for themselves. So long to the internet? Without an ever-improving internet that enabled endless communication, shopping, exercise, work, and food/grocery delivery, it's highly unlikely that politicians would have had the nerve to force lockdowns. The revolts would have been endless.

At the same time, the internet arguably shined a bright light on the mood of Americans. By July 4th they'd had it. That's how John Batchelor, the urbane New York City radio host saw it. He, like tens of millions, had seen the viral video of Californians essentially flipping the finger to the state's politicians. No firework shows? Try to arrest us all! Batchelor viewed it as a *sign*. Never again. No more lockdowns. Americans wouldn't go for something so pointless again. Had the internet Manjoo left for dead in 2017 perhaps revealed an underlying fury within the electorate? Hope springs eternal. Time will tell. Add your clichés here.

The speculation here is that Batchelor will be proven correct. Big time. They fought a virus with mass unemployment, bankruptcy, and desperation. What could they, they being the panicked politicians, have possibly been thinking? The good news is that the truth about the electorate making politicians pay will reveal itself every two years for at least a decade as voters think about what politicians did. Any speculation about the historical meaning of what took place can't be proven in this lifetime, but the view of your author is that historians well into the future will marvel at the abject stupidity of politicians and the hand-wringing experts who surrounded them in 2020: They fought a virus with economic contraction? How could they have been so dim?

Other speculations have unseen qualities to them. To see why, consider Chapter Two once again. Before genius businessmen like John D. Rockefeller, medical science was so very limited. Rockefeller's immense wealth made remarkable advances in medicine possible such that pneumonia was no longer "Captain of Men's Death." Imagine where medicine would have been in the twentieth century, imagine how many more

Americans would have died in the First and Second World Wars, absent the advances that Rockefeller's wealth made possible.

Unseen is what great businesses and business owners were crushed in a global attempt to fight disease with an economic contraction that was followed by a massive, multitrillion-dollar extraction of precious resources from the economy. How much health care experimentation didn't take place as a result, and how much wealth wasn't created to the detriment of future health care experimentation? The aim of politicians was to save lives, but at the expense of how many "excess deaths" in the future—deaths that could have been avoided had there been more wealth being directed toward the creation of knowledge without which life cannot be extended?

It cannot be stressed enough that if better, longer, healthier lives are the goal, then the answer every time is the wealth creation that's a consequence of freedom. Wealth creators make possible the incredibly costly tinkering and *trying* that turns today's killers into tomorrow's afterthoughts. Somehow the political class at all levels, and all over the world, forgot this blindingly simple truth amid the spreading of the new coronavirus. Their forgetful ways meant that hundreds of millions would revisit poverty, starvation, and perhaps death so that politicians could feel good for stalking that which roamed the earth unchecked for months and that few noticed as it roamed.

If it's not apparent to readers yet, the view here is that the reaction by politicians to the coronavirus amounted to the biggest twenty-first century crime against humanity, and nothing else came close.

Important about the above assessment is that it's not meant to blame a collective *we*. The blame lies with politicians who, despite very clear evidence from the other side of the world that the coronavirus wasn't very lethal, chose to rob us of our freedom and prosperity anyway. Politicians erred. *Mightily.* They erred because even if the virus had been lethal, the lockdowns would have made even less sense and for hopefully obvious reasons by now. We suffered their monumental mistakes to varying degrees around the world, most cruelly in places not the United States where poverty amounts to starvation and frequently death.

Strangely, self-hugging *New York Times* columnist David Brooks chose to describe what happened as a "national humiliation" for the United States. He wrote ahead of the July 4th weekend that the year 2020 "humiliated" the American people "as almost never before. We had one collective project this year, and that was to crush Covid-19, and we failed." No, Brooks's assertion wasn't serious. And the previous statement isn't a comment on low death rates from the virus.

While the low death rates and evidence that the virus largely stalked the very old and already ill made, and make, for a good case against broad alarmism about the virus, this book's view as the previous chapter makes plain is that statistical arguments are losing arguments. Statistics can always be twisted, and circumstances can always change. Politicians are ever eager to take our freedoms, so the initial response must always be that our freedoms must not be trampled on, as opposed to, "Yes, but..."

Still, there's a statistic worth bringing up since it came from Brooks's own *New York Times* around the time of his column. Readers are already familiar with it, but it's worth repeating. The newspaper reported that over 40 percent of U.S. coronavirus deaths could be linked to nursing homes.[367] Supposedly the latter existed as pretty powerful evidence that the virus didn't kill the young and healthy, but that the very old, usually with preexisting conditions, tend to die from the virus or with it. It all reads as compelling and certainly an argument against alarmism. But the knowledge about the virus as of the summer of 2020 was once again young. What's obvious now could change. Assumptions don't always age well, which is a long or short of way of saying that the stat cited is not being cited in this instance to dismiss concerns about the coronavirus.

It's being cited here to dispute Brooks's pessimistic assertion of failure, of humiliation. He couldn't have been more incorrect. Brooks thought America was in the midst of embarrassment in the summer of 2020, but in truth it had *thrived*. This was obvious because with or without the coronavirus, more and more Americans were dying of *old age*. *In nursing homes*. What a modern concept. What a *triumph*.

Brooks called for "collective" action to fight the virus that seemingly had him in the proverbial fetal position, biting his nails. No, it was entrepreneurs operating alone (alone because people almost uniformly thought they were nuts) who produced the staggering wealth that enabled scientists and doctors to experiment on the way to the production of information that elongated beautiful life.

Which is why this book will come to an end optimistically. It will because there's reason to be optimistic. Much as politicians erred, this is what they've always done. *It's what they do*. Usually they get us into needless wars that wipe out the young. Luckily, *that* at least didn't happen.

Even better, consider a July 6, 2020, piece for the *Wall Street Journal* that was penned by Andy Kessler. He wrote about a company named Grail in a column titled "Cancer Screening Leaps Forward." Grail is a Menlo Park, CA–based company that through blood sampling "can find cancer well before symptoms show up, in Stage 1 or sooner, when therapies are cheap and effective." As he went on to write, "If Grail can scale, it will be a massive game-changer. Five year survival rates can approach 9 in 10 if cancer is detected early, compared with about 1 in 5 in Stage IV."

Kessler observed that before Grail, cancer screenings produced way too many false positives and false alarms, plus "80% of cancer deaths are from cancers that we don't currently screen for." Grail's false-positive rate is, according to Kessler, less than 1 percent. Even better, the company reports that it's 93 percent accurate in identifying the type of cancer.

To Kessler, a long-time technology analyst who morphed into a hedge fund wizard before becoming a wildly popular author and columnist, "if cancer can be found early, treatment is much easier. You can cut it, heat it, freeze it, or zap it out, especially since you should know where it is."

Crucial for the purposes of this concluding chapter is that the source of Grail's $2 billion cash pile is rich people like Bill Gates and Jeff

Bezos.[368] Think about Gates and Bezos. Ideally for a long time. When information and talent are matched with capital, great strides are made. The truly dense among us routinely bemoan wealth inequality, but as the sketch of Grail reminds us, the rich are the very people who turn what we imagine and what we yearn for into reality. The highly unequal Gates and Bezos may make the elongation of life possible with their wealth.

This cannot be forgotten with *When Politicians Panicked* top of mind. In robbing us of our freedom to live and work as we wanted amid the spreading of the new coronavirus, politicians suffocated wealth creation along with the information necessary to save us from the maladies and death brought by the virus. Tragic. There's so much we didn't, and don't, know, only for politicians to further blind us in the spring and summer of 2020.

So while the speculation about early coronavirus assumptions not aging well stands, readers needn't speculate about the long-term validity of one truth. Specifically, the biggest enemy of life—*by far*—is poverty. Let's never again fight disease with the taking of freedom and wealth so essential to knowledge, prosperity, and, by extension, life.

John Tamny
Bethesda, MD

ACKNOWLEDGMENTS

When Politicians Panicked begins with the great Jeffrey Tucker. There's no way to adequately describe how essential he was and will always be to the coronavirus debate. He sensed realistically before anyone that panic of the political kind was underway when he wrote with horror about the decision in Austin, TX, to cancel South by Southwest. Jeffrey not only sounded a necessary alarm about the tragedy that was set to unfold, he also brought together economic thinkers, doctors, and scientists whose commentary made possible a muscular response to the overnight imposition of command-and-control from the political class, and that culminated in the very essential Great Barrington Declaration. Jeffrey is a hero of mine. Any reasonable history of 2020 will feature him prominently.

John McIntyre is the co-founder with Tom Bevan of *RealClearPolitics* (RCP). I'm editor of *RealClearMarkets*, one of RCP's spawns. John and Tom have long believed that "Fair and Balanced" should be just that. *Pair opposing viewpoints together.* This proved crucial as the lockdowns began. The *RealClear* sites routinely featured both sides of the debate, and often third and fourth sides. What a change this was from the past when the alarmist view of the world was incorrectly billed as the only one.

Bob Reingold was another early skeptic of the political reaction to the virus. He very instinctually sensed from day one that politicians were in the process of mindlessly taking our personal and economic liberty.

Amid all this, Bob e-mailed to express his sadness that politicians had specifically *panicked*. Not only did he perfectly describe what was taking place in March of 2020, his specific words gave me a title for the book you're holding. Bob is extraordinarily insightful, he's taught me a great deal over the years, plus he's an incredibly generous supporter of the freedom movement. I'm very lucky to call him a great friend, but arguably even luckier to be able to routinely consult him on business, public policy, and life matters.

Hall McAdams is the freest thinking person I know. Since 2003 he's been a regular source of wisdom for me, and 2020 was no exception. Hall is so smart on so many levels, but arguably his greatest quality is that of instinct. He knew right away that the "crisis" when it came to the coronavirus was man made. Underlying this man-made disaster was an overreaction that Hall similarly sensed right away. As always, Hall was a huge source of reason and insight when I needed it most. As people all around us were losing their heads, Hall called me for a lengthy talk during which he confirmed my own horror about what was needlessly taking place.

I was on the phone with John Aglialoro and Joan Carter with great regularity as the coronavirus hysteria revealed its ugly self. We were talking in detail about an event that kept being pushed back or canceled thanks to the political reaction to the virus. Great entrepreneurs and wondrously generous benefactors of the freedom movement, Joan and John led by example as they showed extraordinary calm and resolve as an always eccentric world turned upside down. At the height of fear related to the pandemic, they patched me in for one of our conference calls. Interesting about this is that they were driving. They were returning from a restaurant after having picked lunch for all of their employees. John and Joan were and are a reminder of how thoroughly generous and compassionate capitalism is.

Richard and Sue Ann Masson saw up close in Kentucky just how regressive the lockdowns were. Very few in the Bluegrass State were sickened by the virus, but an exponentially greater number of people were sickened economically by a political crack-up that cruelly destroyed jobs and businesses in the service sector. Amid all this the Massons provided verbal and financial support that was crucial to the freedom organizations that chose not to remain silent as politicians got to work on taking our personal and economic freedoms.

The great Ken Fisher was a regular source of insight during the meltdowns of 2020. Ken has a way of keeping a remarkably wise and calm head when all around him are losing theirs. Ken's frequent reminder to clients of his eponymous money management firm kept coming to mind in March and beyond: the market has already priced the bad news, so move on. After that, Ken is an extraordinarily nice man who routinely encourages me as I go about my own work.

Rob Arnott was never fooled. Better yet, Rob spoke out about the injustices taking place related to the virus. He put his thoughts on paper too. He did this despite it being an incredibly difficult year personally for him and his wife Marina.

Bill Walton is a spectacular financial mind who might actually be a better talk-show host. Many of the ideas in this book were first aired on Bill's eponymous show. He and his wife Sarah have been so encouraging for so long, and surely were about the creation of this book.

As these acknowledgments are being written, I'm launching a new show called *The Capitol Brief* with Seth Berenzweig and Tod Castleberry. Seth and Tod are a blast to work with, and our show promises to be a forum for heterodox views of all kinds that have too often not seen the light of day.

Kim Dennis is the president and CEO of the Searle Freedom Trust. Kim has watched me grow up, and lifted me much of the way. She's sick of hearing it, but she supported me when few did. I'm so grateful to her, along with her colleagues at Searle, Courtney Myers and Richard Tren. Kim's daughter Jesse Dennis has similarly been a huge source of encouragement, plus she's made it possible for me to visit her very excellent alma mater in Clemson more than once for speeches. Clemson instructs in countless ways about economics as Jesse well knows.

The freedom movement lost the great Donald Smith way too early last year. It's difficult to contemplate how depleted the world of ideas and action related to freedom would be without Don's amazing support. His daughter Julie continues Don's brilliant work, and does so with great belief and wit.

Adam Brandon is the president of FreedomWorks where I am vice president and head of its Center for Economic Freedom. Adam is unquestionably the best organization head in Washington. It's pure joy coming into the office each day simply because Adam has long surrounded himself with people committed as he is to improving policy in Washington by limiting the power of policymakers. I always tell Adam that with the exception of the Cleveland Browns GM role, he's not allowed to leave FreedomWorks. And even then, he must bring me with him.

To list all my FreedomWorks colleagues would fill too many book pages, so with partial brevity in mind I'll thank Parissa Sedghi and Noah Wall for making the organization operate so smoothly and effectively. The courage the both of you showed when the world was seemingly collapsing around us in March of 2020 was beyond impressive. Thank you to Jason Pye. His ferociously principled view of the world sets an example for everyone in the organization, including me. I always know when I ask Jason a policy question that I can trust his response. The same goes for Josh Withrow, with whom I'm working to change the terms of the monetary discussion. Paul Sapperstein can realistically do everything, and he does just that on a daily basis. Paul is not allowed to leave FreedomWorks either! Kim Drezdon puts up with my "occasional" inattention to detail, and does so with a smile. Jack Scheader is my chief of staff of sorts with whom I look forward to accomplishing many great things.

I know many of the people mentioned so far thanks to Ed Crane. Co-founder of the Cato Institute, Ed typically never lost his head as so many around him did. He never wavered in his view that the more any presumed crisis threatens, the more that political reaction is wholly superfluous. Ed was a regular source of wisdom during the weeks of panic that turned into months.

Richard Rahn, Jeff Erber, and Scott Barbee are weekly members of Crane's lunch club. They brought needed sanity at a time when there was little of it. Richard's writings on the virus routinely informed my own.

Dr. Lawrence Dorr is one of the world's most prominent orthopedic surgeons, yet despite very long hours spent on operations that have literally made it possible for his patients to walk again, he's somehow found time to write novels. Dr. Dorr's ability to combine medical history with fascinating storylines has brought great understanding to his readers. Crucial for the purposes of this book, Dr. Dorr's writings showed me just how primitive medicine was before economic growth rushed an unimaginable future into the present. Before wealth creation people were dying too often and too young. Dr. Dorr has shown his readers and your author that "Die Once, Live Twice" is just the beginning. As the power of medicine expands thanks to economic growth, people will be overcoming all manner of former killers.

Huge thanks to Drs. Jay Bhattacharya, Sunetra Gupta, and Martin Kulldorff for writing the Great Barrington Declaration during that crucial weekend up in Great Barrington. Though *When Politicians Panicked* makes a case that freedom should always take precedence over medicine and science, it was extraordinarily uplifting to be in the company of three prominent doctors willing to risk professional associations, reputations, and careers as they penned their essential Declaration. They could have been aloof, but instead were incredibly available to all in attendance at the American Institute for Economic Research's beautiful headquarters. Their willingness to put their names on the line in support of reason in the face of hysteria lent credibility to a crowd of skeptics that some deemed fringe. I'm so grateful to the doctors, to AIER, to Jeffrey Tucker once again, and to AIER president Edward Stringham for making the Great Barrington Declaration happen.

George Gilder increasingly views AIER as one of his primary ideological homes, and what a wonderful combination of minds this is! George proved crucial during the virus debate. In particular, he wrote a column on April 25 of 2020 that's referenced in *When Politicians Panicked* ("The Pandemic Is Over, Let's Stop the Economic Suicide and Get Back to Work"), and that was a huge confidence booster for those of us fighting what at the time seemed like a losing battle. George gave the lockdown skeptics enormous credibility with his column, but also very important insights used in the fight. George subsequently agreed to write the foreword for this book, for which I'm very grateful.

Holman Jenkins is referenced throughout *When Politicians Panicked*, and with good reason. While he's always an essential read, he became a *crucial* read during the virus crack-up. The Hoover Institution's Scott Atlas similarly brought reason and statistics to a virus discussion that was so unreasonable that the statistics were seemingly obscured.

No book written by me can ever not mention the great Steve Forbes. He's taught me so much, encouraged me even more, plus he's the model human being I aspire to. Steve remains the nicest person I know.

Forbes publisher Rich Karlgaard sniffed out coronavirus hysteria as tragically regressive from day one. It would have been easy for Rich and other prominent names to hide from the controversy, and some did. Not Rich. He saw the horrid injustice of the lockdowns immediately, and he spoke out immediately.

The very excellent McLean Family Restaurant became my near-daily break from the sometimes terrifying process of writing a book. Thank you to Dina Papadis, Litsa Phoutio, and the whole MFR team for giving me something great to look forward to each day in between writing. Thank you to John Grigsby, an MFR regular, with whom I discussed nail-biting politicians with great regularity.

Thank you as always to my parents, Peter and Nancy. Long before the coronavirus reared its ugly head my dad expressed skepticism about the possibility that a virus could be manufactured and spread in lethal fashion in a country or continent. His thoughts informed my own skepticism from day one. More broadly, my parents have always been a strong source of encouragement for me. So has my sister Kim. She saw right through the political panic, plus her always compassionate side had her enraged as those with the least suffered elite hysteria so disproportionately.

Thank you to my wonderful wife Kendall. Some of us need to be pushed. Kendall routinely pushes me to expand my work horizons, and better yet, inspires me. Without her it's no exaggeration to say there are no books. Kendall lives the creation of all of my books, but this one she lived much more than others. Despite having to put up with daily and nightly rants from me about all the injustice taking place, Kendall continued to encourage me, question me, plus she offered insights that can be found throughout this book. To say I'm grateful for all that she does for me and our family brings new meaning to understatement.

Thank you to my daughter Claire. She brings great joy to me every day, and was frequently a lunch partner at MFR during the creation of *When Politicians Panicked.* Very briefly Claire became a minor Twitter star after telling politicians to "Stop It" one day in response to the lockdowns. Claire and I discussed the latter a great deal in 2020, and Kendall would say *too much*. Needless to say, the conversations will continue in the years and decades ahead.

Reed is Claire's baby brother, and the person to whom When Politicians Panicked is dedicated. He arrived just as politicians began to lose their wits. Hopefully Reed's generation, undoubtedly the "COVID-19 Generation," will learn well the egregious errors made by the global political class so that this horrid form of human rights tragedy is not repeated again.

Lastly, the acknowledgments in this book wouldn't be complete without a blanket tribute to the hundreds of millions cruelly rushed to starvation by clueless politicians, the hundreds of millions more needlessly reacquainted with poverty, the tens of millions of Americans who lost jobs owing to their work having a—gasp—*destination* quality, and the millions more honest businessmen and women who lost their life's work so that a self-serious very few who never missed a meal could take a decadent break from reality. What you endured and are enduring is nothing short of tragic. Your stories must be told, *over and over again*, so that history doesn't repeat itself, let alone rhyme.

ENDNOTES

1   Sabrina Tavernise, "As Neon Dims, Despair Grows on Vegas Strip," *New York Times,* April 27, 2020.

2   Ben Kesling, "Farmers Forced to Destroy Their Crops," *Wall Street Journal*, April 27, 2020.

3   Daniel Henninger, "Bring Back Laissez-Faire Capitalism," *Wall Street Journal*, April 15, 2020.

4   Jennifer Medina and Robert Gebeloff, "Trump Stays Quiet on Toll as U.S. Nears a Milestone," *New York Times*, May 25, 2020.

5   Bret Baier, *Special Report with Bret Baier*, March 18, 2020, https://www.youtube.com/watch?v=70A2Px_5m78.

6   Evan Osnos, *Age of Ambition: Chasing Fortune, Truth, and Faith in the New China*, Farrar, Straus & Giroux, 2014, p. 145.

7   Patricia Cohen, "40,767,000: 2.1 Million New Jobless Claims Don't Tell the Full Story," *New York Times*, May 29, 2020.

8   Lionel Shriver, "This is not a natural disaster, but a manmade one," *Spectator*, May 16, 2020.

9   George F. Will, *The Conservative Sensibility*, Hachette Book Group, 2019, p. 239.

10 Lawrence Dorr, M.D., *Die Once, Live Twice*, Silverado Books, 2011, p. 35.

11 Ibid., p. 35.

12 Ibid., p. 194.

13 Ibid., p. 46.

14 Ibid., p. 129.

15 Ibid., p. 130.

16 Ibid., p. 136.

17 Ibid., p. 111.

18 Ibid., pp. 253–54.

19   Ron Chernow, *Titan: The Life of John D. Rockefeller, Sr.*, Vintage Books, 2nd Edition, 2004, p. 470.

20   Ibid., p. 471.

21   Ibid., p. 470.

22   Ibid., p. 476.

23   Ibid., p. 535.

24   Ibid., p. 477.

25   Ibid., p. 491.

26   Ibid., p. 569.

27   Ibid., p. 570.

28   Lawrence Dorr, M.D., *Die Once, Live Twice*, Silverado Books, 2011, p. 188.

29   Matthew Rees, "'Immortality, Inc.' Review: Birthdays without End," *Wall Street Journal*, January 26, 2020.

30   Ludwig von Mises, *Liberalism: The Classical Tradition,* The Liberty Fund, 2005, p. 13.

31   Jason Aten, "Bill Gates to Spend Billions on a Covid-19 Vaccine," *Inc.*, April 6, 2020.

32   Ken Fisher, "'Clarity' Is a Very Costly Word. Stocks Never Wait for It," *RealClearMarkets*, May 26, 2020.

33   Amity Shlaes, *The Forgotten Man*, Harper Collins, 2007, p. 97.

34   John Tamny, "The 1930s Great Depression That Wasn't? A New Look at a Decade That Wasn't All Misery," *Forbes*, November 4, 2016.

35   Caitlin McCabe, "Technology Shares Maintain Their Allure Amid Coronavirus," *Wall Street Journal*, April 21, 2020.

36   Amelia Lucas, "Apple warns on revenue guidance," CNBC, February 17, 2020.

37   Jack Nicas, "New iPhones Fuel Strong Profit for Apple," *New York Times*, January 28, 2020.

38   Emily McCormick, Heidi Chung, and Javier E. David, "Dow jumps 1,290 points in biggest-ever point gain," Yahoo Finance, March 2, 2020.

39   Peggy Noonan, "On Some Things, Americans Can Agree," *Wall Street Journal*, June 6–7, 2020.

40 Robert L. Bartley, *The Seven Fat Years*, Free Press, 1992, p. 212.

41 Ibid., p. 213.

42 Masao Nakamura, *The Japanese Business and Economic System*, Palgrave MacMillan, 2001, p. 230.

43 Robert L. Bartley, *The Seven Fat Years*, Free Press, 1992, p. 212.

44 Ibid., p. 109.

45 Peter Thiel and Blake Masters, *Zero to One*, Currency, 2014, p. 44.

46 Weijian Shan, "American Companies Need Chinese Consumers," *New York Times*, January 7, 2019.

47 Ibid.

48 Phil Knight, *Shoe Dog*, Scribner, 2016, p. 364.

49 Heather Haddon, "Starbucks Reopens Stores in China," *Wall Street Journal*, February 27, 2020.

50 J. Edward Moreno, "Government health agency official: Coronavirus 'isn't something the American public need to worry about,'" *The Hill*, January 26, 2020.

51 Thomas Hazlett, "Policy Diversity Saves Lives: Unmasking Confirmation Bias Caused by a Virus," Truth on the Market, April 8, 2020.

52 Julian E. Barnes and Adam Goldman, "Trump, Diverting Virus Blame, Points Finger at a Messenger," *New York Times*, May 22, 2020.

53 Farhad Manjoo, "Beware the Pandemic Panic," *New York Times*, January 29, 2020.

54 Jonathan S. Tobin, "Conservative Pundits Weren't the Only Ones to Get the Pandemic Wrong," *National Review*, April 3, 2020.

55 Shalini Ramachandran, Laura Kusisto, and Katie Honan, "New York Response Worsened Pandemic," *Wall Street Journal*, June 12, 2020.

56 William K. Rashbaum, J. David Goodman, Jeffery C. Mays, and Joseph Goldstein, "De Blasio Gives Key Virus Role to Ex-Skeptic," *New York Times*, May 15, 2020.

57 Brad Burt, "South by Southwest 2020 Canceled by City of Austin Due to Coronavirus Concerns," KCBD, March 6, 2020.

58 Edward Pinto, "Coronavirus, & the Media's Lies, Damned Lies, and 'Statistics,'" *RealClearMarkets*, April 14, 2020.

59   Kwame Opam, "It's Not 'Shelter-in-Place': What the New Coronavirus Restrictions Mean," *New York Times*, March 24, 2020.

60   Allen C. Guelzo, "A Wolf in Emergency Clothing," *Wall Street Journal*, June 26, 2020.

61   Sareen Habeshian and Mary Beth McDade, "Mayor Garcetti announces water and power will be shut off for nonessential L.A. businesses that don't close," KTLA5, March 24, 2020.

62   Howard Marks, *Mastering the Market Cycle*, Houghton Mifflin Harcourt, 2018, p. 34.

63   Stephen Davis, *Gold Dust Woman: The Biography of Stevie Nicks*, St. Martin's Press, 2017, p. 152.

64   Ibid., p. 146

65   Ibid., p. 163.

66   Ibid., p. 164.

67   Benjamin M. Anderson, *Economics and the Public Welfare*, Liberty Press, 1949, p. 92.

68   Ibid., p. 92.

69   Ibid., p. 92.

70   Edward Pinto, "Coronavirus, & the Media's Lies, Damned Lies, and 'Statistics,'" *RealClearMarkets*, April 14, 2020.

71   Jonathan J. Cooper, "California now world's 5th largest economy, surpassing UK," *USA Today*, May 5, 2018.

72   Edward Pinto, "Coronavirus, and the Media's Lies, Damned Lies, and Statistics," *RealClearMarkets*, April 14, 2020.

73   Lawrence Wright, *God Save Texas: A Journey into the Future of America*, Alfred A. Knopf, 2018.

74   Anemona Hartocollis, "States Seize Chance to Stop College Student Brain Drain," *New York Times*, June 24, 2020.

75   Arthur Brooks, *Who Really Cares*, Basic Books, 2006, p. 54.

76   Diane Coyle, *GDP: A Brief but Affectionate History*, Princeton University Press, 2014, p. 7.

77   Ibid., pp. 14–15.

78   Ibid., p. 16.

79   Ibid., p. 64.

80   Editorial, "Financing an Economic Shutdown," *Wall Street Journal*, March 16, 2020.

81   Ibid.

82   Warren T. Brookes, *The Economy in Mind*, Universe, 1982, p. 172.

83   Allan Smith, "Fauci: Americans are 'going to have to hunker down,'" NBCNews.com, March 15, 2020.

84   Michael Fumento, "CDC director on hot seat over his predictions, agency performance," Just the News, updated May 11, 2020.

85   Dan McConchie, "Limit Governors' Emergency Powers," *Wall Street Journal*, May 1, 2020.

86   Rich Karlgaard, "Living Days Stolen," *Forbes*, April 25, 2020.

87   Andy Kessler, "A War of Meaningless Words," *Wall Street Journal*, June 21, 2020.

88   Jeff Cox, "A record 20.5 million jobs were lost in April," CNBC, May 8, 2020.

89   Mary Williams Walsh, "A Wave of Bankruptcies May Swamp the System," *New York Times*, June 22, 2020.

90   Andy Kessler, "Trump Could Be the First Silicon Valley President," *Wall Street Journal*, February 3, 2017.

91   Thomas Kessner, *Capital City: New York City and the Men Behind America's Rise to Economic Dominance, 1860–1900*, Simon & Schuster, 2004, p. 216.

92   Jason Furman, "The Case for a Big Coronavirus Stimulus," *Wall Street Journal*, March 5, 2020.

93   Jeanna Smialek and Jim Tankersley, "Fed Makes Emergency Rate Cut, but Markets Continue Tumbling," *New York Times*, March 3, 2020.

94   National Taxpayers Union, https://www.ntu.org/foundation/tax-page/who-pays-income-taxes.

95   Peter Thiel and Blake Masters, *Zero to One*, Currency, 2014, p. 133.

96   Andrew Ross Sorkin, "This Is the Only Way to End the Coronavirus Financial Panic," *New York Times*, March 18, 2020.

97   David L. Bahnsen, "Boiling Over," *National Review Online*, May 27, 2020.

98   Samuel Sheetz, "'We Win; They Lose': The Staggering Simplicity of Reagan's Grand Strategy," Daily Signal, December 10, 2011.

99   Katharine Q. Seelye, "Sergei N. Kruschev, 84, Rocket Scientist and the Son of a Former Soviet Premier," *New York Times*, June 25, 2020.

100 Ibid.

101 Ibid.

102 Ibid.

103 Ibid.

104 Jeff Rowe, "Book Review: Disney fans will enjoy Snow's 'Disney's Land,'" Associated Press, December 17, 2019.

105 Thomas Stossel, "What Cancer Doctors Don't Know about Cancer Drugs," *Wall Street Journal*, September 22, 2015.

106 Editorial, "The Assault on Drug Innovation," *Wall Street Journal*, September 22, 2015.

107 Editorial, "The Government Economy," *Wall Street Journal*, April 30, 2020.

108 Casey B. Mulligan and Brian Blase, "Congress Can Still Save the Recovery," *Wall Street Journal*, April 8, 2020.

109 George Gilder, *Knowledge and Power*, Regnery Publishing, 2013, p. 5.

110 Matt Egan, "New threat to the economy: Americans are savings like it's the 1980s," CNN Business, May 12, 2020.

111 Enrico Moretti, *The New Geography of Jobs*, Houghton Mifflin Harcourt, 2012, p. 63.

112 Matt Ridley, "Innovation Can't Be Forced," *Wall Street Journal*, May 16–17, 2020.

113 Jim Tankersley and Ben Casselman, "Inside the Plan to Tweak $600 in Aid," *New York Times*, July 24, 2020.

114 Steve Almasy, "The NCAA is canceling March Madness," CNN.com, March 12, 2020.

115 Mark Feinsand, "Opening day delayed; spring games canceled," MLB.com, March 12, 2020.

116 Rebecca Klar, "Celebrity chef José Andrés closes his DC restaurants," *The Hill*, March 15, 2020.

117 Hannah Yasharoff, "'See you real soon': Disney World officially closes its doors amid coronavirus," *USA Today*, March 16, 2020.

118 Emily Badger and Alicia Parlapiano, "Governmental Orders Won't Rescue Economy," *New York Times*, May 8, 2020.

119 Ibid.
120 Konstantin Kakaes, "New Directions," *Wall Street Journal*, June 25–26, 2016.
121 Ed Catmull, *Creativity, Inc.*, Random House, 2014, p.38.
122 Phil Knight, *Shoe Dog*, Scribner, 2016, p. 160.
123 Peter S. Goodman, "Sweden Stayed Open to Spare Its Economy. It Didn't Succeed," *New York Times*, July 8, 2020.
124 Thomas Erdbrink, "Sweden's Virus Plan Was Called Lax. Can It Be Called a Success?" *New York Times*, September 30, 2020.
125 Alastair Gale, "Japan Eases Curbs in Osaka, but Sustains Them in Tokyo," *Wall Street Journal*, May 22, 2020.
126 Peter S. Goodman and Erik Augustin Palm, "A Safety Net Shows Its Wear," *New York Times*, October 9, 2020.
127 Sarah Chaney and Kim Mackrael, "Limited Virus Restrictions Aid South's Economy," *Wall Street Journal*, October 19, 2020.
128 Yaroslav Trofimov, "A World of Hardening Borders," *Wall Street Journal*, April 17, 2020.
129 Frances Robles, "A 'Scary' Fivefold Surge in Cases Over Two Weeks," *New York Times*, June 29, 2020.
130 Editorial, "Covid Comparisons, Europe and U.S.," *Wall Street Journal*, June 29, 2020.
131 Editorial, "Cuomo's Covid Chutzpah," *Wall Street Journal*, June 27–28, 2020.
132 Holman W. Jenkins Jr., "Angela Merkel's Viral Moment," *Wall Street Journal*, July 1, 2020.
133 Rebecca Everett, "Everything we know about coronavirus curfews, closings and shutdowns in N.J.," NJ.com, March 16, 2020.
134 Greg Weiner, "Are We Sure We Want to Give Trump War Powers?" *New York Times*, March 25, 2020.
135 Joseph A. Ladapo, "The Crucial Reopening Question," *Wall Street Journal*, May 22, 2020.
136 Brooks Barnes, "At Disney World, 'Worst Fears' about Virus Have Not Come True," *New York Times*, October 9, 2020.
137 John Stuart Mill, *Principles of Political Economy*, Prometheus Books, 2004, p. 92.

138 Alan Rappeport, "$1.4 Billion in Stimulus Funds Were Sent to Dead People, Watchdog Finds," *New York Times*, June 26, 2020.

139 John Stuart Mill, *Principles of Political Economy*, Prometheus Books, 2004, p. 92.

140 Tara Siegel Bernard and Ron Lieber, "Checks, Unemployment Benefits and More," *New York Times*, March 27, 2020.

141 Ben Protess and David McCabe, "Prep Schools Face Setback, and a Quandary on Federal Aid," *New York Times*, April 30, 2020.

142 Ibid.

143 Ibid.

144 Editorial, "Harvard University does the right thing…eventually," *Boston Herald*, April 23, 2020.

145 Heather Haddon and Bob Davis, "Shake Shack to Return $10 Million Coronavirus Stimulus Loan," *Wall Street Journal*, April 21, 2020.

146 Alicia Wallace, "Lakers return $4.6 million coronavirus relief loan," CNN Business, April 27, 2020.

147 Esther Fung, "Could a Ski Hill, a Theme Park and 40 Water Slides Save the American Mall?" *Wall Street Journal*, October 25, 2019.

148 Randy Rieland, "The Avenue Gets a Big Boost," *Glover Park Gazette*, March 2020.

149 Randy Rieland, "Avenue Businesses Collaborate on a 'Fix-It Fest,'" *Glover Park Gazette*, October 2018.

150 Stacy Cowley, "Small-Business Owners Are Given Easier Path to Loan Forgiveness," *New York Times*, June 16, 2020.

151 Jessica Young, "US ecommerce sales growth 14.9% in 2019," DigitalCommerce360, February 19, 2020.

152 Yuka Hayashi, "High Rents Curb Benefits of Aid for Small Businesses," *Wall Street Journal*, May 23, 2020.

153 Paul Katzeff, "Smart Warehouses Help Online Retail Companies Outrun Coronavirus," *Investor's Business Daily*, July 2, 2020.

154 Damon Dunn, "Basic Income Guarantees Would 'Warehouse' the Poor, Not Propel Them," *RealClearMarkets*, July 2, 2020.

155 Jerry Bowyer, "Sports Mania Is a Poor Substitute for Economic Success," *Wall Street Journal*, January 17, 2009.

156 Ibid., p. 29.

157 Olivia Horn, "Behind the Boss's Music," *New York Times*, July 3, 2020.

158 Anemona Hartocollis, "States Seize Chance to Stop College Student Brain Drain," *New York Times*, June 24, 2020.

159 Justin Baer, "The Day the Coronavirus Nearly Broke the Markets," *Wall Street Journal*, May 21, 2020.

160 Elizabeth Dilts Marshall, "Exclusive: JPMorgan Chase to raise mortgage borrowing standards as economic outlook darkens," Reuters, April 11, 2020.

161 Hugh Son, "Wells Fargo will no longer accept applications for home equity lines of credit," CNBC, April 30, 2020.

162 Oscar Gonzalez, "Credit card issuers start to lower cardholder limits," CNET, May 6, 2020.

163 Rebecca Elliott, "Pioneer in Shale Industry Files for Chapter 11," *Wall Street Journal*, June 29, 2020.

164 Jeanna Smialek and Alan Rappeport, "Wary Treasury May Constrain Economy's Rise," *New York Times*, May 19, 2020.

165 Editorial, "The Main Street Fakeout," *Wall Street Journal*, May 1, 2020.

166 Jarrett Bellini, "The No. 1 thing to consider before opening a restaurant," CNBC, March 15, 2016.

167 Nathaniel Meyersohn, "Pier 1 files for bankruptcy," CNN Business, February 17, 2020.

168 Shoshy Ciment, "From Forever 21 and Payless to PG&E, here are the biggest bankruptcies of the year so far," Business Insider, October 3, 2019.

169 Glenn Hubbard, "After the Cares Act, Hospitals and Businesses Need Sustained Support," *Wall Street Journal*, April 6, 2020.

170 Ibid.

171 Greg Ip, "Fed Can't Help Much in a Solvency Crisis," *Wall Street Journal*, May 1, 2020.

172 Jeanna Smialek and Alan Rappeport, "Wary Treasury May Constrain Economy's Rise," *New York Times*, May 19, 2020.

173 Todd Leopold, "Your late fees are waived: Blockbuster closes," CNN Business, November 6, 2013.

174 Glenn Hubbard and Hal Scott, "'Main Street' Program Is Too Stingy to Banks and Borrowers," *Wall Street Journal*, July 21, 2020.

175 Paul Kiernan, "Main Street Loan Program Sees Lukewarm Interest," *Wall Street Journal*, July 2, 2020.

176 Editorial, "The Main Street Fakeout," *Wall Street Journal*, May 1, 2020.

177 Paul Kiernan, "Main Street Loan Program Sees Lukewarm Interest," *Wall Street Journal*, July 2, 2020.

178 Reuven Brenner, "Our Muddled Masses," *First Things*, January 2010.

179 Hank Haney, *The Big Miss: My Years Coaching Tiger Woods*, Crown Archetype, 2012, p. 75–76.

180 Steve Williams, *Out of the Rough: Inside the Ropes with the World's Greatest Golfers*, Viking, 2015, p. 21.

181 Ibid., pp. 130, 187.

182 Andrew Beaton, "Mahomes Contract: A Bargain?" *Wall Street Journal*, July 8, 2020.

183 Erin Griffith, "Amazon CEO Jeff Bezos: 'I've Made Billions of Dollars of Failures,'" *Fortune*, December 2, 2014.

184 Matt Phillips, "Investors Bet Giant Companies Will Dominate After Crisis," *New York Times*, April 28, 2020.

185 Ben Smith, "Conde Nast Is Facing an Era's End," *New York Times*, April 24, 2020.

186 Steven Rattner, "The Mystery of High Stock Prices," *New York Times*, July 3, 2020.

187 Ibid.

188 Nick Timiraos, "Fed Slows Buying as Pressures Abate," *Wall Street Journal*, July 27, 2020.

189 Mark Thornton, "Austrian School Scholars Are Right to Be Worried about This Economy," Mises Institute, May 4, 2020.

190 James Dorn, "Why Stock-Market Upheaval Was Inevitable," CNN Opinion, February 7, 2018, updated February 8, 2020.

191 Jeff Cox, "Fed cuts rates by half a percentage point to combat coronavirus slowdown," CNBC, March 3, 2020.

192 Justin Baer, "The Day the Coronavirus Nearly Broke the Markets," *Wall Street Journal*, May 21, 2020.

[193] Fed Funds Rate History, https://www.thebalance.com/fed-funds-rate-history-highs-lows-3306135.

[194] Alexandra Scaggs, "After 20 Years, Has Japan Redefined Monetary Policy Success?" *Barron's*, February 12, 2019.

[195] Katie Allen, "ECB cuts Eurozone interest rate to zero to jump-start economy," *Guardian*, March 10, 2016.

[196] Karen Langley, "U.S. Stocks Are Outpacing the Rest of the World," *Wall Street Journal*, May 31, 2020.

[197] Jeffrey Snider, "Janet Yellen Uses Fed Failures to Expand the Fed's Mandate," *RealClearMarkets*, July 18, 2014.

[198] "10 Year Treasury Rate: Historical Chart," MacroTrends, https://www.macrotrends.net/2016/10-year-treasury-bond-rate-yield-chart.

[199] Tim Arango, "How the AOL-Time Warner Merger Went So Wrong," *New York Times*, January 10, 2010.

[200] Adam Thierer, "A Brief History of Media Merger Hysteria: From AOL-Time Warner to Comcast-NBC," The Technology Liberation Front, December 2, 2009.

[201] Peter Thiel and Blake Masters, *Zero to One*, Currency, 2014, p. 188.

[202] Stephen Johnston, "Largest companies 2008 vs. 2018, a lot has changed," Milford Capital, January 31, 2018.

[203] Matt Phillips, "Markets Are Proving Detachment between Wall and Main Street," *New York Times*, May 11, 2020.

[204] Jason Zweig, "This Bull Market Isn't as Big as You Think," *Wall Street Journal*, June 6–7, 2020.

[205] Gunjan Banerji, "How Stocks Defied the Pandemic," *Wall Street Journal*, September 16, 2020.

[206] Scott W. Atlas, "Adding to Dr. Fauci's diagnosis: The critical case for ending our shutdown," *The Hill*, May 18, 2020.

[207] Roni Caryn Rabin and Chris Cameron, "A False Claim from Trump: 99% of Cases Are Harmless," *New York Times*, July 6, 2020.

[208] Eran Bendavid and Jay Bhattacharya, "Is Covid-19 as Deadly as They Say?" *Wall Street Journal*, April 1, 2020.

[209] David L. Katz, "Is Our Fight against Coronavirus Worse Than the Disease?" *New York Times*, March 20, 2020.

210 Anna Fifield, *The Great Successor: The Divinely Perfect Destiny of Brilliant Comrade Kim Jong Un*, Hachette Book Group, 2019, p. 72.

211 Ibid., p. 72.

212 Ibid., p. 45.

213 Ibid., p. 56.

214 Ibid., p. 144.

215 Jason Rezaian, *Prisoner*, Harper Collins, 2019, p. 11.

216 Scott W. Atlas, "The data is in—stop the panic and end the total isolation," *The Hill*, April 22, 2020.

217 Scott Gottlieb, "America Needs to Win the Vaccine Race," *Wall Street Journal*, April 27, 2020.

218 Matthew Herper, "Cancer Man," *Forbes*, October 9, 2009.

219 Roger Pilon, "Needed: Active Judges—Not to Be Confused with Judicial Activists," *National Review*, November 14, 2002.

220 George Will, *The Conservative Sensibility*, Hachette Books, 2019, p. 164.

221 Ibid., p. 166.

222 Ibid., p. 166.

223 Walter Olson, "Federalism and the Coronavirus Lockdown," *Wall Street Journal*, March 30, 2020.

224 Roger Pilon, "President Trump Cannot 'Order the Nation Back to Work,'" *RealClearMarkets*, April 3, 2020.

225 Andrew Napolitano, "Judge Andrew Napolitano: Coronavirus shutdowns ordered by governors and mayors are unconstitutional," *Fox News*, May 28, 2020.

226 Kimberly Wehle, "Yes, a National Quarantine Is Constitutional…and Necessary," *Politico*, May 15, 2020.

227 Peter Baker and Maggie Haberman, "Crisis Easing, Trump Leaps to Call Shots, Setting Up Standoff with Governors," *New York Times*, April 14, 2020.

228 Rick Rojas, "Trump Criticizes Georgia Governor for Decision to Reopen State," *New York Times*, April 22, 2020.

229 Ken Thomas and Sabrina Siddiqui, "Biden Says President Is Failing on Coronavirus," *Wall Street Journal*, July 1, 2020

230 Michelle Goldberg, "In Some Countries, Normal Life Is Back. Not Here," *New York Times,* July 13, 2020.

231 Kimberley Strassel, "The Obama-Biden Virus Response," *Wall Street Journal,* August 20, 2020.

232 Nicholas Bogel-Burroughs and Jeremy W. Peters, "'You Have to Disobey': Protesting, and Defying, Stay-at-Home Orders," *New York Times,* April 17, 2020.

233 Kristina Peterson, "Work-From-Home Congress Also Can't Figure Out How to Unmute," *Wall Street Journal,* May 7, 2020.

234 Michael Wilson, "What's a New York Drive Like? Tour a Ghost Town of 8 Million," *New York Times,* May 18, 2020.

235 Matthew Haag, "Pandemic Decimates Small Businesses, New York City's Beating Heart," *New York Times,* August 4, 2020.

236 Ted Loos, "Even Art Is Leaving For the Hamptons," *New York Times,* July 13, 2020.

237 Bret Stephens, "The Remote vs. The Exposed," *New York Times,* May 15, 2020.

238 Jonathan Ponciano, "1.3 Million American Households Could Owe $7.2 Billion in Unpaid Rent by End of This Year," *Forbes,* October 23, 2020.

239 David Harrison, "Low-Wage Workers Hit Harder by Layoffs," *Wall Street Journal,* May 15, 2020.

240 Kim Mackrael, "Jobless Claims Surge in Kentucky," *Wall Street Journal,* May 1, 2020.

241 Nicholas Bogel-Burroughs and Jeremy W. Peters, "'You Have to Disobey': Protesting, and Defying, Stay-at-Home Orders," *New York Times,* April 17, 2020.

242 Eric Morath and Amara Omeokwe, "Coronavirus Obliterated Best Black Job Market on Record," *Wall Street Journal,* June 10, 2020.

243 Craig Karmin and Esther Fung, "Hotels Furlough, Cut Thousands of Staff," *Wall Street Journal,* March 23, 2020.

244 Harriet Torry, "Hispanics Take Big Hit in Downturn," *Wall Street Journal,* July 6, 2020.

245 Julie Cresswell, "Learning to Cater to the Unexpected," *New York Times,* August 5, 2020.

246 Justin Baer, "Graduations, Campus Classes Canceled by Coronavirus Shock College-Town Economy," *Wall Street Journal*, May 17, 2020.

247 Rachel Bachman and Laine Higgins, "Small Schools Are Taking a Big Hit," *Wall Street Journal*, July 13, 2020.

248 Kevin Van Valkenburg, "Behold, the Life of Kings," *Baltimore Sun*, March 31, 2008.

249 Sam Kasner, "Both Huntress and Prey," *Vanity Fair*, November 2014.

250 Georgia Pellegrini, "Out of His Shell," *Wall Street Journal*, May 28–29, 2016.

251 Kirk Semple and Natalie Kitroeff, "Crisis Batters Region's Already Fragile Informal Economies," *New York Times*, March 31, 2020.

252 Zia ur-Rehman and Maria Abi-Habib, "Perishing amid Sludge and Waste in Pakistan," *New York Times*, May 5, 2020.

253 Ibid.

254 John D. Gartner, *The Hypomanic Edge*, Simon & Schuster, 2005, p. 12.

255 Kevin Baker, *America the Ingenious*, Artisan, 2016, p. 139.

256 Marian Tupy, "Global Poverty's Defeat Is Capitalism's Triumph," *Investor's Business Daily*, October 10, 2015.

257 Santiago Perez, "Remittances to El Salvador Dry Up," *Wall Street Journal*, June 5, 2020.

258 Anna Fifield, *The Great Successor: The Divinely Perfect Destiny of Brilliant Comrade Kim Jong Un*, Hachette Book Group, 2019, p. 148.

259 Jon Emont, "Countries Lose Billions Sent Home from Workers Abroad," *Wall Street Journal*, July 6, 2020.

260 Ibid.

261 Raja Abdulrahim, "Global Remittances Projected to Decline about 20% in 2020," *Wall Street Journal*, April 23, 2020.

262 Ibid.

263 Jason Gutierrez, "As Lockdown Drags On in a Jam-Packed Slum, Hunger Stalks the Poor," *New York Times*, April 17, 2020.

264 Ibid.

265 John Otis, "Covid-19 Forces 100,000 Venezuelan Migrants Back to Broken Country," *Wall Street Journal*, August 31, 2020.

266 Denise Grady, "'Worst Nightmare' Is Far from Over, Fauci Warns," *New York Times*, June 9, 2020.

267 Abdi Latif Dahir, "135 Million Face Starvation. That Could Double," *New York Times*, April 23, 2020.

268 Jeffrey Gettleman and Suhasini Raj, "Virus Closed Schools, and World's Poorest Children Went to Work," *New York Times*, September 28, 2020.

269 Joseph Epstein, "We've Hardly Gotten to Know You, Coronavirus," *Wall Street Journal*, May 30–31, 2020.

270 Anne Glenconner, *Lady in Waiting: My Extraordinary Life in the Shadow of the Crown*, Hachette Books, 2020, p. 11.

271 Ibid., p. 240.

272 Michael Fumento, "CDC director on hot seat over his predictions, agency performance," Just the News, May 11, 2020.

273 "Rock Hudson Agonized over Kissing Linda Evans on 'Dynasty,'" Associated Press, June 9, 1986.

274 Anne Glenconner, *Lady in Waiting: My Extraordinary Life In the Shadow of the Crown*, Hachette Books, 2020, p. 240.

275 Michael Fumento, "CDC director on hot seat over his predictions, agency performance," Just the News, May 11, 2020.

276 Matt Krantz, "Bill Gates' Coronavirus Manifesto Reveals 5 Forecasts for Investors," *Investor's Business Daily*, April 24, 2020.

277 Sarah Nassauer and Suzanne Kapner, "Target Posts Record Quarter," *Wall Street Journal*, August 20, 2020.

278 Nicole Sperling and Brooks Barnes, "Movie Theaters, Urged to Open, Want to Delay Showtime," *New York Times*, April 23, 2020.

279 David Leonhardt, "U.S. Is Alone Among Peers in Failing to Curb Virus," *New York Times*, August 7, 2020.

280 Samuel Shem, *The House of God*, Dell, 1995 edition, p. 215.

281 Jeffrey A. Tucker, "Woodstock Occurred in the Middle of a Pandemic," American Institute for Economic Research, May 1, 2020.

282 Danny Meyer, *Setting the Table*, Harper, 2006, p. 102.

283 Paul Sullivan, "The Best Medical Care Most Can't Afford," *New York Times*, August 22, 2020.

[284] "RIM half-CEO doesn't see threat from Apple's iPhone," MacDailyNews, February 12, 2007.

[285] Mike Colias and Heather Haddon, "Virus Safety Added to Dining Menus," *Wall Street Journal*, June 13–14, 2020.

[286] Hilary Potkewitz, "How Ready Are Gyms to Reopen?" *Wall Street Journal*, May 19, 2020.

[287] Craig Karmin and Steven Russolillo, "Hotels Are Back. Will Guests Have Any Reservations?" *Wall Street Journal*, June 13–14, 2020.

[288] Natasha Singer, "Farewell to Gummy Bear Jars: Tech Offices Get a Virus Safety Makeover," *New York Times*, June 11, 2020.

[289] Livia Albeck-Ripka, "Australian Soap Opera Returns to Its Drama, But Keeps Lovers Apart," *New York Times*, May 13, 2020.

[290] Editorial, "Small Business Loan Hold Up," *Wall Street Journal*, April 15, 2020.

[291] Holman W. Jenkins Jr., "Sweden Is a Viral Punching Bag," *Wall Street Journal*, April 14, 2020.

[292] Jeffrey A. Tucker, "Woodstock Occurred in the Middle of a Pandemic," American Institute for Economic Research, May 1, 2020.

[293] Brianna Abbott and Jason Douglas, "Research Reveals Fatality Rate for Covid-19," *Wall Street Journal*, July 22, 2020.

[294] Phil Knight, *Shoe Dog*, Scribner, 2016, p. 301.

[295] Alyssia Finley, "The Lockdown Skeptic They Couldn't Silence," *Wall Street Journal*, May 16-17, 2020.

[296] Hannah Critchfield, "Strike Teams Help Nursing Homes Combat Covid-19," *New York Times*, August 18, 2020.

[297] Holman W. Jenkins Jr., "Elon Musk Is Our New ACLU," *Wall Street Journal*, May 12, 2020.

[298] Jared Diamond, "Please Step Away from the Baserunner," *Wall Street Journal*, May 19, 2020.

[299] Lorne Gunter, "Why not include professional athletes in Canada's exemption list?" *Toronto Sun*, July 21, 2020.

[300] Ryan Glasspiegel, "Stephen A. Smith: NBA Players Will 'Struggle' with No Sex in the Bubble," *OutKick*, June 30, 2020.

[301] Josh Christenson, "D.C. Exempts Lawmakers, Federal Employees from New Mask Order," *Washington Free Beacon*, July 23, 2020.

302 Corey Kilgannon,"Lifeguarding in a Pandemic: No-Contact Rescues and CPR Pumps," *New York Times*, August 17, 2020.

303 Joseph A. Ladapo, "The Looming Civil-Liberties Battle," *Wall Street Journal*, April 30, 2020.

304 William McGurn, "The Lockdown Rebellion," *Wall Street Journal*, April 20, 2020.

305 Madeline Wells, "Newsom's office says to keep masks on between bites when eating out," *SFGate*, October 9, 2020.

306 Andy Kessler, "A War of Meaningless Words," *Wall Street Journal*, June 21, 2020.

307 Juliet Isselbacher and Amanda Su, "Harvard to House Freshmen, Select Upperclassmen for Fall Semester," *Harvard Crimson*, July 6, 2020.

308 Nancy Keates, "Virus Mars the College Drop-Off," *Wall Street Journal*, July 8, 2020.

309 Yoree Koh, "Neighbors Resort to Online Shaming," *Wall Street Journal*, April 14, 2020.

310 Jeffrey A. Tucker, "We Were Wrong: So Sorry That We Ruined Your Life," American Institute for Economic Research, March 28, 2020.

311 Editorial, "Government Rules for Restaurants," *Wall Street Journal*, July 22, 2020.

312 Ibid.

313 Ibid.

314 Heather Haddon, "With Indoor Dining Upended, Some Restaurants Call It Quits," *Wall Street Journal*, July 21, 2020.

315 Ruth Simon, Amara Omeokwe, and Gwynn Guilford, "Short on Cash, Small Businesses Brace for Long Crisis," *Wall Street Journal*, July 23, 2020.

316 Ibid.

317 Lisa Birnbach, "A Clothier Woven into the American Fabric Frays," *New York Times*, July 23, 2020.

318 Rolfe Winkler, "Airbnb to Lay Off Quarter of Workforce," *Wall Street Journal*, May 5, 2020.

319 Brooks Barnes, "Disney's Profit Wilts, and Worse Is Ahead," *New York Times*, May 6, 2020.

320 Jeanna Smialek, "No Relief for Larger, Often Debt-Laden, Companies," *New York Times*, June 3, 2020.

321 Kimberley A. Strassel, "The Mnuchin Follies," *Wall Street Journal*, July 24, 2020.

322 Stephen A. Schwarzman, *What It Takes: Lessons in Pursuit of Excellence*, Avid Reader Press, 2019, p. 294.

323 Ibid., p. 108.

324 Michael Ovitz, *Who Is Michael Ovitz?*, Portfolio, 2018, p. 68

325 Ibid., p. 98

326 Phil Knight, *Shoe Dog*, Scribner, 2016, p. 137.

327 Greg Bensinger, "Elon Musk's Latest Gambit," *New York Times*, May 18, 2020.

328 Holman W. Jenkins Jr., "Elon Musk Is Our New ACLU," *Wall Street Journal*, May 12, 2020.

329 Matthew Dalton, "France Identifies Case from Late December," *Wall Street Journal*, May 6, 2020.

330 Allysia Finley, "Herd Immunity May Be Closer Than You Think," *Wall Street Journal*, July 6, 2020.

331 J. David Goodman, "Two Neighborhoods: One Rich, One Poor. One Spared," *New York Times*, July 22, 2020.

332 Hannah Beech, "The Happy Mystery of a Region's Success against the Coronavirus," *New York Times*, July 17, 2020.

333 Apoorva Mandavilli, "Ambitious Study in India of Nearly 85,000 Cases Delivers Many Surprises," *New York Times*, October 1, 2020.

334 Allison Prang and Jennifer Calpas, "Virus Cases Slow but States Struggle," *Wall Street Journal*, July 28, 2020.

335 Jon Emont, "Indonesia Struggles with Low Test Rates," *Wall Street Journal*, October 9, 2020.

336 Holman W. Jenkins Jr., "Why Politicians Despise Us—Continued," *Wall Street Journal*, October 9, 2020.

337 Holman W. Jenkins Jr., "The Other Media Blackout," *Wall Street Journal*, October 30, 2020.

338 Apoorva Mandavilli, "C.D.C. Finds Big Differences in Infections vs. Reported Cases," *New York Times*, July 22, 2020.

339 Norimitsu Onishi and Constant Méheut, "Parisians Embrace a Protest with a Twist," *New York Times*, May 28, 2020.

340 Motoko Rich, "In a 2nd-Wave Lockdown, a Brimming Metropolis Is (a Bit) Less Complacent," *New York Times*, April 20, 2020.

341 Alastair Gale, "Japan Eases Curbs in Osaka, but Sustains Them in Tokyo," *Wall Street Journal*, May 22, 2020.

342 Editors, "Florida Is a Case Study in Media-Induced COVID-19 Panic," *Issues & Insights*, July 27, 2020.

343 Arian Campo-Flores and Alex Leary, "How Florida Dodged Worst Predictions," *Wall Street Journal*, May 4, 2020.

344 Holman W. Jenkins Jr., "Your Covid Crib Sheet, Updated," *Wall Street Journal*, September 30, 2020.

345 Editorial, "The World's Covid Resurgence," *Wall Street Journal*, July 29, 2020.

346 Michael Fumento, "Coronavirus Death Predictions Bring New Meaning to Hysteria," *RealClearMarkets*, April 1, 2020.

347 Edgar Sandoval, "Overwhelmed Funeral Homes in South Texas Struggle to Keep Up," *New York Times*, July 29, 2020.

348 David Leonhardt, "U.S. Is Alone Among Peers in Failing to Curb Virus," *New York Times*, August 7, 2020.

349 James Glanz and Campbell Robertson, "Lockdown Delays Cost at Least 36,000 Lives, Data Show," *New York Times*, May 21, 2020.

350 Jan Hoffman and Ruth Maclean, "New Virus Hastens Spread of Old, Preventable Illness," *New York Times*, June 15, 2020.

351 Apoorva Mandavilli, "'Biggest Monster' Rebounds," *New York Times*, August 3, 2020.

352 Maria Cramer, "Sobering Reality: Many Are Drinking to Excess," *New York Times*, May 27, 2020.

353 Hilary Swift and Abby Goodnough, "Locked Down and Addicted," *New York Times*, September 29, 2020.

354 Andrew Mark Miller, "California doctors say they've seen more deaths from suicide than coronavirus since lockdowns," *Washington Examiner*, May 21, 2020.

355 Dominick Mastrangelo, "Suicides outpacing coronavirus deaths in Tennessee, data says," *Washington Examiner*, March 29, 2020.

356 Sarah Kliff, "Virus Devastates Business Model for Hospitals Both Rich and Poor," *New York Times*, May 16, 2020.

357 Greg Ip, "For Many, Grasping Virus Proves Tricky," *Wall Street Journal*, July 30, 2020.

358 Yves Duroseau, "It's Deadly to Fear the Emergency Room," *Wall Street Journal*, May 20, 2020.

359 Bob Kerrey, "'Elective' Surgery Saves Lives," *Wall Street Journal*, April 21, 2020.

360 Sharon Terlep, "CVS Warns of Nonvirus Health Crisis," *Wall Street Journal*, May 7, 2020.

361 Editorial, "The Lockdown's Destruction," *Wall Street Journal*, July 31, 2020.

362 George Gilder, "This Pandemic Is Over. Let's Stop the Economic Suicide, and Get Back to Work," *RealClearMarkets*, April 25, 2020.

363 Richard W. Rahn, "You Are Not Going to Die from COVID-19," *Washington Times*, May 26, 2020.

364 Michael J. Lewis, "Pandemic as Urban Planner," *Wall Street Journal*, June 8, 2020.

365 Ron Chernow, *Titan: The Life of John D. Rockefeller, Sr.*, Vintage Books, 2nd Edition, 2004, p. 479.

366 Farhad Manjoo, "Without Net Neutrality, Say So Long to the Internet," *New York Times*, November 29, 2017.

367 "More Than 40% of U.S. Coronavirus Deaths Are Linked to Nursing Homes," *New York Times*, July 23, 2020.

368 Andy Kessler, "Cancer Screening Leaps Forward," *Wall Street Journal*, July 6, 2020.